Political Freedom and Social Security

Political Freedom and Social Security

Vimal K Puri

ADHYAYAN

ADHYAYAN PUBLISHERS & DISTRIBUTORS

NEW DELHI (INDIA)

Published by
ADHYAYAN PUBLISHERS & DISTRIBUTORS
4378/4B, 105, J.M.D. House, Murari Lal Street
Ansari Road Darya Ganj, New Delhi - 110002
Ph.: 011-23263018, 011-23277156, Fax: 011-23280028
Email: adhyayanpublishers@yahoo.com

Political Freedom and Social Security

Edition 2011
ISBN 978-81-8435-241-2

Printed in India

Published by Harish Chandra Yadav for Adhyayan Publishers & Distributors, Laser Typeseting at A.V. Rao and Printed at Tarun Offset Printers, Delhi

Preface

Political freedom is the absence of interference with the sovereignty of an individual by the use of coercion or aggression. Freedom is commonly known as a state of being free from government oppression. The opposite of a free society is a totalitarian state, which highly restricts political freedom in order to regulate almost every aspect of behaviour. In this sense 'freedom' refers solely to the relation of humans to other humans, and the only infringement on it is coercion by humans. The concept of political freedom is very closely allied with the concepts of civil liberties and individual rights, which in most democratic societies is characterised by various freedoms which are afforded the legal protection from the state.

Social security is primarily a social insurance program providing social protection, or protection against socially recognised conditions, including poverty, old age, disability, unemployment and others. Social security is more applicable in the conditions, where large numbers of citizens depend on the formal economy for their livelihood. Through a defined contribution, this social security may be managed. But, in the context of wide spread informal economy, formal social security arrangements are almost absent for the vast majority of the working population. Besides, in developing countries, the state's capacity to reach the vast majority of the poor people may be limited because of its limited resources. In such a context, multiple agencies that could provide for social protection is important for policy consideration.

This book elucidates what political freedom is and demonstrates why it should be protected by rights. It will be an essential reading for policymakers involved in reform, researchers , students and all of who interested in the future of political freedom and social security.

Vimal K Puri

Contents

1

Concepts of Political Freedom

Political freedom is the absence of interference with the sovereignty of an individual by the use of coercion or aggression. Freedom is commonly known as a state of being free from government oppression. The opposite of a free society is a totalitarian state, which highly restricts political freedom in order to regulate almost every aspect of behavior. In this sense 'freedom' refers solely to the relation of humans to other humans, and the only infringement on it is coercion by humans The concept of political freedom is very closely allied with the concepts of civil liberties and individual rights, which in most democratic societies is characterized by various freedoms which are afforded the legal protection from the state.

1.1. Freedom of Assembly

Freedom of assembly, sometimes used interchangeably with the freedom of association, is the individual right to come together and collectively express, promote, pursue and defend common interests. The right to freedom of association is recognized as a human right, a political freedom and a civil liberty.

Freedom of assembly and freedom of association may be used to distinguish between the freedom to assemble in public places and the freedom of joining an association. Freedom of assembly is often used in the context of the right to protest, while freedom of association is used in the context of labor rights and the right to collective bargaining, for example by joining a trade union. Freedom of assembly, as guaranteed in the Canadian Constitution and the Constitution of the

United States, is interpreted to mean both the freedom to assemble and the freedom to join an association

The freedom of assembly is enshrined in the following human rights instruments:

— Universal Declaration of Human Rights—Article 20
— International Covenant on Civil and Political Rights—Article 21
— European Convention on Human Rights—Article 11
— American Convention on Human Rights—Article 15

1.1.1. Freedom of Association

Freedom of association is the individual right to come together with other individuals and collectively express, promote, pursue and defend common interests. The right to freedom of association has been included in a number of national constitutions and human rights instruments, including the US constitution and the European Convention on Human Rights and the Canadian Charter of Rights and Freedoms.

Freedom of association in the sense of workers' right to organize and collectively bargain is also recognised in the Universal Declaration of Human Rights and International Labor Organization Conventions.

The right to freedom of association is sometimes used interchangeably with the freedom of assembly. More specifically the freedom of assembly is understood in a political context, although depending on the source (constitution, human rights instrument etc) the right to freedom of association may be understood to include the right to freedom of assembly.

1.1.2. Democracy and Civil Society

Jeremy McBride argues that respect for the freedom of association by all public authorities and the exercising of this freedom by all sections of society are essential both to establish a "genuine democracy" and to ensure that, once achieved, it remains "healthy and flourishing". In this regard he sees the formation of political parties as a significant manifestation of the freedom of association.

The freedom of association is however not only exercised in the political sense, but also for a vast array of interests—such as culture, recreation, sport and social and humanitarian assistance. Jeremey McBride agues that the formation of non-governmental organisations (NGOs), which he equates with civil society, is the "fruit of associational activity".

1.1.3. Libertarian

Freedom of association is a term popular in libertarian literature. It is used to describe the concept of absolute freedom to live in a community or be part of an organization whose values or culture are closely related to one's preferences; or, on a more basic level, to associate with any individual one chooses.

The libertarian concept of freedom of association is often rebuked from a moral/ethical context. Under laws in such a system, business owners could refuse service to anyone for whatever reason. Opponents argue that such practices are regressive and would lead to greater prejudice within society. Right-libertarians sympathetic to freedom of association, such as Richard Epstein, respond that in a case of refusing service (which thus is a case of the freedom of contract) unjustified discrimination incurs a cost and therefore a competitive disadvantage. Left-libertarians argue that such refusal would place those businesses at an economic disadvantage to those that provide services to all, making them less profitable and eventually leading them to close down.

Libertarians also argue that freedom of association, in a political context, is merely the extension of the right to determine with whom to associate in one's personal life. For example, somebody who valued good manners or etiquette may not relish associating with someone who was not decent or was uncouth. Or, those opposed to homosexuality probably would not enjoy associating with gay people. In both instances, a person is voluntarily deciding with whom to associate, based on his/her own volition. Libertarians believe that freedom of association, in the political sphere, is not such a fanciful or unrealistic notion, since individual human beings already choose with whom they would like to associate based on a variety of reasons.

1.1.4. Constitutions

The South African Constitution's Bill of Rights enshrines the right to freedom of association in Section 18, which states "Everyone has the right to freedom of association." Furthermore Section 17 states "Everyone has the right, peacefully and unarmed, to assemble, to demonstrate, to picket and to present petitions", effectively enshrining the right freedom of assembly. While the United States Constitution's First Amendment identifies the rights to assemble and to petition the government, the text of the First Amendment does not make specific mention of a right to association.

1.1.5. Intimate Association

A fundamental element of personal liberty is the right to choose to enter into and maintain certain intimate human relationships. These intimate human relationships are considered forms of "intimate association." The paradigmatic example of "intimate association" is the family.

1.1.6. Expressive Association

Expressive associations are groups that engage in activities protected by the First Amendment—speech, assembly, press, petitioning government for a redress of grievances, and the free exercise of religion. In *Roberts v. United States Jaycees*, the Supreme Court held that associations may not exclude people for reasons unrelated to the group's expression. However, in the subsequent decisions of *Hurley v. Irish-American Gay, Lesbian, and Bisexual Group of Boston* and *Boy Scouts of America v. Dale*, the Court ruled that a group may exclude people from membership if their presence would affect the group's ability to advocate a particular point of view. The government cannot, through the use of anti-discrimination laws, force groups to include a message that they do not wish to convey.

1.1.7. Limitation

However, the implicit First Amendment right of association in the U.S. Constitution has been limited by court rulings. For example, it is illegal in the United States to consider race in the making and enforcement of private contracts other than marriage or taking affirmative action. This limit on freedom of association results from Section 1981 of Title 42 of the United States Code, as balanced against the First Amendment in the 1976 decision of *Runyon v. McCrary*.

The holding of *Runyon* is that the defendant private schools were free to *express* and teach their views, such as white separatism, but could not discriminate on the basis of race in the *provision* of services to the general public. So, if the plaintiff African-American children wished to attend such private schools, *and* were clearly qualified in all respects (but race) and were able to pay the fees, *and* were willing to attend *despite* the fact that the school's professed principles were inconsistent with admitting them, then the schools were required by Section 1981 to admit them. This doctrine rests on the interpretation of a private contract as a "badge" of slavery when either party considers race in choosing the other.

Governments often require contracts of adhesion with private entities for licensing purposes, such as with Financial Industry Regulatory Authority for stock market trading in the 1938 Maloney Act amendments to the Securities Exchange Act of 1934. These contracts often bar association with banned members, as can be seen in *United States v. Merriam*, 108 F.3d 1162.

1.1.8. Workers' Freedom of Association

In the international labour movement, the freedom of association is a right identified under international labour standards as the right of workers to organize and collectively bargain. Freedom of association, in this sense, is recognized as a fundamental human right by a number of documents including the Universal Declaration of Human Rights and International Labor Organization Convention C87 and Convention C98 — two of the eight fundamental, core international labour standards. 'Freedom of association' can also refer to legal bans on private contracts negotiated between a private employer and their employees requiring workers at a particular workplace to join a union as a term and condition of employment. Supporters of this sort of private freedom of association claim that the right to join a union incorporates a right not to join a union. In the United States, the term 'right to work' is more common for this type of law.

1.2. Freedom of Movement

Freedom of movement, mobility rights or the right to travel is a human rights concept that the constitutions of numerous states respect. It asserts that a citizen of a state, in which that citizen is present has the liberty to travel, reside in, and/or work in any part of the state where one pleases within the limits of respect for the liberty and rights of others, and to leave that state and return at any time. Some immigrants' rights advocates assert that human beings have a fundamental human right to mobility not only across states but across nations.

1.2.1. Common Limitations

Nevertheless, restrictions on international freedom of movement (immigration or emigration) are commonplace. Within countries, freedom of movement is often more limited for minors, and penal law can modify this right as it applies to persons charged with or convicted of crimes (for instance, parole, probation, registration). In some countries, freedom of movement has historically been limited for women, and for members of disfavored racial and social groups. Circumstances, both legal and practical, may operate to limit this freedom. For example, a nation that is generally permissive with respect to travel may restrict that right during time of war. In some instances, the laws of a nation may assert a guarantee of this right, but lawless conditions may make unfettered movement impossible. In other instances, a nation whose written laws codify such rights may fail to actually provide them. Other common political-legal restrictions on freedom of movement are:

- national and regional official minimum wage tariff barriers to labour market entry (free movement or migration of workers);
- official identity cards (internal passports, citizenship licenses) that must be carried and produced on demand;
- obligations on persons to register change of address or partner with the state authorities;
- protectionist local-regional barriers to housebuilding and therefore settlement in particular districts; and
- road toll barriers to the free movement of persons by motor cars.

Scholars have attempted to base a universal "right to move" on several philosophical grounds, including the idea of a common ownership of the earth, a natural right of movement existing prior to the advent of nation states, an ethics of cosmopolitanism, and utilitarian notions of the benefits of immigration to both receiving countries and immigrants.

1.2.2. Freedom of Movement between Private Parties

Freedom of movement is not construed as a right to permit an individual to enter private property of another. Such an unauthorized entry constitutes a trespass, often punishable as a tort or a crime, for which the private landowner can summon public officials to remove a trespasser from the landowner's property. In some jurisdictions, questions have arisen as to the extent to which a private owner of land can exclude certain persons from land used for public purposes, such as a shopping mall or a park. There is also a rule of law that a landowner whose property is completely boxed in by that of other private landowners shall have the right to cross private land if that is necessary to reach a public thoroughfare. The concept is also used as the basis for enacting laws to prevent alternate use of streets, roads and right-of-ways from blocking or restricting freedom of movement such as block parties and playing basketball.

There is a converse duty for a private person not to impede the free movement of another. Where a person prevents another from freely leaving an area, either by physically imprisoning them or by threats, that person may be subject to a lawsuit for false imprisonment, and to criminal charges for kidnapping.

Some countries, such as the former Soviet Union, required that their citizens, and sometimes foreign travelers, obtain an exit visa to be allowed to leave the country. Currently, foreign students in Russia are issued only an entry visa on being accepted to University there, and must obtain an exit visa to return home. The United States requires foreign students to receive permission from the school to exit. This is done by official signature on an I-20 form. Without the signature the student will not be allowed to exit (if checked) or re-enter.

Sometimes restrictions are placed on leaving that are specific to the intended destination. In the United States travel to Cuba is restricted with the ostensible goal of putting pressure on Cuba by denying it income from American travelers

1.3. Freedom of Religion

Freedom of religion is a principle that supports the freedom of an individual or community, in public or private, to manifest religion or belief in teaching, practice, worship, and observance; the concept is generally recognized also to include the freedom to change religion or not to follow any religion. Freedom of religion is considered by many people and nations to be a fundamental human right. Thomas Jefferson said (1807) "among the inestimable of our blessings, also, is that...of liberty to worship our Creator in the way we think most agreeable to His will;..." In a country with a state religion, freedom of religion is generally considered to mean that the government permits religious practices of other sects besides the state religion, and does not persecute believers in other faiths

Historically *freedom of religion* has been used to refer to the tolerance of different theological systems of belief, while *freedom of worship* was defined as freedom of individual action. Each of these have existed to varying degrees. While many countries have accepted some form of religious freedom, this has also often been limited in practice through punitive taxation, repressive social legislation, and political disenfranchisement.

1.3.1. Antiquity

In Antiquity a syncretic point-of-view often allowed communities of traders to operate under their own customs. When street mobs of separate quarters clashed in a Hellenistic or Roman city, the issue was generally perceived to be an infringement of community rights. Cyrus the Great established the Achaemenid Empire ca. 550 BC, and initiated a general policy that can be described as a policy of permitting religious freedom throughout the empire, documenting this on the Cyrus Cylinder. Some of the historical exceptions have been in regions where one of the revealed religions has been in a position of power: Judaism, Zoroastrianism, Christianity and Islam. Others have been where the established order has felt threatened, as shown in the trial of

Socrates in 399 BC or where the ruler has been deified, as in Rome, and refusal to offer token sacrifice was similar to refusing to take an oath of allegiance. This was the core for resentment and the persecution of early Christian communities.

Freedom of religious worship was established in the Maurya Empire of ancient India by Asoka the Great in the 3rd century BC, which was encapsulated in the Edicts of Ashoka. Greek-Jewish clashes at Cyrene in 73 AD and 117 AD and in Alexandria in 115 AD provide examples of cosmopolitan cities as scenes of tumult.

1.3.2. Middle Ages

Following a period of fighting lasting around a hundred years before 620 AD which mainly involved Arab and Jewish inhabitants of Medina (then known as *Yathrib*), religious freedom for Muslims, Jews and pagans was declared by Muhammad in the Constitution of Medina. The Islamic Caliphate later guaranteed religious freedom under the conditions that non-Muslim communities accept *dhimmi* (protected) status and their adult males pay the *jizya* tax as a substitute for the *zakat* paid by Muslim citizens.

Religious pluralism existed in classical Islamic ethics and Sharia law, as the religious laws and courts of other religions, including Christianity, Judaism and Hinduism, were usually accommodated within the Islamic legal framework, as seen in the early Caliphate, Al-Andalus, Indian subcontinent, and the Ottoman Millet system. In medieval Islamic societies, the *qadi* (Islamic judges) usually could not interfere in the matters of non-Muslims unless the parties voluntarily choose to be judged according to Islamic law, thus the *dhimmi* communities living in Islamic states usually had their own laws independent from the Sharia law, such as the Jews who would have their own *Halakha* courts.

Dhimmis were allowed to operate their own courts following their own legal systems in cases that did not involve other religious groups, or capital offences or threats to public order. Non-Muslims were allowed to engage in religious practices that was usually forbidden by Islamic law, such as the consumption of alcohol and pork, as well as religious practices which Muslims found repugnant, such as the Zoroastrian practice of incestuous "self-marriage" where a man could marry his mother, sister or daughter. According to the famous Islamic legal scholar Ibn Qayyim (1292–1350), non-Muslims had the right to engage in such religious practices even if it offended Muslims, under the conditions that such cases not be presented to Islamic Sharia courts and that these religious minorities believed that the practice in question is permissible according to their religion.

1.3.3. India

Ancient Jews fleeing from persecution in their homeland 2,500 years ago settled in India and never faced Anti-Semitism. Freedom of religion edicts have been found written during Ashoka the Great's reign in 3rd Century BC. Freedom to practise, preach and propagate any religion is a constitutional right in Modern India. Indians celebrate and respect the holy festivals of all major religions. India is a 80% Hindu country yet its Prime Minister is a Sikh (Manmohan Singh), the chairperson of the ruling alliance is a Catholic woman of Italian origin (Sonia Gandhi), three out of the twelve Presidents of India have been Muslims. Still, though some argue that India's predominant religion, Hinduism, has long been among the most tolerant of religions, others assert that tolerance only appeared in India with the emergence of modern Republic of India as a secular nation in 1947.

The Hindu-nationalist Bharatiya Janata Party (BJP) emerged as a major national political party in the 1980s, and formed the core of the government from 1998 to 2004. It is the biggest constituent of the National Democratic Alliance which as of 2009[update] is in the opposition. Some Christians charge that the rise of the BJP and the emergence of Hindu nationalism have been accompanied by the repression of Christianity and assaults on Christians and their institutions. In the year 2000, the government in India's north-eastern state of Tripura has accused The local Baptist Church to have supplied the National Liberation Front of Tripura (NLFT) with explosives. The NLFT is accused of forcing Tripura's indigenous tribes to become Christians and give up Hindu forms of worship in areas under their control. In 1999, they issued a ban on the Hindu festivals of Durga Puja and Saraswati Puja.

Freedom of religion in contemporary India is a fundamental right guaranteed by the country's constitution. Every citizen of India has a right to practice and promote their religions peacefully. However, there is tension between Muslim (and Christian) minorities and the Hindu majority. It has been alleged that the tension is mainly due to the fact that Muslims and Christians actively involve in proselytism, which is disliked by the Hindus.

Freedom of religion in the Indian subcontinent is exemplified by the reign of King Piyadasi (304 B.C to 232 B.C) (Asoka). One of King Asoka's main concerns was to reform governmental institutes and exercise moral principles in his attempt to create a just and humane society. Later he promoted the principles of Buddhism, and the creation of a just, understanding and fair society was held as an important principle for many ancient rulers of this time in the East.

Religious freedom and the right to worship freely was a practice that had been appreciated and promoted by most ancient India dynasties. As a result, people fleeing religious persecution in other parts of the world including Christians, Jews and Zoroastrians fled to India as a place of refuge where they could enjoy religious freedom. This had been the underlying attitude of most rulers of India until 1200 AD.

The initial entry of Islam into South Asia came in the first century after the death of the Islamic Prophet Muhammad. When around 1210 AD the Islamic Sultanates invaded India from the north-west, gradually the principle of freedom of religion deteriorated in this part of the world. They were subsequently replaced by another Islamic invader in the form of Babur. The Mughal empire was founded by the Mongol leader Babur in 1526, when he defeated Ibrahim Lodi, the last of the Delhi Sultans at the First Battle of Panipat. The word "Mughal" is the Indo-Iranian version of Mongol.

On the main Asian continent, the Mongols were tolerant of religions. People could worship as they wished freely and openly.

1.4. Freedom of Speech

Freedom of speech is the freedom to speak without censorship or limitation, or both. The synonymous term freedom of expression is sometimes used to indicate not only freedom of verbal speech but any act of seeking, receiving and imparting information or ideas, regardless of the medium used. In practice, the right to freedom of speech is not absolute in any country and the right is commonly subject to limitations, such as on "hate speech".

The right to freedom of speech is recognized as a human right under Article 19 of the Universal Declaration of Human Rights and recognized in international human rights law in the International Covenant on Civil and Political Rights (ICCPR). The ICCPR recognizes the right to freedom of speech as "the right to hold opinions without interference. Everyone shall have the right to freedom of expression". Furthermore freedom of speech is recognized in European, inter-American and African regional human rights law.

Concepts of freedom of speech can be found in early human rights documents and the modern concept of freedom of speech emerged gradually during the European Enlightenment. England's Bill of Rights 1689 granted 'freedom of speech in Parliament' and the Declaration of the Rights of Man and of the Citizen, adopted during the French Revolution in 1789, specifically affirmed freedom of speech as an inalienable right. The Declaration provides for freedom of expression in Article 11, which states that: "The free communication of ideas and opinions is one of the most precious of the rights of man. Every citizen may, accordingly, speak, write, and print with freedom, but shall be responsible for such abuses of this freedom as shall be defined by law."

Article 19 of the Universal Declaration of Human Rights, adopted in 1948, states that: "Everyone has the right to freedom of opinion and expression; this right includes freedom to hold opinions without interference and to seek, receive and impart information and ideas through any media and regardless of frontiers."

Today freedom of speech, or the freedom of expression, is recognized in international and regional human rights law. The right is enshrined in Article 19 of the International Covenant on Civil and Political Rights, Article 10 of the European Convention on Human Rights, Article 13 of the American Convention on Human Rights and Article 9 of the African Charter on Human and Peoples' Rights. Based on John Stuart Mill's arguments, freedom of speech is understood as a multi-faceted right that includes not only the right to express, or disseminate, information and ideas, but three further distinct aspects:

— the right to seek information and ideas;
— the right to receive information and ideas;
— the right to impart information and ideas.

International, regional and national standards also recognize that freedom of speech, as the freedom of expression, includes any medium, be it orally, in written, in print, through the Internet or through art forms. This means that the protection of freedom of speech as a right includes not only the content, but also the means of expression.

1.4.1. Relationship to other Rights

The right to freedom of speech and expression is closely related to other rights, and may be limited when conflicting with other rights. The right to freedom of expression is also related to the right to a fair trial and court proceeding which may limit access to the search for information or determine the opportunity and means in which freedom of expression is manifested within court proceedings. As a general principle freedom of expression may not limit the right to privacy, as well as the honor and reputation of others. However greater latitude is given when criticism of public figures is involved. The right to freedom of expression is particularly important for media, which plays a special role as the bearer of the general right to freedom of expression for all. However, freedom of the press is not necessarily enabling freedom of speech. Judith Lichtenberg has outlined conditions in which freedom of the press may constrain freedom of speech, for example where the media suppresses information or stifles the diversity of voices inherent in freedom of speech. Lichtenberg argues that freedom of the press is simply a form of property right summed up by the principle "no money, no voice".

1.4.2. Origins and Academic Freedom

Freedom of speech and expression has a long history that predates modern international human rights instruments. It is thought that ancient Athens' democratic ideology of free speech may have emerged in the late 6th or early 5th century BC. In Islamic ethics, freedom of speech was first declared in the Rashidun period by the caliph Umar in the 7th century AD. In the Abbasid Caliphate period, freedom of speech was also declared by al-Hashimi (a cousin of Caliph al-Ma'mun) in a letter to one of the religious opponents he was attempting to convert through reason. According to George Makdisi and Hugh Goddard, "the idea of academic freedom" in universities was "modelled on Islamic custom" as practiced in the medieval Madrasah system from the 9th century. Islamic influence was "certainly discernible in the foundation of the first deliberately-planned university" in Europe, the University of Naples Federico II founded by Frederick II, Holy Roman Emperor in 1224.

1.4.3. Freedom of Speech, Dissent and Truth

Before the invention of the printing press a writing, once created, could only be physically multiplied by the highly laborious and error-prone process of manual copying out and an elaborate system of censorship and control over scribes existed. Printing allowed for multiple exact copies of a work, leading to a more rapid and widespread circulation of ideas and information. The origins of copyright law in most European countries lie in efforts by the church and governments to regulate and control the output of printers. In 1501 Pope Alexander VI issued a bull against the unlicensed printing of books and in 1559 the Index Expurgatorius, or *List of Prohibited Books*, was issued for the first time. While governments and church encouraged printing in many ways, which allowed the dissemination of Bibles and government information, works of dissent and criticism could also circulate rapidly. As a consequence, governments established controls over printers across Europe, requiring them to have official licences to trade and produce books.

The notion that the expression of dissent or subversive views should be tolerated, not censured or punished by law, developed alongside the rise of printing and the press. *Areopagitica*, published in 1644, was John Milton's response to the Parliament of England's re-introduction of government licensing of printers, hence publishers. Milton made an impassioned plea for freedom of expression and toleration of falsehood, stating: "Give me the liberty to know, to utter, and to argue freely according to conscience, above all liberties."

Milton's defence of freedom of expression was grounded in a Protestant worldview and he thought that the English people had the mission to work out the truth of the Reformation, which would lead to the enlightenment of all people. But Milton also articulated the main strands of future discussions about freedom of expression. By defining the scope of freedom of expression and of "harmful" speech Milton argued against the principle of pre-censorship and in favour of tolerance for a wide range of views.

As the "menace" of printing spread governments established centralised control mechanism. The French crown repressed printing and the printer Etienne Dolet was burned at the stake in 1546. In 1557 the British Crown thought to stem the flow of seditious and heretical books by chartering the Stationers' Company. The right to print was limited to the members of that guild, and thirty years later the Star Chamber was chartered to curtail the "greate enormities and abuses" of "dyvers contentyous and disorderlye persons professinge the arte or mystere of pryntinge or selling of books." The right to print was restricted to two universities and to the 21 existing printers in the city of London, which had 53 printing presses. As the British crown took control of type founding in 1637 printers fled to the Netherlands. Confrontation with authority made printers radical and rebellious, with 800 authors, printers and book dealers being incarcerated in the Bastille in Paris before it was stormed in 1789.

A succession of English thinkers developed the idea of a right to freedom of expression, starting with John Milton (1608–74), then John Locke (1632–1704) and culminating in John Stuart Mill (1806–1873). Locke established the individual as the unit of value and the bearer of rights to life, liberty, property and the pursuit of happiness. It was the role of Government to protect these rights and this belief was first enshrined in the US Constitution, with the First Amendment adding the guarantee that "Congress shall make no law... abridging the freedom of speech, or of the press". John Stuart Mill argued that human freedom is good and without it there can be no progress in science, law or politics, which according to Mill required free discussion of opinion. Mill's On Liberty, published in 1859 became a classic defence of the right to freedom of expression. Mill argued that truth drives out falsity, therefore the free expression of ideas, true or false, should not be feared. Truth is not stable or fixed, but evolves with time. Mill argued that much of what we once considered true has turned out false. Therefore views should not be prohibited for their apparent falsity.

Mill also argued that free discussion is necessary to prevent the "deep slumber of a decided opinion". Discussion would drive the onwards march of truth and by considering false views the basis of true views could be re-affirmed.

1.4.4. Democracy

The notion of freedom of expression is intimately linked to political debate and the concept of democracy. The norms on limiting freedom of expression mean that public debate may not be completely suppressed even in times of emergency. One of the most notable proponents of the link between freedom of speech and democracy is Alexander Meiklejohn. He argues that the concept of democracy is that of self-government by the people. For such a system to work an informed electorate is necessary. In order to be appropriately knowledgeable, there must be no constraints on the free flow of information and ideas. According to Meiklejohn, democracy will not be true to its essential ideal if those in power are able to manipulate the electorate by withholding information and stifling criticism. Meiklejohn acknowledges that the desire to manipulate opinion can stem from the motive of seeking to benefit society. However, he argues, choosing manipulation negates, in its means, the democratic ideal.

Eric Barendt has called this defence of free speech on the grounds of democracy "probably the most attractive and certainly the most fashionable free speech theory in modern Western democracies". Thomas I. Emerson expanded on this defence when he argued that freedom of speech helps to provide a balance between stability and change. Freedom of speech acts as a "safety valve" to let off steam when people might otherwise be bent on revolution. He argues that "The principle of open discussion is a method of achieving a moral adaptable and at the same time more stable community, of maintaining the precarious balance between healthy cleavage and necessary consensus." Emerson furthermore maintains that "Opposition serves a vital social function in offsetting or ameliorating (the) normal process of bureaucratic decay."

Research undertaken by the Worldwide Governance Indicators project at the World Bank, indicates that freedom of speech, and the process of accountability that follows it, have a significant impact in the quality of governance of a country. "Voice and Accountability" within a country, defined as "the extent to which a country's citizens are able to participate in selecting their government, as well as freedom of expression, freedom of association, and free media" is one of the six dimensions of governance that the Worldwide Governance Indicators measure for more than 200 countries.

1.4.5. Limitations on Freedom of Speech

According to the Freedom Forum Organization, legal systems, and society at large, recognize limits on the freedom of speech, particularly when freedom of speech conflicts with other values or rights. Limitations to freedom of speech may follow the "harm principle" or the "offense principle", for example in the case of pornography or "hate speech". Limitations to freedom of speech may occur through legal sanction or social disapprobation, or both.

In "On Liberty" (1859) John Stuart Mill argued that "...there ought to exist the fullest liberty of professing and discussing, as a matter of ethical conviction, any doctrine, however immoral it may be considered." Mill argues that the fullest liberty of expression is required to push arguments to their logical limits, rather than the limits of social embarrassment. However, Mill also introduced what is known as the harm principle, in placing the following limitation on free expression: "the only purpose for which power can be rightfully exercised over any member of a civilized community, against his will, is to prevent harm to others.

In 1985 Joel Feinberg introduced what is known as the "offence principle", arguing that Mill's harm principle does not provide sufficient protection against the wrongful behaviours of others. Feinberg wrote "It is always a good reason in support of a proposed criminal prohibition that it would probably be an effective way of preventing serious offense (as opposed to injury or harm) to persons other than the actor, and that it is probably a necessary means to that end." Hence Feinberg argues that the harm principle sets the bar too high and that some forms of expression can be legitimately prohibited by law because they are very offensive. But, as offending someone is less serious than harming someone, the penalties imposed should be higher for causing harm. In contrast Mill does not support legal penalties unless they are based on the harm principle. Because the degree to which people may take offense varies, or may be the result of unjustified prejudice, Feinberg suggests that a number of factors need to be taken into account when applying the offense principle, including: the extent, duration and social value of the speech, the ease with which it can be avoided, the motives of the speaker, the number of people offended, the intensity of the offense, and the general interest of the community at large.

1.5. Freedom of the Press

Freedom of the press is the freedom of communication and expression through vehicles including various electronic media and published materials. While such freedom mostly implies the absence of interference from an overreaching state, its preservation may be sought through constitutional or other legal protections.

With respect to governmental information, any government may distinguish which materials are public or protected from disclosure to the public based on classification of information as sensitive, classified or secret and being otherwise protected from disclosure due to relevance of the information to protecting the national interest. Many governments are also subject to sunshine laws or freedom of information legislation that are used to define the ambit of national interest.

The Universal Declaration of Human Rights states: *"Everyone has the right to freedom of opinion and expression; this right includes freedom to hold opinions without interference, and impart information and ideas through any media regardless of frontiers"*

This philosophy is usually accompanied by legislation ensuring various degrees of freedom of scientific research (known as scientific freedom), publishing, press and printing the depth to which these laws are entrenched in a country's legal system can go as far down as its constitution. The concept of freedom of speech is often covered by the same laws as freedom of the press, thereby giving equal treatment to spoken and published expression.

Besides legal definitions, some non-governmental organizations use other criteria to judge the level of press freedom around the world:

— Reporters Without Borders considers the number of journalists murdered, expelled or harassed, and the existence of a state monopoly on TV and radio, as well as the existence of censorship and self-censorship in the media, and the overall independence of media as well as the difficulties that foreign reporters may face.

— The Committee to Protect Journalists (CPJ) uses the tools of journalism to help journalists by tracking press freedom issues through independent research, fact-finding missions, and firsthand contacts in the field, including local working journalists in countries around the world. CPJ shares information on breaking cases with other press freedom organizations worldwide through the International Freedom of Expression Exchange, a global e-mail network. CPJ also tracks journalist deaths and detentions. CPJ staff applies strict criteria for each case; researchers independently investigate and verify the circumstances behind each death or imprisonment.

— Freedom House likewise studies the more general political and economic environments of each nation in order to determine whether relationships of dependence exist that limit in practice the level of press freedom that might exist in theory. So the concept of independence of the press is one closely linked with the concept of press freedom.

Every year, Reporters Without Borders establishes a ranking of countries in terms of their freedom of the press. The Worldwide press freedom index list is based on responses to surveys sent to journalists that are members of partner organisations of the RWB, as well as related specialists such as researchers, jurists and human rights activists. The survey asks questions about direct attacks on journalists and the media as well as other indirect sources of pressure against the free press, such as pressure on journalists by non-governmental groups. RWB is careful to note that the index only deals with press freedom, and does not measure the quality of journalism.

In 2009, the countries where press was the most free were Finland, Norway, Ireland, Sweden and Denmark. The country with the least degree of press freedom was Eritrea, followed by North Korea, Turkmenistan, Iran and Myanmar (Burma).

Freedom of the Press is a yearly report by US-based non-governmental organization Freedom House, measuring the level of freedom and editorial independence enjoyed by the press in every nation and significant disputed territories around the world. Levels of freedom are scored on a scale from 1 (most free) to 100 (least free). Depending on the basics, the nations are then classified as "Free", "Partly Free", or "Not Free".

1.5.1. Non-democratic States

According to Reporters Without Borders, more than a third of the world's people live in countries where there is no press freedom. Overwhelmingly, these people live in countries where there is no system of democracy or where there are serious deficiencies in the democratic process. Freedom of the press is an extremely problematic problem/concept for most non-democratic systems of government since, in the modern age, strict control of access to information is critical to the existence of most non-democratic governments and their associated control systems and security apparatus.

To this end, most non-democratic societies employ state-run news organizations to promote the propaganda critical to maintaining an existing political power base and suppress (often very brutally, through the use of police, military, or intelligence agencies) any significant attempts by the media or individual journalists to challenge the approved "government line" on contentious issues.

In such countries, journalists operating on the fringes of what is deemed to be acceptable will very often find themselves the subject of considerable intimidation by agents of the state. This can range from simple threats to their professional careers (firing, professional blacklisting) to death threats, kidnapping, torture, and assassination. Reporters Without Borders reports that, in 2003, 42 journalists lost their lives pursuing their profession and that, in the same year, at least 130 journalists were in prison as a result of their occupational activities. In 2005, 63 journalists and 5 media assistants were killed worldwide.

According to the Press Freedom Index for 2007, Iran ranked 166th out of 169 nations. Only three other countries—Eritrea, North Korea and Turkmenistan—had more restrictions on news media freedom than Iran. The government of Ali Khamenei and the Supreme National Security Council had imprisoned 50 journalists in 2007 and had all but eliminated press freedom. Reporters Without Borders (RWB) has dubbed Iran the "Middle East's biggest prison for journalists."

1.6. Freedom of Thought

Freedom of thought (also called the freedom of conscience or ideas) is the freedom of an individual to hold or consider a fact, viewpoint, or thought, independent of others' viewpoints. It is different from and not to be confused with the concept of freedom of expression.

'Freedom of thought' is the derivative of and thus is closely linked to other liberties: freedom of religion, freedom of speech, and freedom of expression. It is a very important concept in the western world but nearly all democratic constitutions protect these freedoms. For instance, the U.S. Bill of Rights contains the famous guarantee in the First Amendment that laws may not be made that interfere with religion "or prohibiting the free exercise thereof". A US Supreme Court Justice (Benjamin Cardozo) reasoned in *Palko v. Connecticut* (1937) that:

> Freedom of thought... is the matrix, the indispensable condition, of nearly every other form of freedom. With rare aberrations a pervasive recognition of this truth can be traced in our history, political and legal.

Such ideas are also a vital part of international human rights law. In the Universal Declaration of Human Rights (UDHR), which is legally binding on member states of the International Covenant on Civil and Political Rights, *freedom of thought* is listed under Article 18:

> Everyone has the right to freedom of thought, conscience and religion; this right includes freedom to change his religion or belief, and freedom, either alone or in community with others and in public or private, to manifest his religion or belief in teaching, practice, worship and observance.

The Human Rights Committee states that this, "distinguishes the freedom of thought, conscience, religion or belief from the freedom to manifest religion or belief. It does not permit any limitations whatsoever on the freedom of thought and conscience or on the freedom to have or adopt a religion or belief of one's choice. These freedoms are protected unconditionally." Similarly, Article 19 of the UDHR guarantees that "Everyone has the right to freedom of opinion and expression; this right includes freedom to hold opinions without interference..."

1.6.1. Suppression

The obvious impediment to censoring thought is that it is impossible to know with certainty what another person is thinking, and harder to regulate it. Many famous historical works recognize this. The Bible summarizes in Ecclesiastes 8:8: "There is no man that has power over the spirit, to retain it; neither has he power in the day of death." A similar sentiment is expressed in the teachings of Jesus in the New Testament, where he likens those who attempt to control the emotions of their neighbours to "the children in the marketplace" who try to produce dancing with a happy song and mourning with a dirge, and then express frustration at their futility in trying to do so. Queen Elizabeth I revoked a thought censorship law in the late sixteenth century, because, according to Sir Francis Bacon, she did "'not [like] to make windows into men's souls and secret thoughts".

However, freedom of expression can be limited through censorship, arrests, book burning, or propaganda, and this tends to discourage freedom of thought. Examples of effective campaigns against freedom of expression are the Soviet suppression of genetics research in favor of a theory known as Lysenkoism, the book burning campaigns of Nazi Germany, the radical anti-intellectualism enforced in Cambodia under Pol Pot, and the strict limits on freedom of expression imposed by the Communist governments of the Peoples Republic of China and Cuba.

Freedom of expression can also be stifled without institutional interference when majority views become so widely accepted that the entire culture represses dissenting views. For this reason, some condemn political correctness as a form of limiting freedom of thought. Although political correctness aims to give minority views equal representation, the majority view itself can be politically correct;

for example, college student Max Karson was arrested following the Virginia Tech shootings for politically incorrect comments that authorities saw as "sympathetic to the killer." Karson's arrest raised important questions regarding freedom of thought and whether or not it applies in times of tragedy.

The Sapir–Whorf hypothesis, which states that thought is inherently embedded in language, would support the claim that an effort to limit the use of words of language is actually a form of restricting freedom of thought. This was explored in George Orwell's novel *1984*, with the idea of Newspeak, a stripped-down form of the English language lacking the capacity for metaphor and limiting expression of original ideas.

1.6.2. Internet censorship

Some countries, like Iran, Saudi Arabia, Egypt, China, and others attempt to control and censor information on the World Wide Web. In October 2006, Iranian mullahs ordered internet service providers to reduce connection speeds for home and cafe computers.

1.7. Suffrage

Suffrage, political franchise, or simply the franchise is the civil right to vote, or the exercise of that right. In English, *suffrage* and its synonyms are sometimes also used to mean the right to run for office (to be a candidate), but there are no established qualifying terms to distinguish between these different meanings of the term(s). The right to run for office is sometimes called (*candidate*) *eligibility*, and the combination of both rights is sometimes called *full suffrage*. In many other languages, the right to vote is called the *active right to vote* and the right to be voted for (to run for office) is called the *passive right to vote*. In English, these are rarely called *active suffrage* and *passive suffrage*.

Suffrage may apply to elections, but also extends to initiatives and referendums. Suffrage is used to describe not only the legal right to vote, but also to the practical question of the opportunity to vote, which is sometimes denied those who have a legal right. In the United States, extension of suffrage was part of Jacksonian democracy.

In most democracies, eligible voters can vote in elections of representatives. Voting on issues by initiative may be available in some jurisdictions but not others. For example, Switzerland permits initiatives at all levels of government whereas the United States does not offer initiatives at the federal level or in many states. That new constitutions must be approved by referendum is natural law.

Typically citizens become eligible to vote after reaching the age of legal adulthood. Most democracies no longer extend different voting rights on the basis of sex or race. Resident aliens can vote in some countries and in others exceptions are made for citizens of countries with which they have close links (e.g. some members of the Commonwealth of Nations, and the members of the European Union).

Where Universal suffrage exists, the right to vote is not restricted by race, gender, belief, sexual orientation, gender identity, wealth, or social status. It typically does not extend a right to vote to all residents of a region; distinctions are frequently made in regard to citizenship, age, and occasionally mental capacity or criminal convictions.

The short-lived Corsican Republic (1755-1769) was the first country to grant limited universal suffrage for all inhabitants over the age of 25. This was followed by other experiments in the Paris Commune of 1871 and the island republic of Franceville (1889), and then by New Zealand in 1893. Finland was the first European country to grant universal suffrage to its citizens in its 1906 elections, and the first country in the world to make every citizen eligible to run for parliament.

1.7.1. Forms of Exclusion from Suffrage

1.7.1.1. Religion

In the aftermath of the Reformation it was common in European countries for people of disfavored religious denominations to be denied civil and political rights, often including the right to vote, to stand for election or to sit in parliament. In the United Kingdom and Ireland, Roman Catholics were denied the right to vote from 1728 to 1793, and the right to sit in parliament until 1829. The anti-Catholic policy was justified on the grounds that the loyalty of Catholics supposedly lay with the Pope rather than the national monarch.

In England and Ireland, several Acts practically disenfranchised non-Anglicans or non-Protestants by imposing an oath before admission to vote or to run for office. The 1672 and 1678 Test Acts forbade non-Anglicans from holding public offices, the 1727 Disenfranchising Act took away Catholics' (*Papists'*) voting rights in Ireland, which were restored only in 1788. Jews could not even be naturalized. An attempt was made to change this situation, but the Jewish Naturalization Act 1753 provoked such reactions that it was repealed the next year. Nonconformists (Methodists and Presbyterians) were only allowed to run for elections to the British House of Commons in 1828, Catholics in 1829 (following the Catholic Relief Act 1829), and Jews in 1858 (with the Emancipation of the Jews in England). Benjamin Disraeli could only begin his political career in 1837 because he had been converted to Anglicanism at the age of 12.

In several British North American colonies, even the Declaration of Independence, Jews, Quakers or Catholics were denied voting rights and/or forbidden to run for office. The Delaware Constitution of 1776 stated that "Every person who shall be chosen a member of either house, or appointed to any office or place of trust, before taking his seat, or entering upon the execution of his office, shall (...) also make and subscribe the following declaration, to wit: *I, A B. do profess faith in God the Father, and in Jesus Christ His only Son, and in the Holy Ghost, one God, blessed for evermore; and I do acknowledge the holy scriptures of the Old and New Testament to be given by divine inspiration.*". This was repealed by article I, section 2 of the 1792 Constitution: "No religious test shall be required as a qualification to any office, or public trust, under this State.". The 1778 Constitution of the State of South Carolina stated that "No person shall be eligible to sit in the house of representatives unless he be of the Protestant religion", the 1777 Constitution of the State of Georgia (art. VI) that "The representatives shall be chosen out of the residents in each county (...) and they shall be of the Protestent *(sic)* religion". In Maryland, voting rights and eligibility were extended to Jews in 1828.

In Canada, several religious groups (Mennonites, Hutterites, Doukhobors) were disenfranchised by the war-time Elections Act of 1917, mainly because they opposed military service. This disenfranchisement ended with the end of the First World War, but was renewed for Doukhobors from 1934 (*Dominion Elections Act*) to 1955.

The first Constitution of modern Romania in 1866 provided in article 7 that only Christians could become Romanian citizens. Jews native to Romania were declared stateless persons. In 1879, under pressure of the Berlin Peace Conference, this article was amended granting non-Christians the right to become Romanian citizens, but naturalization was granted on a case-by-case basis and was subject to Parliament approval. An application took over ten years to process. Only in 1923 was a new constitution adopted, whose article 133 extended Romanian citizenship to all Jewish residents and equality of rights to all Romanian citizens.

1.7.1.2. Wealth, tax class, social class

Until the nineteenth century, many Western democracies had property qualifications in their electoral laws; e.g. only landowners could vote, or the voting rights were weighed according to the amount of taxes paid (as in the Prussian three-class franchise). Most countries abolished the property qualification for national elections in the late nineteenth century, but retained it for local government elections for several decades. Today these laws have largely been abolished, although the homeless may not be able to register because they lack regular addresses.

In the United Kingdom, prior to the House of Lords Act 1999, peers who were members of the House of Lords were excluded from voting for the House of Commons because they were not commoners. The sovereign is also ineligible to vote in British parliamentary elections.

1.7.1.3. Knowledge

Sometimes the right to vote has been limited to people who had achieved a certain level of education or passed a certain test, e.g. "literacy tests" in some states of the US. In practice, the composition and application of these tests were frequently manipulated so as to functionally limit the electorate on the basis of other characteristics like wealth or race.

1.7.1.4. Race

Various countries, usually with large non-white populations, have historically denied the vote to people of particular races or to non-whites in general. This has been achieved in a number of ways:

— Official—laws and regulations passed specifically disenfranchising people of particular races (for example South Africa under apartheid).

— Indirect—nothing in law specifically prevents anyone from voting on account of their race, but other laws or regulations are used to exclude people of a particular race. In southern states of the U.S. before the passage of the 1965 Voting Rights Act, literacy and other tests were used to disenfranchise African-Americans. Property qualifications have tended to disenfranchise non-whites, particularly if tribally-owned land is not allowed to be taken into consideration. In some cases (such as early colonial New Zealand) property qualifications were deliberately used to disenfranchise non-whites; in other cases this was an unintended (but usually welcome) consequence.

— Unofficial—nothing in law prevents anyone from voting on account of their race, but people of particular races are intimidated or otherwise prevented from exercising this right.

1.7.1.5. Age

All modern democracies require voters to meet age qualifications to vote. Worldwide voting ages are not consistent, differing between countries and even within counties, usually between 16 and 21 years.

1.7.1.6. Criminality

Many countries restrict the voting rights of convicted criminals. Some countries, and some U.S. states, also deny the right to vote to those convicted of serious crimes after they are released from prison. In some cases (e.g. the felony disenfranchisement laws found in many U.S. states) the denial of the right to vote is automatic on a felony conviction; in other cases (e.g. France and Germany) deprivation of the vote is meted out separately, often limited to certain crimes such as those against the electoral system. In the Republic of Ireland, prisoners are not specifically denied the right to vote, but are also not provided access to a ballot station, so are effectively disenfranchised. Canada allowed only prisoners serving a term of less than 2 years the right to vote, but this was found unconstitutional in 2002 by the Supreme Court of Canada in *Sauvé v. Canada (Chief Electoral Officer)*, and all prisoners were allowed to vote as of the 2004 Canadian federal election.

1.7.1.7. Residency

Under certain electoral systems elections are held within subnational jurisdictions, preventing persons who would otherwise be eligible from voting because they do not reside within such a jurisdiction, or because they live in an area which cannot participate. In the United States, residents of Washington, DC receive no voting representation in Congress, although they have (de facto) full representation in presidential elections. Residents of Puerto Rico have neither. Sometimes citizens become ineligible to vote because they are no longer resident in their country of citizenship. For example, Australian citizens who have been outside Australia more than one and less than six years may excuse themselves from the requirement to vote in Australian elections while they remain outside Australia.

1.7.1.8. Nationality

In most countries, suffrage is limited to citizens and, in many cases, permanent residents of that country. However, some members of supra-national organisations such as the Commonwealth of Nations and the European Union have given voting rights to citizens of all countries within that organisation. Until the mid-twentieth century, many Commonwealth countries gave the vote to all British citizens in the country, regardless of whether they were normally resident there. In most cases this was because there was no distinction between British and local citizenship. Several countries qualified this with restrictions preventing non-white British citizens such as Indians and British Africans from voting. Under European Union law, citizens of European Union countries can vote in each others' local and European Parliament elections on the same basis as citizens of the country in question.

1.7.1.9. Naturalization

In some countries, naturalized citizens do not enjoy the right of vote and/or to be candidate, either permanently or for a determined period.

Article 5 of the 1831 Belgian Constitution made a difference between ordinary naturalization, and *grande naturalisation*. Only (former) foreigners who had been granted *grande naturalisation* were entitled to vote or be candidate for parliamentary elections or to be appointed as minister. However, ordinary naturalized citizens could vote for municipal elections. Ordinary naturalized citizens and citizens who had acquired Belgian nationality through marriage were only admitted to vote, but not to be candidate, for parliamentary elections in 1976. The concepts of ordinary and grande naturalization were suppressed from the Constitution in 1991.

In France, the 1889 Nationality Law barred those who had acquired the French nationality by naturalization or marriage from voting, eligibility and access to several public jobs. In 1938 the delay was reduced to 5 years. These discriminations, as well as others against naturalized citizens, were gradually abolished in 1973 (9 January 1973 law) and 1983.

In Morocco, a former French protectorate, and in Guinea, a former French colony, naturalized citizens are prohibited from voting for 5 years after their naturalization. In the Federated States of Micronesia, Micronesian citizenship for a minimum of 15 years is an eligibility condition to be elected to the parliament.

1.7.1.10. Scientific freedom

Scientific freedom is the idea of freedom (in the sense of Freedom of thought and Freedom of the press) applied to natural science, in particular the practices of scientific research and discourse, mainly by publication. The ideal is promoted by many organizations of scientists, and is the subject of article 15 of the International Covenant on Economic, Social and Cultural Rights.

One classic defence of the idea is in Michael Polanyi's book, *Personal Knowledge* (1958). Polanyi criticized the common view that the scientific method is purely objective and generates objective knowledge. Polanyi cast this view as a misunderstanding of the scientific method and of the nature of scientific inquiry, generally. He argued that scientists do and must follow personal passions in appraising facts and in determining which scientific questions to investigate. He concluded that a structure of liberty is essential for the advancement of science—that the freedom to pursue science for its own sake is a prerequisite for the production of knowledge through peer review and the scientific method. Polanyi subsequently co-founded the Society for Freedom in Science.

1.8. Academic Freedom

Academic freedom is the belief that the freedom of inquiry by students and faculty members is essential to the mission of the academy, and that scholars should have freedom to teach or communicate ideas or facts (including those that are inconvenient to external political groups or to authorities) without being targeted for repression, job loss, or imprisonment.

Still, academic freedom has limits. In the United States, for example, according to the widely recognized "1940 Statement on Academic Freedom and Tenure", teachers should be careful to avoid controversial matter that is unrelated to the subject. When they speak or write in public, they are free to express their opinions without fear from institutional censorship or discipline, but they should show restraint and clearly indicate that they are not speaking for their institution. Academic tenure protects academic freedom by ensuring that teachers can be fired only for causes such as gross professional incompetence or behavior that evokes condemnation from the academic community itself.

Proponents of academic freedom believe that the freedom of inquiry by students and faculty members is essential to the mission of the academy. They argue that academic communities are repeatedly targeted for repression due to their ability to shape and control the flow of information. When scholars attempt to teach or communicate ideas or facts that are inconvenient to external political groups or to authorities, they may find themselves targeted for public vilification, job loss, imprisonment, or even death. For example, in North Africa, a professor of public health discovered that his country's infant mortality rate was higher than government figures indicated. He lost his job and was imprisoned.

1.8.1. Academic Freedom for Colleges and Universities

A prominent feature of the English university concept is the freedom to appoint faculty, set standards and admit students. This ideal may be better described as institutional autonomy and is distinct from whatever freedom is granted to students and faculty by the institution.

The Supreme Court of the United States said that academic freedom means a university can "determine for itself on academic grounds:

— who may teach,
— what may be taught,
— how it should be taught, and
— who may be admitted to study."

In a 2008 case, a Federal court in Virginia ruled that professors have no academic freedom; *all* academic freedom resides with the university or college. In that case, *Stronach v. Virginia State University*, a district court judge held "that no constitutional right to academic freedom exists that would prohibit senior (university) officials from changing a grade given by (a professor) to one of his students." The court relied on mandatory precedent of the U.S. Supreme Court case of *Sweezy v. New Hampshire* and a case from the fourth circuit court of appeals. The *Stronach* court also relied on persuasive cases from several circuits of the courts of appeals, including the first, third, and seventh circuits. That court distinguished the situation when a university attempts to coerce a professor into changing a grade, which is clearly in violation of the First Amendment, from when university officials may, in their discretionary authority, change the grade upon appeal by a student. The *Stronach* case has gotten significant attention in the academic community as an important precedent.

1.8.2. Relationship to Freedom of Speech

Academic freedom and free speech rights are not coextensive, although this widely accepted view has been recently challenged by an "institutionalist" perspective on the First Amendment. Academic freedom involves more than speech rights; for example, it includes the right to determine what is taught in the classroom. In practice, academic freedom is protected by institutional rules and regulations, letters of appointment, faculty handbooks, collective bargaining agreements, and academic custom.

References

Acton, John D. 1907. *The History of Freedom and Other Essays*. London: Macmillan. p. 4.

Andrew Puddephatt. 2005. *Freedom of Expression, The essentials of Human Rights*, Hodder Arnold.

Brett, Sebastian. 1999. *Limits to tolerance: freedom of expression and the public debate in Chile*. Human Rights Watch.

Marlin, Randal . 2002. *Propaganda and the Ethics of Persuasion*. Broadview Press.

Guibault, Lucy; & Bernt Hugenholtz . 2006. *The future of the public domain: identifying the commons in information law*. Kluwer Law International.

2

Social Security: Issues and Challenges

In many parts of the world, in the closing years of the twentieth century, social security systems have been under challenge. Some consider that the systems are too expensive, and that they harm the process of economic growth and development. Others point to deficiencies in the level of protection and the scope of coverage, and argue that in times of increased unemployment and other forms of labour insecurity, social security is more needed than ever. Particularly in the industrialised countries (including the transition economies of Central and Eastern Europe), social security systems must respond to new demographic challenges, such as ageing and changing family structures, with important implications for the financing of social protection.

In some countries, there is dissatisfaction with the administration of social security, and calls for reform involve a review of the role of the State, the responsibilities of the social partners and the desirability of greater participation of the private sector. One of the key global problems facing social security today is the fact that more than half of the world's population (workers and their dependants) is excluded from any type of social security protection. They are covered neither by a contribution based social insurance scheme nor by tax-financed social benefits, while a significant additional proportion are covered for only a few contingencies.

In sub-Saharan Africa and South Asia, statutory social security personal coverage is estimated at 5 to 10 per cent of the working population and in some cases is decreasing. In Latin America, coverage lies roughly between 10 and 80 per cent, and is mainly stagnating. In South-East and East Asia, coverage can vary between 10 and almost 100 per cent, and in many cases was until recently increasing. In most industrialised countries, coverage is close to 100 per cent, although in a number of these countries, especially those in transition, compliance rates have fallen in recent years.

In most of its standard-setting and technical cooperation activities on social security, the International Labour Organisation (ILO) had expected that an increasing proportion of the labour force in developing countries would end up in formal-sector employment or self-employment covered by social security. It implicitly assumed that past economic and social development patterns of the industrialised countries would replicate themselves in other regions. However, experience in developing countries and more recently in the industrialised countries has shown that this proportion is in many cases now stagnating or declining. Even in countries with high economic growth, increasing numbers of workers often women are in less secure employment, such as casual labour, home work and certain types of self-employment.

The growth of informal, unprotected work creates dangers for formal and informal economy workers alike. The area of social protection illustrates the very real and direct interest, on the part of workers with "normal" employment status and of their organisations, in bringing informal economy workers into the mainstream of formal employment. With shrinking formal employment, workers bear an increasing direct burden of financing social needs, with adverse effects on their quality of life. That burden may also undermine the capacity of enterprises to compete in the global economy.

2.1. Global Context

Globalisation, either alone or in combination with technological change, often exposes societies to greater income insecurity. Research on the developed countries suggests that income transfers tend to be largest in economies that are simultaneously very open and subject to substantial price risk in world markets. Other observers claim that reductions in income security and social protection arise from the attempts of governments to promote competitiveness and attract foreign direct investment. Some of them also foresee that tax competition will lead to further reductions in taxes, particularly on returns to capital, and lower the ability of governments to finance social protection. The structural adjustment policies pursued in most developing countries have often contributed to a decline in the small percentage of the working population in the formal sector. The successive waves of structural adjustment programmes have also led to wage cuts in the public and private sectors, thereby eroding the financial base of statutory social insurance schemes.

Simultaneously, many such schemes in developing countries have suffered from bad management and bad governance, which have often strongly reduced the trust of their members. In addition, structural adjustment programmes have often resulted in severe cuts in social budgets. In Begin, for example, health expenditure's share in the total government budget dropped from 8.8 to 3.3 per cent between 1987 and 1992. As most governments can no longer guarantee access to free health and education, there is apart from national systems greater demand for international and local arrangements to finance and organise these social services.

Particularly in low-income countries, structural adjustment and socioeconomic changes have also produced large vulnerable groups that cannot contribute to social insurance schemes. The most vulnerable groups outside the labour force are people with disabilities and old people who cannot count on family support, and who have not been able to make provisions for their own pensions. Some countries, such as China and India, have taken specific social assistance measures to meet the needs of these groups.

The world today also faces a large number of complex crises, often with global repercussions. One of the most visible recent examples has been the Asian financial crisis, which led to massive job losses in the formal sector of the economy, rapidly rising unemployment, and an expansion of employment in the informal economy. Then there have been many armed conflicts in recent years, particularly in sub-Saha-34ran Africa (Angola, Congo, Liberia and Rwanda, for example) but also in Europe (Bosnia and Herzegovina, Kosovo). Numerous countries around the world continue to be afflicted by health disasters, such as the HIV/AIDS pandemic, leaving many children orphans.

Natural disasters, such as recurrent droughts and floods (in Africa and Asia), earthquakes and hurricanes (for example in Turkey and Central America) have not only left many communities without homes and sources of income but have also wiped away years of their countries' efforts at development. Lastly, some countries are facing the difficult process of making economic as well as political transitions, whether from a centrally planned economy to a market-oriented system, or from a politically restrictive regime like apartheid to a multiracial and democratic society. Ran Africa (Angola, Congo, Liberia and Rwanda, for example) but also in Europe (Bosnia and Herzegovina, Kosovo).

Numerous countries around the world continue to be afflicted by health disasters, such as the HIV/AIDS pandemic, leaving many children orphans. Natural disasters, such as recurrent droughts and floods (in Africa and Asia), earthquakes and hurricanes have not only left many communities without homes and sources of income but have also wiped away years of their countries' efforts at development. Lastly, some countries are facing the difficult process of making economic as well as political transitions, whether from a centrally planned economy to a market-oriented system, or from a politically restrictive regime like apartheid to a multiracial and democratic society.

The transition in Central and Eastern European countries led to unprecedented unemployment, which still persists in some of these countries. In these countries and in the former USSR the responsibility for income security and certain social services has often shifted from enterprises in the context of centrally planned economies to other, often weak and inadequate, schemes, a situation which threatens to leave many workers with reduced benefits or no protection whatsoever. In South Africa, the peaceful transition from an apartheid political regime to a democratic and inclusive one has not as yet yielded decent jobs, appropriate incomes and improved economic conditions for the majority of the population.

2.2. Social Security and Decent Work

People wish to secure a decent standard of living, within a context of security and of freedom to express their opinion and to associate. They can achieve this income security not only through productive employment, savings and accumulated assets (such as land and housing), but also through social protection mechanisms. These mechanisms function not only as a protective but also as a productive factor. Workers need income security to make long-term plans for themselves and their families. Workers' income security is also good for the economy, since it makes effective demand more predictable and provides enterprises with a more productive and flexible work force.

The objective of most social security schemes is to provide access to health care and income security, i.e. minimum income for those in need and a reasonable replacement income for those who have contributed in proportion to their level of income. The Income Security Recommendation, 1944, for instance, focuses on compulsory national social insurance schemes, which in principle also cover the self-employed, and provides for social assistance. In practice, however, it has been very difficult to implement this concept in the case of workers, such as many of the self-employed, who have irregular patterns of income, for whom the concept of earnings itself is difficult to measure and who generally have different social security needs and priorities.

The emergence of new contributory schemes for workers in the informal economy has highlighted this need for a wider concept. A broader social security concept could cover, for example, some housing, food security and child education benefits, in addition to the contingencies foreseen in the Social Security (Minimum Standards) Convention, 1952 (medical care and family benefits, as well as benefits in the event of sickness, unemployment, old age, employment injury, maternity, invalidity and death of the breadwinner).

Various authors and institutions, in particular those with experience in developing countries, have pleaded for a broader definition of social security. Some claim that within the context of a developmental anti-poverty strategy social security could also include policies, for example on access to productive assets, employment guarantee, minimum wages and food security. Others distinguish two aspects of social security, which are defined as the use of social means to prevent deprivation (promote living standards) and vulnerability to deprivation (protect against falling living standards).

Many international organisations, including the ILO, also use the broader concept of "social protection", which covers not only social security but also non-statutory schemes; the Statistical Office of the European Communities (Eurostat) includes in its figures for social protection certain social services such as creches and home help. The goal and concept of decent work match this broader concept of social security. In his first Report to the International Labour Conference, the Director-General of the International Labour Office, Mr. Juan Synovia, introduced the "decent work for all" strategy, which established as the primary goal of the ILO "to promote opportunities for women and men to obtain decent and productive work, in conditions of freedom, equity, security and human dignity".

The decent work strategy adopts a broad perspective on work, which includes not only (paid) employment, but also work at home so as to take gender roles into consideration. Decent social protection can therefore play an important role in achieving gender equality , if all people working men and women (remunerated or not), as well as children and the elderly can have independent access to social protection. One of the essential features of the decent work approach is that everybody is entitled to basic social protection.

The right to social security for everyone is already laid down in article 9 of the International Covenant on Economic, Social and Cultural Rights. A decent work strategy therefore aims at universality of coverage, which has now been translated into the official goal of the Social Protection Sector: enhancing the coverage and effectiveness of social protection for all. As noted earlier, this goal is far from being achieved.

It is obvious that not all societies can afford the same level of social security. Yet it is inhuman anywhere to live and work in permanent insecurity threatening the material security and health of individuals or families. An essentially rich world can afford a minimum of security for all its inhabitants. That minimum might range from basic health services and basic food, shelter and educational rights in the poorest countries to more elaborate income security schemes in the industrialised countries. Everyone of working age has a responsibility to contribute to the social and economic progress of the community or country he or she lives in and should be given the opportunity to do so. In exchange, all have the right to a fair share of the country's or community's income and wealth.

In a globalising world, where people are increasingly exposed to global economic risks, there is growing consciousness of the fact that a broad-based national social protection policy can provide a strong buffer against many of the negative social effects of crises. However, such a policy might need to be complemented by new international and possibly global financing mechanisms, as proposed by the recent "Social Summit Special Session of the United Nations General Assembly in Geneva. These proposals concern, inter alia, the possible establishment of a (voluntary) World Solidarity Fund, international cooperation in tax matters, debt relief, living up to development aid commitments and the provision of more concession financing.

2.3. Social Security, Employment and Development

There is considerable controversy about the social and economic effects of social security, and most of the current debate is focused on its supposedly negative effects. Social security is said to discourage people from working and saving, to reduce international competitiveness and employment creation, and to encourage people to withdraw from the labour market prematurely. On the other hand, social security can also be seen to have a number of very positive economic effects. It can help to make people capable of earning an income and to increase their productive potential; it may help to maintain effective demand at the national level; and it may help create conditions in which a market economy can flourish, notably by encouraging workers to accept innovation and change.

Social protection and decent employment are both necessary components for a market economy to provide income security for all. Social protection is also designed to have important positive effects on society as a whole, by promoting social cohesion and a general feeling of security among its members.

Unemployment is one of the greatest social risks facing people who depend for their livelihood on the sale of their labour power. Yet unemployment benefit systems exist only in a minority of countries and many workers, including almost all the self-employed, are not covered by them. Protection against the risk of unemployment is provided not only by benefits but also by measures of employment protection (such as protection against dismissal and promotion.

2.4. Socioeconomic Impact of Social Security

The mechanisms by which social protection influences socioeconomic development involve the behaviour of individuals, as workers and job seekers, as savers, as portfolio investors and as members of civil society. They involve the decisions of firms and enterprises, and the operation of markets, including the determination of wages and prices.

In the case of the labour market, social protection has an impact on labour force participation. Benefits can encourage people to leave the labour force, for example where there is provision for early retirement. Conversely, social protection may induce people to participate in the formal economy, on account of the prospective entitlement to pensions and other benefits. Social protection can also have an impact on employment. Do benefits cause people to be slower about finding a new job when they are unemployed? Does unemployment benefit allow better worker/ employer matches? Then there is the question of the extent of productive labour input.

Do sickness benefits reduce hours worked, by encouraging absence from work, or is such an effect offset by the way they help promote quick recovery and prevent the spread of infection among the work force? Does social protection form part of a package which causes workers to be more productive? Answering these questions is not easy, as other variables have to be held constant in order to isolate the effects of social protection. It may be added that, if effects on worker productivity are considered here, this in no way disregards the fact that social protection finds its primary justification in the impact it has on workers' well-being. In the capital market, the existence of state pensions is held by some economists to have reduced the rate of personal savings.

2.4.1. Productivity and Social Stability

It has been suggested by various commentators that social security contributes to economic growth by raising labour productivity and enhancing social stability.

Various types of social security are particularly relevant to labour productivity:

—Health-care systems help to maintain workers in good health and to cure those who become sick. Poor health is a major cause of low productivity in many developing countries where workers do not have access to adequate health care. Not only does it limit their ability to cope with the physical demands of their jobs, but it also leads to sickness absence and can seriously undermine efficiency even among workers who do not absent themselves from work. Care for workers' family members helps to ensure the good health of the future labour force.

— Pension systems ease the departure of older workers from the labour force, thereby helping to avoid the problem of workers remaining in employment when their productivity has fallen to a low level.

— Cash sickness benefit contributes to the recovery of sick workers by removing the financial pressure to carry on working when ill. It also helps to maintain the productivity of other workers by countering the spread of infection.

— Maternity insurance is of particular importance for the reproduction of a healthy work force, as well as for the maintenance of the health of working mothers.

— Work injury schemes the oldest and most widespread form of social security are playing an increasingly important role in preventing work-related accidents and sickness and in rehabilitating workers who fall victim to these. Such activities are of considerable relevance to productivity, given the enormous numbers of days off work attributable to avoidable health risks.

— Unemployment benefit provides unemployed workers with the breathing space they need in order to find suitable work which makes full use of their talents and potential; the associated employment and training services are also highly relevant in this respect.

— Child benefits (and other cash benefits provided when the breadwinner is unable to work) help to ensure that families with children have enough income to provide proper nutrition and a healthy living environment for their children. In developing countries, child benefits can also be a powerful instrument to combat child labour and promote school attendance. Children can thus receive an education that will permit them in the long run to attain much higher levels of productivity and income.

More indirect effects on productivity may also be important. The existence of a good unemployment insurance system creates a feeling of security among the work force which can greatly facilitate structural change and technological innovations that workers might otherwise perceive as a great threat to their livelihoods. The link between these issues was graphically illustrated in the Republic of Korea by the Tripartite Accord of 1998 under which workers' organisations accepted greater labour market flexibility, including layoffs, in exchange for better social protection.

Social security helps create a more positive attitude not just to structural and technological change, but also to the challenges of globalisation and to its potential benefits in terms of greater efficiency and higher productivity. Countries with relatively open national economies (a high ratio of trade to GDP) and high exposure to external risks (high variability in the relative prices of imports and exports) have been observed to provide high levels of social security. It appears that societies which expose themselves to more external risk demand a higher degree of social protection.

Globalisation and social security thus tend to be mutually reinforcing. Social security can be an important factor in the maintenance of effective demand and of business confidence. This effect is most obvious in the case of unemployment benefits, which help to maintain the purchasing power of workers who have lost their jobs. However, other social security benefits also act as an economic buffer during a recession or crisis. Without them, the multiplier effects of the first round of job losses could be followed by second and third rounds that could cut deep into the social fabric of the community, as well as leaving much of the economy working well below capacity. Social security thus helps to prevent production from falling too far and to keep companies in business, with their work force intact, ready to participate in the upswing when it comes.

2.4.2. Employer Contributions

Widespread concern has been expressed in business and political circles that high employer contributions to social security make national economies less competitive, a claim frequently heard in discussions of globalisation. Most economists, however, have taken the view that in the long run, through the normal working of market forces, these costs will be borne by workers in the form of lower wages (lower, that is, than they would receive in an identical economy without any payroll tax or employer social security contributions).

Social security contributions do not have any long-run impact on unemployment. This helps to explain why Denmark, the only country in Europe with virtually no employer contributions, has over the years had unemployment on a par with the European average and appears to derive no special employment advantage from its lack of such contributions. Governments often believe that a reduction in social security contributions will reduce labour costs. The experience of Chile before and after its social security pension reform has been investigated in order to establish the impact of the sharp reduction in contributions.

The average payroll tax rate in the sample of manufacturing firms covered by the research fell from 30 per cent to 5 per cent over the period between 1979 and 1985. Strong evidence is found that the reduction was fully offset by higher wages, leaving labour costs unreduced. All this should not be taken to suggest that there is no limit to the level of social security contributions. In any democratic society the political preferences of the majority most certainly impose a limit. Depending on what people perceive as desirable and fair, that limit is much lower in some countries than others. Moreover, if the level of contributions rises very high, this creates strong incentives for noncompliance, which if not controlled will seriously undermine the system.

Much research has been carried out to investigate the hypothesis that the average duration of unemployment benefit receipt is positively related both to the level of unemployment benefits (the replacement ratio) and to the maximum duration of benefit. Various studies have confirmed that significant relationships exist, but that their effects are modest. An important question left unanswered by many of these studies is what happens to people once they cease to receive unemployment benefit. It cannot simply be assumed that they find regular employment.

Recent work has investigated this issue. In Bulgaria those without unemployment benefit are more likely to leave registered unemployment, but it is to inactivity rather than to employment. In Slovakia, changes in eligibility periods result in people leaving unemployment not so much to take up regular jobs as for "other reasons". People in Sweden not receiving unemployment benefit were found to be much more likely to leave the labour market or to take up places in active labour market programmes. In other countries those who cease to receive unemployment benefit often move into informal or even criminal activities, resulting in massive tax evasion and other costs to society.

Since lack of benefit entitlement may simply be causing people to quit the labour force, it may be more important to examine the relationship between unemployment benefit and employment: after all the real concern is that people may be drawing unemployment benefit when they could be employed instead. A recent study concluded, on the basis of cross-country evidence, that there is in fact no connection between unemployment benefits and total employment. This study also found that high unemployment was associated with the absence of complementary active labour market policies.

2.4.2.1. Early Retirement

In recent years there has been great concern about the adverse effects which early retirement provisions may have upon employment as well as upon pension costs. These had been introduced during periods of high unemployment, particularly among older workers, in the hope of creating more job openings for younger workers. As unemployment has fallen, early retirement provisions in numerous social security systems have been tightened or even abolished. However, there has been little or no change in retirement behaviour. This paradox is explained by a number of factors:

- The proportion of older workers receiving unemployment benefits remains relatively high and includes many who have, for all intents and purposes, retired.
- Employer pension schemes often contain strong incentives to retire early.
- Even workers without unemployment benefits or private pension entitlements are quitting the labour force before standard

pensionable age, many of them manual workers for whom demand is low and who are often in poor health.

2.4.2.2. Unemployment Benefits

It was estimated that at the end of 1998 some 1 billion workers or one-third of the world's labour force were either unemployed or underemployed. The actual number of unemployed people that is, seeking or available for work but unable to find it was about 150 million. In addition, 25 to 30 per cent of the world's workers were underemployed, that is, either working substantially less than full time, but wishing to work longer, or earning less than a living wage. It is striking to see not only how many workers are affected in absolute terms, but also how rapidly the situation can change.

For example, as a result of the Asian financial crisis, one in 20 workers in the Republic of Korea lost their jobs during the nine months from November 1997 to July 1998 and open unemployment jumped from 2.3 to 8 per cent between the end of 1997 and the beginning of 1999. Unemployment benefit systems protect employees in the industrialised countries and in a number of middle-income developing countries. In most developing countries no unemployment benefits exist as such, but some of the unemployed may be able to get a limited amount of paid work in labour-intensive programmes. Of the world's unemployed, probably not more than a quarter are entitled to unemployment benefit.

2.4.2.3. International Labour Standards

The most recently adopted instruments are the Employment Promotion and Protection against Unemployment convention, 1988, and Recommendation. The contingencies covered by the Convention include full unemployment "defined as the loss of earnings due to inability to obtain suitable employment in the case of a person capable of working, available for work and actually seeking work". Member States shall in addition endeavour to extend the protection of the Convention to two other contingencies:

— Loss of earnings due to partial unemployment (short-time working).

— Suspension or reduction of earnings due to a temporary suspension of work; as well as to part-time workers who are actually seeking full-time work.

Persons protected under the Convention "shall comprise prescribed classes of employees, constituting not less than 85 percent of all employees". Compared with previous Conventions dealing with unemployment benefit, an innovative feature of Convention No. 168 is that it requires the payment of "social benefits" to at least three of the following ten categories of new applicants for employment:

— Young persons who have completed their vocational training; young people who have completed their studies.

— Young people who have completed their compulsory military service.

— People seeking work after a period devoted to bringing up a child or caring for someone who is sick, disabled or elderly.

— People whose spouse had died, when they are not entitled to a survivor's benefit.

— Divorced or separated persons.

— Released prisoners; adults, including disabled persons, who have completed a period of training.

— Migrant workers returning to their home country (except in so far as they have acquired rights under the legislation of the country where they last worked).

— Previously self-employed persons.

The benefits under the Convention are not less than 50 per cent of previous earnings in earnings-related systems, while in other types of system they must be fixed at not less than 50 per cent of the minimum wage or of the wage of an ordinary labourer, or at a level that provides the minimum essential for basic living expenses, whichever of the three is the highest.

2.4.3. Industrialised Countries

Within the industrialised countries there is substantial variation in unemployment benefit systems. One group of countries is characterised by the high level and long duration of their unemployment insurance benefits, by extensive coverage and by the existence of a fall-back benefit system of unemployment assistance for workers who have exhausted their insurance entitlements. These countries include Austria, Belgium, Denmark, Finland, France, Germany, Iceland, Luxembourg, Netherlands, Norway, Portugal, Spain, Sweden and Switzerland. They generally have not only good benefits, but also a high level of employment protection. A second group of countries, including Australia, Canada, Japan, New Zealand, the United Kingdom and the United States, have systems which provide lower benefits.

According to the OECD employment protection ranking, the legal arrangements in these countries apparently provide relatively little statutory employment protection. The countries of Central and Eastern Europe introduced unemployment benefit systems about the end of the 1980s which were initially rather generous, but have since been reduced, particularly in terms of benefit duration. Benefit levels as a percentage of wages are similar to those in Western Europe, but a much lower proportion of the unemployed receive benefits in these countries for example, about one-third of the registered unemployed in Poland.

Unemployment benefit schemes have become more and more inadequate as individual employment patterns have become increasingly uncertain. These schemes therefore have to be flexible enough to cover new uncertainties and changes facing workers and have to form part of larger strategies for employment and economic development. Employment protection policies in the industrialised countries have been concerned in particular with the high rates of unemployment affecting unskilled workers.

One approach has stressed the need for better education and training to ensure that workers have the skills that are in demand in a high-wage, high-productivity economy. Another approach has been to use social protection to subsidise unskilled labour, either through the payment of income-tested benefits to the working poor or through the (partial or total) exemption of their employers from paying social insurance contributions on their behalf (with the cost being borne by the State).

2.4.4. Middle-Income Developing Countries

Unemployment benefit systems are at best in their formative stages in the middle-income developing countries: the duration and level of benefits are generally low and coverage is much more limited than in the industrialised countries. On the other hand, formal-sector employees are covered by various forms of employment protection legislation in a number of middle-income developing countries, including some that do not have any unemployment benefits. The legislation typically includes severance pay, which can help to tide redundant workers over a period of unemployment.

However, these are lump-sum payments, the size of which depends on the length of previous service, not on the occurrence or duration of unemployment. Severance payments have traditionally been an employer's liability. However, in some Latin American countries in the 1990s they were replaced by mandatory severance savings schemes. This change has meant that the funds are invested in the capital market rather than retained within the firm. While this introduces uncertainty as to the amount of benefit that workers will receive, it guards against the risk that an insolvent employer may fail to provide severance pay.

Most unemployment benefit schemes in the developing countries, as in the industrialised world, are financed by employer and worker contributions, but in certain Latin American countries such as Brazil and Chile they are financed from tax revenue. Where unemployment benefits exist, the proportion of the total unemployed receiving them tends to be low. The replacement rate (benefits as a proportion of previous wages) varies between 40 and 80 per cent in Latin America and the Caribbean and is 45 per cent in South Africa.

Benefit duration tends to be fairly limited and is often related to the length of time that the worker has been insured. In China the locally set rates of unemployment benefit are generally low. Hong Kong, China, provides benefits on a means-tested basis as part of its social assistance system to registered unemployed persons with at least one year's residence. The Republic of Korea has expanded its unemployment insurance system to cover about half of all employees, but those in small enterprises who are often the most vulnerable are still excluded.

The recent Asian financial crisis has made it clear that unemployment insurance schemes could have played a substantial role in coping with the unacceptable levels of hardship caused by rapidly escalating unemployment. They would also have helped to limit the collapse of consumer demand and business confidence which made the crisis much more acute than it would otherwise have been. As was shown in an ILO feasibility study carried out for the Government of Thailand, the contribution rate necessary to finance a modest unemployment insurance scheme would in the long run be less than 1 per cent of earnings.

Implementing unemployment insurance in the context of a developing country represents a considerable challenge. Employment services, where they exist, tend to be rudimentary and have to be upgraded in order to provide meaningful help to unemployed workers to find other work, as well as to monitor whether they are in fact willing and available to take up employment.

A second problem is that much employment in these countries is not effectively covered by social security either because it is excluded from the legislation, which may apply only to workers in firms above a certain size, or because employers and workers do not comply with the legislation. The reality for most workers in developing countries, even countries in the middle-income category, is that their jobs are not covered, because they are self-employed or because they are employed in the informal economy or in small enterprises. To help protect them in the event of unemployment, other measures are needed, such as the opportunity to obtain employment in labour-intensive public works. It is important to note that when people lose their jobs and have no access to benefits, they must usually resort to informal-sector activity in order to survive: they may therefore be more accurately described as underemployed than unemployed.

2.4.5. Other Developing Countries

In so far as other developing countries have taken measures to provide some protection for the unemployed and underemployed, these have tended to take the form of employment-intensive programmes. These are undertaken mainly during the lean season, when small farmers and landless workers are not engaged in agricultural activities and have no alternative sources of employment. In an urban setting they can also be implemented during periods of recession or economic crisis.

These programmes can both generate employment and reduce poverty by using labour-based techniques for mainstream investment programmes and by directing investments increasingly towards the productive and social needs of the low-income groups in the population. Some programmes of this type operate on a large scale. For example, the Jawahar Rozgar Yojana (JRY) programme in India by the mid-1990s covered over one-third of the country's underdeveloped districts and provided some 20 days' work a year to each participant. Similar programmes operate on a smaller scale in countries such as Bolivia, Botswana, Chile, Honduras, Kenya, the United Republic of Tanzania and (recently) South Africa, and the umbrella organisation AFRICATIP groups together some 18 executing agencies in French- and Portuguese-speaking African countries which organise public works for implementation by small local contractors, with a view to boosting employment.

A salient feature of employment-intensive programmes is that they "self-select" the people who participate in them. Since they pay only the going agricultural wage in the region (or the minimum wage if this is set realistically), only low-income workers are attracted to them. This avoids the cumbersome and costly administrative arrangements that would be necessary if assistance were to be provided to such people on a means-tested basis. The programmes have the advantage that they are open both to wage earners and to people who normally work on their own account (whose needs may in some cases be just as great). Employment under a labour-intensive programme can be organised so that workers can obtain an employment guarantee for a certain number of days per year, which thus provides a kind of income security. The guarantee is most extensive where employment is provided on demand.

Social security policies are part of and interact with a wide range of social policies, such as investments in basic social services, protective labour legislation and the enforcement of basic rights. They are also intimately related to employment policies, because most social insurance schemes are financed out of labour incomes and protect against risks related to employment capacity, such as unemployment, sickness, disability and old age. Favourable social security and employment outcomes are strongly influenced by economic development, and all of them contribute to the process of socioeconomic development.

Docial security is increasingly seen as an integral part of the development process. It is therefore necessary to look for asynergies between policies for social protection, employment and development. These asynergies exist in various areas of social policy, such as health, education, housing and social welfare, but also in areas of economic policy, such as macroeconomic and sectorial policies (for instance, small-scale enterprise development). However, the potential asynergies are probably strongest with regard to employment and labour market policies.

References

Modigliani, Franco. 2004. *Rethinking pension reform* . Franco Modigliani, Arun Muralidhar. Cambridge, UK ; New York : Cambridge University Press,

Muralidhar, Arun S. 2001. *Innovations in pension fund management* / Arun S. Muralidhar. Stanford, Calif.Stanford Economics + Finance.

Arno Tausch, (Ed) 2003. "The Three Pillars of Wisdom? A Reader on Globalization, World Bank Pension Models and Welfare Society" Nova Science Hauppauge, New York.

Peter Middlebrook , 2009. *When the Public Works: Generating Employment and Social Protection in Ethiopia*. Lambert Academic Publishing.

3

Right to Social Security

International instruments adopted by the ILO and the United Nations affirm that every human being has the right to social security. In the Declaration of Philadelphia the International Labour Conference recognised the ILO's obligation as regards "the extension of social security measures to provide a basic income to all in need of such protection and comprehensive medical care". The ILO's Income Security Recommendation, 1944, provides that "social insurance should afford protection, in the contingencies to which they are exposed, to all employed and self-employed persons, together with their dependants".

The Universal Declaration of Human Rights, 1948, states that "everyone, as a member of society, has the right to social security", and refers specifically to the right to medical care and necessary social services, to security in the event of sickness, disability, widowed, old age and unemployment, and to special care and assistance for motherhood and childhood. The International Covenant on Economic, Social and Cultural Rights, 1966, recognises "the right of everyone to social security, including social insurance".

It goes without saying that the practical implementation of this right requires a major undertaking by the State and the community. The ILO's social security Conventions recognise that in practice the ideal may be difficult to attain. For example, the Social Security (Minimum Standards) Convention, 1952 requires in the case of sickness and old-age benefits, for instance, that persons covered shall comprise:

— Prescribed classes of employees, constituting not less than 50 per cent of all employees.
— Prescribed classes of the economically active population, constituting not less than 20 per cent of all residents.
— All residents whose means during the contingency do not exceed prescribed limits.

These alternatives are intended to facilitate ratification of the Convention by countries, whatever type of social security system they may have. Later Conventions such as the Invalidity, Old-Age and Survivors' Benefits Convention, 1967, contain more exacting standards, but provide a similar choice. The Plantations Convention, 1958, applies to workers hired by agricultural undertakings in the tropical or subtropical regions of the world. In terms of social security its standards are less exacting than those of Convention No. 102. It requires that plantation workers be covered by workers' compensation and maternity protection, including a minimum of 12 weeks' paid leave. The Convention also contains provisions relating to medical care.

During the 1990s new ILO instruments have sought to promote social security coverage for persons outside regular wage employment. Thus, the Home Work Convention, 1996, provides that national policy on home work shall promote, as far as possible, equality of treatment between home workers and other wage earners in areas including statutory social security protection and maternity protection. The accompanying Recommendation proposes that social protection can be achieved through the extension and adaptation of existing social security schemes and/or through the development of special schemes or funds.

The Job Creation in Small and Medium-Sized Enterprises Recommendation, 1998, recommends that labour and social legislation be reviewed inter alia to determine whether social protection extends to workers in these enterprises, whether there are adequate provisions to ensure compliance with social security regulations covering the standard contingencies and whether there is a need for supplementary social protection measures for workers in these categories. The Part-Time Work Convention, 1994, states that social security schemes shall be adapted so that part-time workers enjoy conditions equivalent to those of comparable full-time workers.

3.1. Problem of Non-Coverage

A very large proportion of the population in most regions of the world still does not enjoy any social protection or is covered only very partially. This is the case for the vast majority of people in developing countries, and even in some of the richest industrialised countries there are large and growing gaps in social protection. Informal economy workers are not covered by social security for a variety of reasons. One is the extreme difficulty of collecting contributions from them and, as the case may be, from their employers.

Another problem is that many of these workers are unable to contribute a relatively high percentage of their incomes to financing social security benefits and unwilling to do so when these benefits do not meet their priority needs. Their most immediate priorities tend to include health care, in particular where structural adjustment measures have reduced access to free services. They feel less need for pensions, for example, as for many of them old age appears very remote and the idea of retirement perhaps unreal. Unfamiliarity with social security schemes and distrust of the way they are managed add to their reluctance to contribute.

The problem of low coverage is of course not new, especially in countries where large numbers of people work in subsistence agriculture. However, in recent years, prospects of resolving or at least mitigating it have taken a dramatic turn for the worse, as an increasing proportion of the urban labour force is working in the informal economy, inter alia as a result of structural adjustment. In Latin America and many other parts of the developing world in recent years most of the increase in the urban labour force has taken place in the informal economy. In most countries of Africa, a growing proportion of the urban labour force is active in the informal economy, reflecting the (at best) sluggish growth of wage employment, the massive migration to the cities and the need for workers to supplement falling wages with earnings from the informal economy. For example, in the case of Kenya, informal employment accounted for almost two-thirds of total urban employment in 1996, compared with just 10 per cent in 1972.

Several developing countries of Asia have expanded wage employment substantially but the informal economy remains very important almost everywhere. In India, for example, if agriculture is included, more than 90 per cent of workers are to be found in the informal economy. It should be noted that the informal economy is not a "sector" as such. It is in fact a phenomenon to be found in almost all sectors. And it includes workers of all different categories: employees, self-employed, home workers, unpaid family workers, etc. Informations is not restricted to small-scale enterprises; in many countries it includes unregulated wage labour throughout the economy: in Argentina and Brazil, for example, approximately 40 per cent of urban wage earners are in informal employment.

In many countries a higher proportion of women work in the informal economy, to some extent because there they can more easily combine work with their heavier burden of family responsibilities, and partly for other reasons related, for example, to discrimination encountered in the formal economy. ILO statistics show that in two-thirds of the countries for which separate figures are available, the informal economy accounts for a higher share of total female urban employment than is the case for men. There is a widespread tendency for women to remain trapped in the informal economy for much of their working lives, whereas for men in the industrialised countries at any rate it is less likely to be permanent. For long-term income security (in old age for instance), this difference has especially important implications, as women tend to live longer than men.

- Informal economy workers have little or no security of employment or income.
- Their earnings tend to be very low and to fluctuate more than those of other workers.
- A brief period of incapacity can leave the worker and her or his family without enough income to live on.
- The sickness of a family member can result in costs which destroy the delicate balance of the household budget.
- Work in the informal economy is often intrinsically hazardous and the fact that it takes place in an unregulated environment makes it still more so.
- Women face additional disadvantages due to discrimination related to their reproductive role, such as dismissal when pregnant, or upon marriage.

Women in the informal economy do not benefit from safeguards and benefits related to child-rearing that in principle apply to women in formal wage employment (such as family allowances, paid maternity leave, nursing breaks or assistance with the cost of child care). It is now widely recognised that there is a pressing need to find effective ways to extend social protection. The recent past has seen a stagnation in the proportion of the labour force covered. Given current economic trends, failure to take action is very likely to lead to a reduction in the rate of coverage or even in the absolute numbers of workers protected, as has occurred in parts of sub-Saharan Africa.

3.2. Policies to Achieve the Extension of Coverage

Outside the industrialised world, policy-makers have found few remedies for the lack of social protection. This may be because existing social protection policies are inappropriate. It may be because insufficient efforts have been made to implement these policies. Or it may be because the lack of social protection is related to much wider economic, social and political problems. If policy-makers define the problem too narrowly, their chances of finding feasible solutions may be greatly reduced. It is therefore necessary to give due consideration to the wider context in which social security systems have to operate.

3.2.1. Economic, Social and Political Context

The first point to consider is the nature of a country's governance. Among market economies, experience shows that, with few exceptions, there tends to be a correlation between the level of democracy and the adequacy of social protection. For the most vulnerable members of the population to have their needs for health care and basic income security met, it is vital that they should at least be able to make their voices heard. In the long run a democracy which does not ensure adequate social protection is unlikely to survive.

The second issue which must be considered is the macroeconomic situation and the state of the labour market. The scope of social protection is likely to extend naturally (the means by which it may do so are considered below) if and only if the labour market is strong. So long as demand for labour remains weak, few people will obtain decent jobs and most will depend on ill-paid and unprotected work in the informal economy. Conversely, if the demand for labour increases, more workers may look forward to better-paid and generally better-protected employment in the formal economy. However, the informal economy in its many manifestations is hardly likely to disappear either naturally or quickly, and it is of the greatest importance that governments work towards social protection policies, which must be both innovative and imaginative, that will promote improved conditions for such workers.

A third point is that excessive demands should not be placed on social security systems. They are no substitute for adequate macroeconomic, regional education and housing policies and they cannot be expected to achieve a fair distribution of income on their own. Many social security systems redistribute from the rich to the poor, but this is not their main objective. The prime objective is to provide security for people when they are sick, disabled, unemployed, retired, etc.

Schemes which represent reasonable value for money for all the insured have the best chance in practice of achieving high compliance rates, that is, of ensuring that legislation providing for wide coverage is actually implemented. Social security is just part albeit an important part of the broader package of measures necessary to reduce poverty and improve income distribution.

Finally, public confidence in social security systems is crucial if they are to attain and maintain wide coverage. This requires not only efficient administration and high standards of financial probity, but also a strong degree of commitment by the government itself to ensure the long-run health of the system. Where this confidence is lacking, people will always find ways to avoid contributing, even though their need for social protection may be very high.

3.2.2. Strategies for Extending Social Protection

There are essentially four ways to extend social protection:

— Extending social insurance schemes.

— Encouraging micro insurance.

— Introducing universal benefits or services financed from general state revenues.

— Establishing or extending means-tested benefits or services (social assistance), also financed from general state revenues.

None of these approaches should be excluded a priori. The appropriate mix of different mechanisms will depend on the national context and on the national strategy adopted. Careful thought has to be given to their respective roles and to the linkages between them. Achieving a better understanding of these is essential if progress is to be made. There is a need for research, experimentation and innovation.

No doubt, in this process, distinctions will be drawn between groups of countries, depending on their level of economic and social development. Within the developing countries, there are those in the middle-income category, some of which already have well-developed social security institutions. These countries, and indeed the industrialised countries where coverage is incomplete, may aim at extending compulsory coverage to all or most of the population, using the existing social insurance schemes or modifying them to suit the needs of the new categories of the population to be covered. Secondly, there is the large group of low-income countries where, if any real increase in coverage is to be achieved, it will almost certainly have to be by some of the other means mentioned above.

3.2.3. Extending Social Insurance Schemes

Whenever social insurance schemes have been made compulsory for a limited section of the labour force in the formal economy, legislators have usually envisaged extending their coverage at a later stage. The initial restriction of coverage has almost invariably been justified by invoking practical constraints: for example, the administrative infrastructure did not exist which would permit the collection of contributions from workers in small firms or from the self-employed, or health-care facilities did not exist in rural areas, so workers there could not be required to contribute. These reasons were and, in many cases, remain perfectly valid. However, the question that should always be asked is what is being done to remove these constraints. Unfortunately, the answer in many cases is that very little has been or is being done, and this for a variety of reasons:

— A lack of effective political pressure from those who are not protected and limited awareness of the benefits that social protection can bring.

— A lack of effective and efficient social partnership within certain countries and at the international level.
— The unwillingness or inability of governments to assume new and potentially costly commitments.
— Institutional inertia.

The first and, to some extent, the second reasons reflect the relatively low level of organisation among people who are unprotected. The third reason has to do with the fact that subsidies, which governments sometimes provide for the minority of the population covered by the existing system, would become very much more expensive if protection were significantly extended.

As for the fourth, the institutions which prepare proposals to extend coverage are often those responsible for administering the existing system and often have to do so in difficult conditions; they may have little incentive to propose extensions of coverage where these would make it still harder for them to discharge their existing responsibilities. Removing constraints on freedom of association and strengthening democratic institutions would help address the first problem and measures to foster collective bargaining and tripartite institutions would be relevant to the second.

The adverse implications for the state budget of extending social insurance coverage could be attenuated by a reduction or re-orientation or, if necessary, the elimination of state subsidies particularly where they benefit only a minority and could not conceivably be extended to the majority of the work force. As for institutional inertia, this may be at least partially remedied by government action, for example to release the social security institution from civil service rules when these impose unrealistic limits on staffing and on pay levels, and to give it clear instructions to formulate, within a certain time frame, legislative proposals to extend coverage.

Most commonly, compulsory coverage is extended in stages by bringing into the scheme successively smaller enterprises. Each extension naturally expands the number of insured workers, but disproportionately increases the number of enterprises with which the social security system must deal. The smaller enterprises may present additional problems, given their rudimentary accounts and arrangements for paying workers and their stronger tendency to noncompliance. Many less developed social security systems understandably hesitate to try covering all employees, including those in the smallest enterprises.

However, experience in numerous countries has now shown that it is feasible. Indeed, it can be advantageous to abandon any threshold and so remove an incentive for employers to report artificially low numbers of workers. Many enterprises usually claim to be just below the threshold, and it is very difficult in practice to prove otherwise. Besides, a rule which encourages enterprises to remain small can seriously hamper their development and constrain productivity growth. The most compelling reason for covering even the smallest enterprises is that it is their workers who tend to be the lowest paid and to have least job security they need social security even more than other employees.

Attempts to extend existing social insurance schemes to cover the self-employed have met with mixed success. Few join these schemes on a voluntary basis, as they are unwilling and indeed frequently unable to pay the combined worker and employer contribution. Only in some cases do people not subject to compulsory coverage have a strong incentive to contribute voluntarily, for example in order to preserve their pension entitlements or to complete the minimum period required to qualify for a pension.

As for compulsory coverage of the self-employed, this is difficult to achieve, given the problems involved in identifying who the self-employed are and what they earn. Some special schemes for self-employed workers tend to have more success, particularly if the government is willing to subsidise them. Specially adapted social insurance schemes can take account of the lower contributory capacity of most self-employed workers by providing a more limited benefit package than the employees' scheme.

Lower contributions and concentration on benefits which are of greatest interest to the self-employed (recent ILO work in several developing countries suggests that these include not only health care, but also survivors' and invalidity insurance) make it easier to achieve compliance. Most of the financial support currently given (via tax concessions) to voluntary coverage tends to go to supplementary private pension and health insurance schemes and thus to favour the higher-income groups. It is important to quantify the support that the State gives to such schemes. Such data will inform the public debate on social protection and help to define priorities in the use of public resources, so that in future state support for voluntary coverage could be much better targeted than it is now.

3.4. Examples of Extensions of Compulsory Coverage

In 1995 Namibia launched a new scheme covering maternity, sickness and death (funeral) benefits. By 1999 an estimated 80 per cent of formal sector workers were covered and the scheme enjoyed wide popularity. The scheme provides three months of maternity benefit at 80 per cent of covered wages, and up to two years of sickness benefit at 60 per cent of wages for six months and 50 per cent thereafter. The success of the scheme is attributed to its efficient administration, its low contributions and the absence of organised financial interests opposing it.

Following Bill Clinton's first election as President of the United States, one of his nominees for a senior administration appointment was asked during her confirmation hearing whether she had paid social security contributions for the person she employed to look after her young child. It turned out that she had not and the same was the case of many other nominees. Congress then rewrote the law in order to improve enforcement. The changes made it easier to pay the contributions and increased the penalties for not doing so. Many more domestic workers were subsequently covered.

The Republic of Korea's national pension system, which previously covered 7.8 million workers, was extended in 1999 to cover a further 8.9 million persons, comprising the urban self-employed and employees of firms with fewer than five workers. The previous year the unemployment insurance scheme, initially applicable from 1995 only to employees in firms with 30 or more workers, was extended, as planned, to firms with ten or more workers; later the same year, as a result of an agreement reached in the Tripartite Commission, the scheme was further extended to workers in enterprises with five or more workers and in 1999 to part-timers. In Spain the 1986 legislation establishing a national health service extended health care to 99.8 per cent of the population by the 1990s, bringing in all dependants of insured persons (regardless of age), recipients of social pensions and those who had previously had to have their health care financed out of poor relief.

3.5. Specific Schemes for Informal Economy Workers

In recent years various groups of workers in the informal economy have set up their own micro insurance schemes. In these schemes, the insurance is independently managed at the local level and sometimes the local unit links into larger structures that can enhance both the insurance function and the support structures needed for improved governance. Such schemes typically have the advantages of cohesion and direct participation, although this is not true of provider-based systems.

They can also achieve low administrative costs, but views differ widely about their cost-effectiveness. They may operate within the context of a credit scheme, such as the Grameen Bank, which has already had experience with the collection of contributions and administration of payments. On the other hand, as in Argentina, mutual benefit organisations may set up credit schemes in order to subsidise their activity in the field of health care.

They have in some cases developed jointly with organisations such as the Self-Employed Women's Association (SEWA) of India which have a good understanding of the needs of their members. The term "micro insurance" refers to the ability to handle small-scale cash flows (by way of both income and expenditure), not to the size of the scheme, although often such schemes are in fact local and have a very small membership. The primary aim of many of these schemes is to help their members meet unpredictable out-of pocket medical expenses. They do not usually aspire to provide comprehensive health insurance, still less to pay income replacement benefits.

It is estimated that these schemes usually attract about 25 per cent or less of the target population in the localities where they exist. The only schemes which manage to achieve high penetration rates (between 50 and 100 per cent) are those in particularly close-knit communities or those that all members of the target group (such as a trade union or professional association) are required to join. This percentage, though far from satisfactory, is much higher than that achieved by social insurance schemes open on a voluntary basis to all the self-employed, no doubt because micro insurance contributions are very much lower and because the schemes focus on providing only those benefits which are perceived by people as most urgently necessary.

These schemes may have the potential to increase social protection coverage substantially, by collaborating with each other and by working together with statutory social insurance schemes, local and national government and other large-scale organisations. There are various ways in which the State can promote micro insurance schemes:

— Financial support: help with setup costs, facilitating re-insurance options, payment of subsidies in the form of matching contributions, etc.

— Creation of a legislative and regulatory framework within which such schemes may operate, for example ensuring democratic and economically sound management. It remains to validate the potential of micro insurance schemes in practice. Arguably there is justification for these schemes to receive more support and certainly they should be the subject of further research.

Examples of specific government-supported schemes for workers in the informal economy are the labour welfare schemes in India, financed from resources derived from a tax on the output of about 5 million workers in the cigarette (beady) and cinema industries as well as in certain mines. A similar scheme operates in the Philippines for sugar workers. In general, however, the level of resources generated is low and only limited social protection is provided.

3.6. Services Financed from General State Revenues

Universal cash benefits are to be found in a number of industrialised countries, but only rarely in developing countries, one example being Mauritius. Universal services, particularly public health services, are more common. However, in recent years the universal character of these health services has been greatly eroded by the imposition of user charges, from which only the destitute tend to be exempt. By definition, universal schemes extend coverage to 100 per cent of the target population, for instance those over a certain age, without any contribution condition or income test. They avoid many of the problems involved in contributory systems.

Naturally, they will tend to cost more to the extent that they are providing benefits to more people. However, it must be borne in mind that eligibility conditions, such as pension age, may be quite restrictive and benefit levels rather low. Universal health-care systems are able to achieve much more effective cost control than other types of health-care systems and do not need to spend money on administering systems of insurance and patient billing. Another difference between contributory schemes and universal schemes is that the latter do not provide higher cash benefits to higher earners, but a single flat-rate amount to all who qualify. This too helps to hold down the cost of universal schemes.

Universal schemes can greatly enhance gender equality. They cover people regardless of their employment status and work history, and women receive the same rate of benefit as men. The benefits typically provided by universal schemes are all of particular importance to women: old-age pensions (as women have a longer average life expectancy); child benefits (as women are typically more involved in caring for children); and health care (as the health of children and issues of reproductive health are of special concern to women).

The real problem with the existing universal schemes, which are mainly to be found in the industrialised world, is not so much their aggregate cost (which is usually less than that of contributory schemes), but the fact that unlike contributory schemes they have to be financed from general government revenue and therefore have to compete every year with all the government's other expenditure priorities. What may be perceived as affordable one year may be less so the next, if policies or economic conditions have changed.

The widest possible form of universal cash benefit is the citizen's income, which would be provided not only for groups such as children and the elderly who are not expected to earn their living but also for the able-bodied of working age. This type of proposal has excited much interest in recent years. According to some of its proponents it would replace income-tested benefits such as social assistance; for others it would replace all existing social security schemes, including social insurance. Establishing or extending means-tested benefits or services.

Social assistance is to be found in virtually all industrialised countries, where it serves to plug at least some of the gaps left by other social protection schemes and thus to relieve poverty. In developing countries social assistance is much less widespread. Where it exists, it is usually restricted to just one or two categories of the population, such as the elderly.

The relative paucity of social assistance schemes in the developing world testifies to the problems which many governments have in devoting adequate resources to it. This should not be seen purely as a reflection of the low absolute level of national income or of government revenue. It may be questioned whether governments, in establishing their priorities, always give sufficient weight to their social assistance schemes, whose beneficiaries are rarely in a position of political strength.

Social assistance is targeted only at those in need and the means test can in theory be made rigorous enough to exclude all but those whose needs are greatest. In practice things tend to be different, even in the most sophisticated social assistance systems. On the one hand, no means test is foolproof, so some people who are not eligible nevertheless succeed in obtaining benefits particularly in countries where there is a thriving informal economy. Such errors are serious not only because they cost money, but above all because they undermine public confidence in the system. On the other hand, social assistance benefits fail to reach many of those in greatest need for one or more of the following reasons:

— They are unwilling to apply because of social stigma.
— They may be unaware of their rights under the legislation.
— They find it difficult to submit an application for benefit, as procedures are often complicated and time-consuming.
— Social assistance is often subject to considerable administrative discretion, opening the way to favouritism, clientelism and discrimination.

The more rigorous the means test, the greater the likelihood that people will be put off from applying and that those in real need will fail to obtain benefit. Self-selection mechanisms are often more appropriate than means testing, especially in the context of developing countries. These tend to be used, for example, in the provision of paid work in labour-intensive projects and of basic food aid. Means-tested social assistance has another major drawback, as it can discourage people from saving (or encourage deceiving) if they think that any savings they have will simply be deducted from the benefit that they would otherwise receive. Similarly, it may act as a disincentive from contributing to other forms of social protection. Thus it can help to create situations of need because of the perverse incentives inherent in means testing.

On the other hand, social assistance can be useful for specific vulnerable groups, such as the elderly and children. It may well be the only solution for widows who have not been able to contribute themselves to pension schemes or whose husbands were not covered by survivors' insurance. It is often also a way of helping poor households with children; in various countries the provision of such benefits is now linked to school attendance.

3.7. Components of Social Protection

Most social protection systems are mixed and there are linkages between their different components. One obvious linkage is that certain benefits are designed to supplement others. Compulsory contributory benefits may supplement universal benefits. Voluntary contributory benefits may be intended to supplement one or both of these. The linkage between social assistance and the other components of social protection is of course quite different. If a person receiving social assistance is eligible for other social benefits, then the latter will be deducted from what would otherwise have been paid by social assistance. If these other benefits are contributory, the result is that the person has contributed for nothing.

This suggests that the relationship between means-tested schemes and contributory schemes has to be carefully thought through. Among the issues which deserve attention are: the sequence in which social assistance and contributory schemes should be established; the relative levels of benefits provided by each; and whether eligibility conditions (such as pension age) should be different. These issues give rise to real dilemmas. As policy-makers become more aware of them, they may be more prepared to give universal schemes serious consideration, in order to minimise perverse incentives.

Social protection is constantly changing and the direction in which it is likely to change is often highly dependent on what has gone before. Policy-makers should be conscious of these dynamic linkages, since otherwise the final result of their decisions may diverge significantly from their intentions. For example, they may be very keen to encourage the establishment of contributory schemes, in view of the many advantages which such schemes obviously have.

However, if these schemes fail and with non-statutory schemes in an unregulated environment this is quite likely to happen then people's trust in such ventures may be destroyed for a long time to come. Or to take another example, tax policies may result in the establishment of voluntary contributory schemes for some workers, creating vested interests (notably among the financial institutions involved in managing them) which would stand in the way of establishing a national social security scheme covering all workers.

The existence of these various linkages serves to underline the need to develop an overall public policy concerning social protection, defining priorities and the financial involvement of the State. The key issues are to determine the institutions through which to channel state subsidies and the categories of the population which are to benefit. It is also important to recognise possible complementarities, for example, support for the creation of health-care facilities and support for the development of insurance mechanisms.

References

Norton, A.; Conway, T.; and Foster, M. 2001. *Social protection concepts and approaches: Implications for policy and practice in international development.* London, Overseas Development Institute; Working Paper 143.

Ortiz, I. (ed.). 2001. *Social protection in Asia and the Pacific.* Manila, Asian Development Bank.

Panda, P. 1998: "The elderly in rural Orissa. Alone in distress", in *Economic and Political Weekly.* Mumbai, June 20th, pp. 1545-1550.

Reynaud, E. 2002: *The extension of social security coverage: The approach of the International Labour Office.* Geneva, ILO, Extension of Social Security, ESS - Paper No. 3.

Rodrik, D. 1997: *Has globalization gone too far?* Washington DC, Institute for International Economics.

Ron, A. 1998: "Health care in Asia and the Pacific: increasing the focus on social health insurance", in *International Social Security Review* Geneva, ISSA. Vol.51, No. 2, pp.17-37.

4

Gender Equality in Social Security Systems

Gender equality issues are to be found in virtually all aspects of social protection. Gender equality in social protection is more than a question of securing equal treatment of men and women in the formal sense. It is also a matter of taking account, in an appropriate way, of gender roles in society, roles which differ between societies and have in recent years undergone immense change in very many countries. Thus social protection schemes should be designed, on the one hand, to guarantee equality of treatment between men and women and, on the other hand, to take into account different gender roles and serve as a tool for the promotion of gender equality.

Gender equality in social security systems is a complex matter which involves two types of discrimination, direct and indirect. Direct discrimination can be traced to:

— Differences in treatment between economically active married women and men, based on the idea that the woman is dependent on her husband, so that her social insurance entitlements are derived rights based on his insurance rather than personal rights based on her own.

— Differences in rates of benefits or contributions based on actuarial calculations made separately for men and women, taking into account factors such as different life expectancy, risks of morbidity and disability, anticipated work patterns, etc., such differences being found in systems of individual savings accounts in which there is no pooling of risk or solidarity.

Indirect discrimination results from measures which, although often defined without distinction as to sex, do in practice affect women and men differently because of the nature of their occupational activity, marital status or family situation. Women workers predominate in the sectors not covered by social security, such as domestic, part-time or occasional work or in the informal economy. Certain conditions, such as long qualifying periods, also penalise women.

Many women spend much of their lives outside paid employment and are thus economically dependent on their husbands. In social security systems based on gainful employment, derived rights allow a dependent spouse to benefit from health care and survivors' benefits. The issues to be considered here include: the adaptation of derived rights to changing family structures such as common-law unions, divorce and separation; the change in the concept of social protection which implies equal treatment of widows and widowers; the introduction of measures for all single parents (of which widows are but a subcategory).

4.1. International Standards and Gender Equality

In the ILO's early years, standards related to women aimed primarily at protecting female workers in terms of health and safety, conditions of work and special requirements related to their reproductive function. Over time, there has been a change in the types of standards relevant to women from protective Conventions to Conventions aimed at giving women and men equal rights and equal opportunities.

The adoption of the Equal Remuneration Convention, 1951, the Discrimination (Employment and Occupation) Convention, 1958, and the Workers with Family Responsibilities Convention, 1981, marked a shift in traditional attitudes concerning the role of women, and a recognition that family responsibilities affect not only women workers but the family and society as well. The mid-1970s marked the emergence of a new and more ambitious concept aimed at equality of opportunity between men and women in all fields. This concept found its expression in the debates and texts that came out of the 60th Session of the International Labour Conference held in 1975. Since then the protection of working women has been based on the principle that women must be protected against the risks inherent in their job and profession on the same basis and according to the same norms as men. The special protective measures which remain permissible are those aimed at protecting women's reproductive function.

Most of the ILO social security instruments contain no provision forbidding discrimination on the basis of sex, having been adopted at a time when the prevailing opinion (often at variance with reality even then) was that men were the breadwinners and that women would normally stay at home to take care of the family. Two social security Conventions do however prohibit discrimination. One is the Maternity Protection Convention (Revised), 1952, which states that any contribution shall be paid in respect of all men and women employed by the enterprise without distinction on the basis of sex. The other is the Employment Promotion and Protection against Unemployment Convention, 1988, which requires equality of treatment for all persons protected, without discrimination on the basis inter alia of sex, while allowing member States to adopt special measures to meet the specific needs of categories of persons who have particular problems in the labour market.

Other ILO Conventions not specifically relating to social security do of course expressly prohibit discrimination on the basis of sex, namely Conventions Nos. 100, 111 and 156 mentioned above. With a view to creating effective equality of opportunity and treatment for men and women workers, Convention No. 156 prescribes that all measures compatible with national conditions and possibilities shall be taken to take account of the needs of workers with family responsibilities in social security.

The Discrimination (Employment and Occupation) Recommendation, 1958, recommends that all persons should, without discrimination, enjoy equality of opportunity and treatment in respect of social security measures. The protection of the reproductive function of women is intimately linked with the promotion of gender equality. Maternity insurance benefits are critical for allowing women and their families to maintain their standard of living when the mother is unable to work. Throughout its history the ILO has been concerned to ensure that women workers enjoy this entitlement, from the adoption in 1919 of the Maternity Protection Convention to the adoption in 2000 of the Maternity Protection Convention and Recommendation.

4.2. Social Protection and Gender

Most social security schemes were initially set up on the basis of the male breadwinner model. Thus, for example, they usually provided widows' but not widowers' benefits and, in some countries, wives who engaged in paid employment did not have to contribute to the scheme. A lower pensionable age for women was also in some ways a reflection of a model in which the labour force participation of women was regarded as secondary. As more and more women have joined the paid labour force, ideas about gender roles have evolved and social security schemes are gradually being reformed. Within social protection there are two complementary approaches leading towards gender equality:

— Prescriptions/measures to level the playing field and ensure that equal treatment is granted to men and women. The goal is to eliminate discriminatory practices in programme design; but women remain in a disadvantaged position in terms of social protection as long as social security benefits are tied to labour market employment, where pervasive gender inequalities persist.

— Prescriptions/measures to equalise outcomes and compensate for discrimination and inequalities generated outside the social security systems, for example in the labour market.

4.3. Labour Market Inequalities

Women are often in a disadvantaged position in the labour market. Their situation is determined by the division of labour, in which they undertake a very large share of unpaid caring work. The latter role often prevents women from taking up or remaining in full-time employment. It affects the type of work they can undertake and the number of years they spend in employment covered by social security. It often has an adverse effect on their earnings, on their ability to pursue their training and on their prospects for professional advancement. Even women who currently have no caring responsibilities may be affected, if employers assume that they will have in future.

These labour market inequalities affect the position of women in some types of social protection much more than others. Some of the strongest effects are to be seen in company pension and health plans: women are more often excluded from these schemes than men, because they are in lower grades, or have insufficient years of service, or work part time. Company schemes also exclude those workers who, for one reason or another, are not covered by social insurance schemes. Company schemes provide benefits that are related to the level of previous earnings and to length of service, both factors which tend to favour men.

In addition, some are final pay schemes, which are particularly advantageous for employees who have moved up most in the company and for those who have long periods of uninterrupted service. Again this is more likely to be the case for men than for women. All sorts of savings schemes for old age tend to reflect, and indeed to amplify, labour market inequalities. Workers in low-paid and precarious jobs, among whom women are disproportionately represented, cannot afford to save much and often fail to do so, even in countries where the law has supposedly made retirement savings schemes mandatory. Those whose savings are small or irregular typically get a lower net return, as a greater proportion of their savings is eaten up by administrative costs, owing to the higher costs of small accounts.

In savings systems there is no solidarity or redistribution. Because of their greater life expectancy, women's pensions are lower than those of men, even if their savings are of the same value. Social insurance schemes frequently do not cover categories such as home workers, domestic workers and part-time workers, in which women are heavily represented. Workers in the informal economy where so many women spend much of their working life are also unprotected. Interrupted careers, shorter contribution records and lower pay adversely affect women's entitlements under social insurance as in other employment-related schemes.

This affects not only pensions but also unemployment benefits, which many unemployed women do not receive. (If they are single they may be able to obtain social assistance benefits, but these are usually lower and subject to numerous restrictions. If they have a partner, the household means test usually disqualifies them from social assistance, as explained below.) However, social insurance schemes do have certain features which attenuate labour market inequalities, such as minimum pensions or weighted benefit formulae favouring the lower paid.

For workers in the informal economy, notably in developing countries, micro insurance schemes can help to fill the gap in social protection, and some of them cater especially for women; given the voluntary character of such schemes, however, there tends to be little systematic redistribution from men to women. Universal schemes national health services, child benefits, universal old-age benefits usually give women the same rights as men, regardless of employment and earnings history.

As for social assistance schemes, these may, in formal terms, provide for equality of treatment and, since they cater for the poor, tend to redistribute income in favour of women (at least to those who are single). However, social assistance benefits are means-tested against the earnings of a spouse or partner; given that men usually have higher earnings than women, the result in practice is likely to be that a married woman has less chance of receiving benefit than a married man. And where a male partner succeeds in establishing entitlement to social assistance, the element of the benefit intended to meet the needs of his female partner will be paid to him, not to the woman.

Finally, it should be borne in mind that not only do labour market inequalities affect social protection, but social protection also has an impact on labour market inequalities. For example, a well-functioning system of unemployment benefits (including both unemployment insurance and unemployment assistance for those without insurance entitlements) helps to minimise the problems of low-paid, low productivity jobs. Child care and other social services are also of crucial importance in helping women to compete in the labour market on a more equal footing with men.

4.4. Promoting Gender Equality through Social Protection

A wide range of social protection measures have been used or may potentially be used to promote gender equality. These and some other issues relevant to gender equality are examined below under the following headings:

— Survivors' pensions.

— Divorce and pension-splitting.

— Pensionable age.
— Pension credits for persons with caring responsibilities.
— Sex-differentiated annuity rates.
— Parental leave and benefits and child care services.
— Child benefit.

4.4.1. Survivors Pensions

Survivors' pensions are based on the notion of dependency: they link benefit entitlements to the contributions paid by (or on behalf of) the deceased spouse, they insure against the loss of the breadwinner and (in many countries) they may be suspended if the recipient remarries. Traditionally survivors' benefits were provided only to the widow and to orphans, not to the widower (unless he had a disability and was for that reason dependent on his wife). This discrimination has been abolished in the social security systems of many countries, including the United States and most Member States of the European Union. Discrimination against widowers was ruled to be unlawful in occupational pension schemes by the European Court of Justice in 1993.

Mainly as a result of the developments described above, elements of income testing have been introduced in the statutory survivors' benefits schemes, for example in France, Greece, Italy, the Netherlands and Sweden. Other countries have restricted the payment of benefit to survivors above a certain age (at which it is judged to be difficult to enter employment) and to those caring for young children. As a result of such restrictions, some women are worse off than they would have been under the old legislation.

Those who are younger than the specified age may experience real difficulty finding employment. And even for many who are employed, the death of the husband may lead to serious financial difficulties, if no widow's pension is payable: the household budget in most cases is then less than half of what it was. The main aim of these restrictive measures has been to limit the increase in the cost of survivors' benefits resulting from their extension to widowers. It is no doubt significant that equal treatment of survivors was introduced at a time when social security systems already faced financial problems.

The issue has given rise to a debate between those who feel it is reasonable that women should nowadays normally be expected to earn their living and those who point out that this was not what was expected of many women entering married life in past decades. Should those becoming widows now suffer because values and attitudes have changed? In numerous pension systems, women who are not legally married do not qualify for a survivor's pension upon the death of their partner. However, some countries do grant a pension provided that there is evidence of dependency or cohabitation. Such is the case, for example, in Costa Rica, Denmark, Luxembourg, the Netherlands, Norway, the United Kingdom and Venezuela.

The position of widows in developing countries, particularly in Africa and South Asia, is very much more difficult than in the industrialised economies, not only because the social security systems are more rudimentary, but also because widows are often subject to discrimination, social isolation and even physical violence. If a country has a universal pension (or a social assistance pension available on conditions that are not too restrictive), this is of immense assistance to older widows, few of whom will have any contributory entitlements whatsoever.

However, it should be remembered that many widows are not nearly old enough to qualify for an old-age pension, particularly in societies with a tradition of child brides and in countries seriously affected by AIDS and by wars. (High mortality rates from AIDS, among both men and women, are also leaving many orphans, most of whom have no benefit entitlements.) Various states in India have extended means-tested pensions to cover destitute widows, but problems of implementation have limited the impact of such measures.

4.5. Divorce and Pension Splitting

The last three or four decades of the twentieth century saw a rapid rise in the rate of divorce in many industrialised countries. For example, in both Canada and the United Kingdom they were six times higher in 1990 than in 1960. Between the mid-1970s and the mid-1990s the rate doubled in the Republic of Korea, Thailand and Venezuela. This trend has profound implications for the old-age security of divorced women, particularly where they have not themselves been in pensionable employment. If the former husband remarries as is most often the case they may lose some or all of their entitlement to a widow's pension.

To deal with this problem, pension systems in various countries have introduced a refinement commonly known as "pension splitting". All the pension entitlements earned by both partners while they were married to each other are added up, then divided equally between them. Such a system has existed in the social security schemes of Canada and Germany for almost a quarter of a century. More recently, it has been introduced in Ireland, South Africa and Switzerland. It has recently also attracted attention in relation to occupational pension schemes.

4.5.1. Pensionable Age

Numerous countries either have or have had until recently a lower pensionable age for women than for men. Why did legislators in these countries (the overwhelming majority of whom were men) decide to make this difference? It has been suggested that it may be related to the tendency for men to marry somewhat younger women and for them to wish to retire about the same time. Another possible explanation is that the age for women is lower to compensate for the double burden they have borne, by going out to work and also doing most of the work in the home.

A lower pensionable age for women constitutes formal discrimination against men. The difference, where it still exists, is now widely questioned. That women do bear a double burden is undeniably true, but whether this affects their ability to remain in employment until the same age as men is far from evident. Indeed their higher life expectancy might even suggest the opposite.

A consensus is tending to emerge in favour of a common pensionable age, as already exists in Canada, France, Germany, Japan, the United States and many other countries. However, what that age should be is often the subject of heated debate. Many women are understandably reluctant to see their pensionable age increase or to receive reduced pensions at the existing pensionable age. On the other hand, if the age for men were to be reduced, the cost would be enormous. This would in any case be inadvisable, since the projected rise in the ratio of pensioners to workers suggests that pensionable age should rise rather than fall.

Many countries which are increasing pensionable age have introduced an element of flexibility that allows workers to continue drawing their pension from the previous pensionable age, subject to an actuarial reduction. Generally speaking, women have opposed proposals to increase their pensionable age and/or to reduce the benefits granted at the existing pensionable age. However, some women workers may stand to gain, if the increase means that they can stay longer than before in employment and build up bigger pension entitlements.

For women who have taken time out of the labour force to raise a family, this may be a real advantage, assuming of course that they do wish to carry on working and that they are actually obliged to retire at the standard pensionable age. To be regarded as equitable, increases in pensionable age usually have to be introduced gradually. For example, a formula commonly suggested in Central and Eastern European countries has been to raise the age each year by three months — thereby phasing in a five-year increase over a 20-year period. This is necessary, not only to give the working population time to adjust to quite a profound change, but also to allow time for the labour market to adjust: a more rapid increase could lead to significantly higher unemployment.

4.5.2. Pension Credits for Persons with Caring Responsibilities

Many women reach retirement age with low or even zero pension entitlements in their own right either because their unpaid work as careers has prevented them from participating in the paid labour force or because their caring responsibilities have obliged them to participate only in peripheral forms of employment, which are poorly remunerated and not covered by social security systems. In order to help remedy this problem, numerous countries have introduced provisions under which persons staying at home to care for young children (and for others unable to look after themselves) are awarded pension credits for the period in question as if they had been employed and paying social security contributions.

Among the countries with such provisions are Germany, Norway, Sweden and Switzerland. Ireland and the United Kingdom have implemented a variant of the caring credit through a procedure called home responsibilities protection which provides for years of low or zero earnings to be disregarded in the calculation of the pension amount. In 1996 Ireland increased the number of years for which such protection could be available by raising the age of qualifying children from six to 12. These measures contribute to gender equality not only as they help to provide better income security for the many women who leave the labour force to raise a family, but also as they are available to husbands who look after the children while their wives pursue their careers. Another approach, which in practice helps more to promote labour market equality, is the provision of child care services.

4.5.3. Sex-Differentiated Annuity Rates

In most of the mandatory retirement savings systems that have been introduced to date, particularly in Latin America, workers upon retirement have the option between the purchase of an annuity and a phased withdrawal of the money in their account. Under this type of system unlike the existing social insurance schemes there is no pooling of risk or solidarity between men and women (who have a substantially longer average life expectancy). Hungary and Poland, however, have provided in their legislation for mandatory lifetime annuities using unisex rates. It remains to be seen how easy it will be to enforce such legislation upon competitive annuity companies, all of which will have a strong preference for male customers.

The male/female pension differentials in the Latin American countries concerned may be widened not only by the introduction of gender-specific parameters, such as lower annuity rates for women, but also perhaps by the increase in the standard pensionable age for women and the associated actuarial reductions for women unwilling or unable to postpone retirement.

4.6. Childcare Services

Social security can promote gender equality not only by compensating unpaid careers for lost periods of pensionable employment, but also by making it easier for either men or women to assume the caring role and for them to do so without abandoning their careers. Parental leave and parental benefits (which replace their lost earnings) contribute significantly to this objective:

— As they are available to the mother or the father or can be shared by both.
— As they usually also provide for a number of days per year on which either parent may take time off work to look after a child who is sick.

The provision of high-quality and affordable child care services, often under the aegis of social security institutions or social service agencies, also plays an important role in promoting gender equality. The need for these services has risen as the participation of women in paid work has increased. In many countries a higher proportion of the work force is faced with the competing demands of work and family responsibilities.

4.6.1. Child Benefit

Child benefit is also a measure that favours gender equality in more ways than one. It is a benefit that is nowadays usually paid to the parent effectively caring for the child. This is an important consideration as the distribution of income within the single-breadwinner family is often highly unequal and breadwinners sometimes abuse the dominant position that receipt of the household income confers. While common in industrialised countries, child benefits are to be found in very few developing countries.

Recent years have seen a large rise in the proportion of families that are headed by a lone parent. Since 1960 this has more than doubled in countries such as the United Kingdom and the United States. This trend is related to the enormous increase in births to unmarried mothers (up more than fivefold in these and other countries), as well as to rising divorce rates. The vast majority of lone parents are women, most of them young. Given the high cost of child care in many countries and the limited access of young mothers to reasonably well-paid jobs, many of those concerned find that they have little choice but to stay at home with the child and live on social assistance or other means-tested benefits. But if child benefit is paid, this can, in combination with earnings from employment, provide them with a viable alternative. For those who are trying to develop a career and are often at an early and crucial stage, having the option to enter or remain in employment may be extremely important for their future earnings potential.

In developing countries the provision of child benefit conditional upon school attendance can be a powerful instrument for ensuring that both girls and boys receive an education and for combating the scourge of child labour. Such benefits can take the form of waivers of school fees, which is probably the most powerful incentive for children to go to school. The experience with cash grants to families and children shows that they are a useful initial incentive for families to withdraw their children from work and send them to school.

If possible these should be reinforced by other provisions such as school lunches, books, uniforms, pads and pencils, transport, accommodation and counselling, which encourage children to attend school and to remain in school. The Balsa Escola programme in Brazil, for example, has shown how cash grants can help very poor families to keep their children in school. Its major impact is to allow poor children to remain in school when they would otherwise be excluded owing to inadequate academic performance. Although only a minute number of families has benefited so far from the programme and the amount they receive does not eliminate poverty, in-depth assessments have indicated a significant impact on beneficiary families.

References

Ron, A.; Abel-Smith, B.; and Tamburi, G. 1990: *Health insurance in developing countries. The social security approach.* Geneva, ILO.

Sabates-Wheeler, R. and Kabeer, N. forthcoming: *Gender equality and the extension of social protection.* Geneva, ILO, Extension of Social Security (ESS) paper series).

Sankaran, T.S. 1998: "Social assistance: Evidence and policy issues", in W. van Ginneken (ed.) *Social security for all Indians.* New Delhi, Oxford University Press.

Save the Children UK. 2001. *The bitterest pill of all: The collapse of Africa's health care* system.

Schleberger, E. 2002: *The universal pension scheme in Namibia.* Geneva, ILO, Extension of Social Security, ESS - Paper No. 6.

5

Social Security Expenditure

Many contemporary national social security systems financed largely on a pays-you-go (PAYG) basis are presently criticised on the grounds that they will become unaffordable, inefficient or ineffective in the face of ageing population, or owing to the competitive forces in the new global economy and to the growth of the informal economy.

Worldwide social security expenditure has been on the increase for decades. In market economy countries sharp increases were observed in the overall social expenditure ratio (i.e. social security expenditure measured as a percentage of GDP) in the 1960s and 1970s, followed by a stagnation during the second half of the 1980s and most of the 1990s. Social security expenditure reached an average of about 18 per cent in the mid-1990s in the OECD countries.

In the former planned economies, economic transition placed a heavy strain on the badly prepared social transfer systems during the 1990s, yet total social security expenditure was maintained at about 15 to 20 per cent (excluding subsidies on certain goods and services) albeit of contracting levels of GDP. In the developing world the picture is more heterogeneous. As a general rule expenditure has increased in recent decades. But it grew from a level which on the whole was about ten times lower than in developed countries in the 1960s and is still three to five times lower.

In the more developed economies overall social security expenditure could grow further if dependency ratios were to continue to rise. Dependency will remain high or will increase further if female labour force participation in some major economies remains relatively low (compared to that of males), if the average age of entry into the labour market continues to rise and if de facto retirement ages continue to drop. It is often maintained that there is a simple relationship between social security expenditure and GDP levels. In other words, as countries get richer they tend to spend more on social security.

5.1. Social Security and its Challenges

Contemporary social protection financing systems face three major challenges. They are said to be ill-equipped to deal with the ageing of the population and with globalisation, and the financial burden placed on contributors and taxpayers in all countries is said to have reached the limits of affordability.

5.1.1. Ageing Crisis

Ageing often misrepresented as the key challenge for the financing of formal social transfer systems will pose a major problem only if rapidly ageing societies cannot contain overall social dependency. However, even in Europe where the ageing process is at a relatively advanced stage dependency could be reduced substantially through increased retirement ages and greater labour force participation of women. An ageing society need not face any crisis, as long as it is able to provide jobs for its ageing work force.

After decades of heavy investment in health care through social protection, people are remaining fit and healthy until later in life and should be able to work longer. In addition, modern and more flexible lifetime working patterns should be able to accommodate employment patterns needed by parents and older workers. ILO model calculations show that in a typical rapidly ageing European country with a de facto retirement age of 60 and a female labour force participation rate like that of the Netherlands, the combined unemployment and old age pensioner dependency ratio would have been on the order of 62 dependants per 100 employed persons in 1995.

If the country were to (a) raise the de facto retirement age to 67 by 2030 and (b) increase female labour force participation to the present highest levels in Europe (i.e. the Swedish level) then the combined dependency ratio in 2030 would amount to about 68 per 100 employed.

Under status quo conditions (i.e. unchanged de facto retirement age of 60 and unchanged labour force participation of women) that ratio would be 80 to 100, or about 18 per cent higher. Employment is the key to the future financing of social protection in all societies. Ageing is not so much a threat for social security systems as a challenge for economic and social policy-making and for the labour market.

5.1.2. Globalisation Crisis

Up to now some of the countries with the most open economies have the highest levels of social spending (for example, most of the Nordic countries, Austria, Germany, the Netherlands). Open national economies in a global economy do not have to have lower social spending. On the contrary, a higher level of social protection would appear to be necessary in countries that are more exposed to external risks or which have to undergo difficult structural adjustments. However, the data reflect economic realities in the mid-1990s.

In the meantime political realities appear to have changed to some extent. Globalisation not only channels liquid financial resources from one part of the world to another, it also exposes whole industries to new competitive pressures; which subsequently trickle down as pressures on wages and non-wage labour costs to employees. Credible threats to relocate enterprises or actual closures due to competitive forces can in practice limit the power of the nation State to tax or collect contributions.

National fiscal policies may react by seeking to move to income sources which are not exposed to globalisation pressures or do not negatively affect the country's competitive position, or by taking measures to curb expenditures in systems that are seen to affect labour costs. Containing overall labour costs is an explicit policy objective in most highly industrialised countries as well as many developing countries. There is wide agreement among economists that social security contributions and taxes are not driving labour costs.

Labour markets determine the price of the overall compensation package of employees. Nevertheless, since wages the major component of that package are often hard to change directly, the labour cost debate often concentrates on other elements of labour costs, notably on social insurance contributions. If alternative sources of financing cannot be found, benefit levels in public social security schemes tend to be reduced. The diminishing fiscal sovereignty of the nation State as a result of globalisation is one of the major new challenges for national social protection systems.

5.1.3. Limits of Affordability

It is the case in all societies (assuming the intention to treat their members with decency) that income is shared, to a greater or lesser extent and by more or less transparent means, between those who have the capacity to earn it and those who are unable to do so. However, the levels of transfers recorded in national statistics do not appear to correspond very closely to the economic potential of different countries. This suggests that the measurement of transfers, in most countries, is very inexact.

In countries where extended family and kinship structures remain relatively strong, these may well provide the major vehicles for transfers, on an informal basis, whereas other countries have moved towards more formal redistributed mechanisms, such as national pension schemes. Overall, it seems certain that the differentials between countries in total (informal and formal) transfers are much smaller than shown in national and international social statistics.

A simple quantitative exercise may illustrate the point. It is assumed here that the economically active population (including the unemployed) earn all the income in a country (i.e. profits and wages) and would share this income with children, inactive persons in the active age group and persons beyond active age. It is assumed also that the ratio of consumption of an active person to that of an economically inactive person (in any decent society) is 1 to 0.666.4 Based on these assumptions a hypothetical transfer ratio can be calculated for selected regions.

Most countries (except possibly the poorest) are redistributing more socialite resources than formal social transfer statistics indicate. There is no reason to believe that formal social transfer levels have anywhere become excessive in terms of the income redistribution which societies find necessary. The debate on the affordability of social protection is thus really a debate on policy preferences for particular redistribution mechanisms.

5.2. National Financing Options

Each country has to adapt its overall social protection financing systems to its economic circumstances, its demographic situation and most importantly the preferences of its citizens. Each country has a limited set of possible transfer mechanisms at its disposal, ranging from completely informal intra-family transfers to universal systems financed from general government revenue, with many intermediate possibilities. National policy choices and objectives are embodied in the selected financing systems and the role of governments versus the private provision of social transfers.

5.2.1. Financing Systems

Financing systems can be described in terms of the following parameters:

— The extent of group solidarity.

— The level and pattern of funding.

— The sources of financing.

5.2.1.1. The extent of group solidarity

The smallest group within which transfers occur is obviously the nuclear family. The next smallest group is the extended family or the immediate neighbourhood, followed by the community or by occupational groups. Unless mandated by specific legal provisions (such as alimony provisions in family law), transfers within families and/or small communities are most often of an informal nature. The extent of solidarity within these groups varies greatly, depending on values and on specific family or community circumstances.

There are often no clear entitlements to benefits, even in community-based schemes. Just as in informal family settings, community based transfer levels often depend on the level of income of the group as a whole rather than on the precise needs of potential transfer recipients. The theory of insurance suggests that the viability of a scheme increases with the size of the insured group. National schemes or social insurance schemes with a wide coverage generally have more stable income than schemes restricted to smaller groups.

The variance of the benefit experience of large groups (i.e. their financial risk) is inevitably more stable than that of smaller groups, which in turn stabilises their financial position. Small groups also often face joint risks, such as unemployment in an occupational group, poverty in a family, or epidemics in a community. In other words larger schemes can usually cope better with most risks, provided they are well governed. The disaggregation of national solidarity into smaller solidarity groups inevitably leads to a wider disparity of benefit levels. In various parts of the world, a trend may be observed towards greater disaggregation of solidarity groups, the extreme case being that of individual accounts. This inevitably creates greater benefit inequalities and uncertainties.

5.2.1.2. Level and Pattern of Funding

Short-term benefit schemes (with the notable exception of private health insurance schemes) are generally financed on a PAYG basis on all levels of group risk-pooling. The rationale is that short-term benefits are short-term promises and can be adapted relatively quickly to changing demographic or economic circumstances and hence do not need to build up huge reserves for distant future liabilities. In the case of pension schemes three financing methods are commonly distinguished:

— PAYG, i.e. virtually no advance funding.

— Full advance funding.

— Intermediate or partial funding.

Private pension systems usually are fully funded, i.e. they have to have sufficient resources to honour their obligations should the insurance company, the occupational pension scheme or the sponsor of an occupational scheme be dissolved. If this condition is met, the scheme is fully funded. Public pension schemes, which are backed by a socialite promise guaranteeing their liquidity and ideally indefinite existence, do not require the same level of funding. The level of funding in social security schemes is determined by considerations other than the exclusive financial safeguarding of pension promises. Most social security pension systems are in practice partially funded.

Even systems which were originally designed to be fully funded often became partially funded when inflation undermined the value of reserves. Recently several countries with old PAYG schemes have begun to introduce defined contribution funded second-tier schemes (Hungary, Latvia, Poland). Others are introducing reserve funds in their PAYG schemes (e.g. Canada, France and the Netherlands). From a purely financial point of view, there is no real difference between a partially funded defined benefit scheme and a pension system which consists of an unfunded and a funded tier. In aggregate terms, both are partially funded.

Recent years have seen an intense international debate on the merits or demerits of increased advance funding of national pension schemes. While social security pension schemes do not really require the financial security that a high level of funding may provide for small private systems, extraneous reasons for advance funding of pension schemes are frequently invoked. Funding, it is claimed, can increase national savings. The evidence does not support that contention. High levels of national savings may well coincide with low levels of pension reserves and vice versa. Funding is often said to stimulate the growth of capital markets. But, here again, the evidence is far from compelling: emerging stock markets have notched up very impressive growth rates in various countries where there are few, if any, funded pension schemes.

It is often claimed that funding will help to insulate pension schemes against the negative effects of ageing. While this is possibly true for small insured communities within a society or a small country in a global economy, the same does not apply to whole national societies or to global society as a whole. A society has to allocate a certain amount of resources to provide a certain level of consumption for its elderly. The shift from wage-based to capital-based financing does not change that fundamental equation. Ultimately the consumption of the retired population has to be financed out of the current GDP produced by the active population (unless it sells real assets to the rest of the world).

It must be expected that advance funded and PAYG financed pension schemes will both be vulnerable to demographic change. Funded schemes operate on the principle that pensioners are able in effect to sell their assets to (or use them as collateral to borrow from) active generations in order to generate cash income. If the buyer generation contracts, then one must expect asset prices to drop, thereby reducing the retirement income of the selling generation.

Table 5.1. National savings rates and occupational pension assets

Country	National savings (as % of GDP)	Pension assets (as % of GNP)
Australia	18	39
Canada	15	35
Denmark	19	60
France	21	3
Germany	23	4
Ireland	20	37
Japan	34	8
Netherlands	25	76
Switzerland	30	70
United Kingdom	14	73
United States	15	66

Heavy strain on national finances (as opposed to the real amount of transfers needed to finance the consumption of the elderly) may arise if a country moves from PAYG financing to advance funding (for example by replacing its social insurance scheme wholly or partially with private funding arrangements), as a (long) transitional period will be necessary during which funds must be accumulated by current workers to finance future pensions while at the same time pensions must be paid to current pensioners. There is then a real risk that the value of the social insurance benefits may be allowed to fall, in order to achieve economies and to limit the amounts that government would otherwise have to raise through taxation or borrowing or the sale of assets.

If funding per se does not increase the resources that can be allocated to the dependent population and economic advantages of funding are uncertain, then the only policy rationale for switching from PAYG defined benefit schemes to funded defined contribution schemes (as in Latin America and parts of Eastern Europe) lies in the stabilisation of social security contribution or tax rates. As benefit levels are then dependent on long-term capital market performance, certainty concerning contribution or tax levels is achieved at the cost of uncertain benefit levels. This represents a complete reversal of previous policy objectives. Sources of financing National social security systems are generally financed through the following main sources of revenue:

— Social security contributions paid by employers and/or workers.

— Taxes, which may be either part of general government revenue or earmarked taxes.

— Investment income.

— Private out-of-pocket outlays or insurance premiums.

However, most national social security systems are in practice financed by a mix of sources. This even applies to subsystems such as pension schemes. The present debate about high public spending on social protection may disguise the fact that many government budgets have substantially benefited from the existence of national social security schemes.

Young pension schemes and unemployment benefit schemes during periods of high growth normally produce large surpluses when contributions are collected but no or few pensions are paid. These surpluses might have simply been absorbed into the general government budget either through straight transfers (as was the case in Central and Eastern Europe) or through lending (as was the case in many African schemes). Many of these transfers were never returned and low interest rates (often negative in real terms) were paid on the loans. In such cases, social security contributions were thus to a large extent another form of taxation.

Governments often feel unable to finance social protection expenditure from general tax revenue. The traditional solution has been to provide special legislation for social security to be financed from compulsory contributions which have to be used only for the purposes specified in the legislation. However, governments may also explicitly mandate private agencies to finance and provide social security, or they may choose to leave any such provision up to voluntary initiative. Private provision, mandatory or voluntary, is often regarded as a convenient way of keeping down public expenditure (broadly defined to include social security expenditure financed from contributions). It is, however, incorrect to think that private provision has no effect on public finances.

There is an obvious indirect linkage between all public and private social protection financing instruments. In addition to the counting entliabilities of the government as ultimate guarantor of most social transfers, that linkage is defined by the overall limit of aggregate social charges (both public and private) that is accepted by the population. It seems probable that most people, if obliged to make payments on a mandatory basis, will be indifferent subject to equivalent guarantees as to whether these take the form of contributions (or taxes) to a public institution or premiums to private institutions.

They are prepared to accept a certain aggregate level of social charges in return for a certain level of protection. If charges increase beyond the acceptable level, tax avoidance strategies begin to take their toll on public revenues. There is no general rule as to what combined level of social security contributions and taxes is acceptable. This has to be tested on a trial and error basis in long-term political consensus-building processes. However, there are indications that the differences between countries at least between countries at the same level of development are less pronounced than commonly assumed.

5.3. Government as Financial Guarantor

In addition to assuming direct financial costs on a regular basis, governments may bear indirect costs or be liable for potential costs. Governments play an important role as financial guarantor, or ultimate underwriter, of social security schemes or even of privately administered social security systems. The liabilities of governments can take several explicit and implicit forms. An explicit liability exists when the social insurance law stipulates that the government will cover any deficit of the scheme. Guarantee payments of this type exist in several countries, both in Western Europe and in Central and Eastern Europe (for example, Bulgaria).

Governments also have an explicit liability when the State guarantees a minimum benefit, by supplementing pensions falling below that level for any beneficiary fulfilling prescribed conditions. The magnitude of such contingent liabilities may be considerably affected by systemic declines in the rate of return on pension assets and by market turmoil-induced falls in asset prices. An implicit guarantee exists if as a result of public political pressure the government is obliged to bail out non-performing private, community-based or social security schemes (as, for example, Baô-Kur, the public system for the self-employed in Turkey). Even if governments resist pressure to bail out schemes in serious financial trouble, they may well end up paying far more in social assistance benefits to the people whose other benefits (i.e. pensions or short-term cash benefits) go unpaid or have to be reduced.

Thus, through explicit or implicit financial guarantees, governments provide re-insurance for public and private social transfer systems, even if they do not directly finance benefits. Governments remain the ultimate guarantor of national social security schemes and have to exercise their supervisory function accordingly.

5.4. Globalisation and Social Security Financing

While for a long time the choice of the actual national mix of social protection and public finance instruments was a matter of national preferences and consensus, today global pressures leave their mark on many national policy choices. For the time being such pressures can only be relieved albeit imperfectly by domestic policy measures. Governments may not have exhausted all domestic policy means to increase revenues and contain costs without an outright reduction of protection levels. Financing could be switched to general income taxation and specific consumption taxes. In addition measures to reduce dependency could be introduced, for example by raising the retirement age. Simultaneously production processes have to be adapted to accommodate an older work force.

And yet it is not difficult to foresee that the increasing interconnections of world markets may further modify the architecture of social protection financing. Financial globalisation has proceeded apace in recent years, at the same time as the role of financial markets in the financing of pension schemes has increased. Major second-tier pension schemes and in future the reserve funds of public pension schemes (for example those in Canada, France and Ireland) will be or are already leading players on the international financial markets.

As the performance of these markets is interconnected, pension entitlements of many workers around the world are already highly interdependent. If one major stock exchange crashes, or if stock markets collectively mark down asset prices, millions of workers around the world are simultaneously affected. Conversely, many jobs depend, directly or indirectly, on the investment decisions of the pension schemes of the industrialised world. The international financial institutions are increasingly lending money for the inception or reform of social security systems. International loan and grant moneys go into national and regional social funds. International aid is providing disaster relief and subsidies to national health systems, etc.

In their Heavily Indebted Poor Countries (HIPC) debt initiative the IMF and the World Bank are now tying debt relief to the development of sound national anti-poverty policies. All these developments and initiatives are so far proceeding in an uncoordinated manner. According to recent ILO estimates it would take only a small fraction of the world GDP to lift most people out of most severe poverty in the poorest countries. Organising or canalising transfers and delivering benefits still constitute an enormous challenge for global and national governance. With their debt relief campaign the international financial institutions have made a first step. In 2000 the "Social Summit Special Session of the United Nations General Assembly encouraged interested governments to consider the establishment of a World Solidarity Fund to be financed on a voluntary basis in order to contribute to the eradication of poverty and promote social development in the poorest regions of the world.

It must nevertheless be stressed that the extension of social security remains fundamentally the responsibility of each nation. While the international community may provide crisis-related social assistance (and of course development assistance) the continuing effort required to provide social protection must rest with individual countries.

References

Messel, E. 2001: *Social protection strategy.* Geneva, ILO; paper presented to an ADB seminar in Tokyo.

Standing, G. 1999. *Global labour flexibility. Seeking distributive justice* London, MacMillan Press.

Thuy, P; Hansen, E.; and Price, D. 2001. *The public employment service in a changing labour market* ILO, Geneva.

WHO. 2001. *Macroeconomics and health: Investing in health for economic development.* Geneva.

World Bank, 2000: *World Development Report 2000-1. Attacking poverty.* Oxford University Press.

Zeller, M. 2000. "The safety net role of micro-finance for income and consumption smoothing", in Lustig, N. (ed.) *Shielding the poor. Social protection in the developing world.* Washington DC, Brookings Institution Press and Inter-American Development Bank.

6

Actors in Social Protection

People and societies have developed different forms of social protection, depending on their needs and their pattern of social and economic development. Social protection can be provided within family and community networks, as well as by institutions of civil society, by enterprises and the commercial market, and by public institutions. In more recent years, the international community as was made clear by the World Summit for Social Development (Social Summit) in Copenhagen in 1995 and "Social Summits held in Geneva in 2000 has become more concerned with global social policies.

The main function of social protection is to provide income security and access to health care and basic social services. There are various actors involved here, such as family and local solidarity networks, institutions of civil society, enterprises and the commercial market, government and social security institutions, as well as the international community.

The social partners employers' and workers' organisations often play an important role in the development and management both of social security and of occupational or complementary schemes within the formal sector of the economy. Trade unions need to be committed to expanding their activities to include the informal economy. Can informal economy workers join existing unions and, if not, what changes are needed? Are special structures and recruitment strategies required ? In order to be relevant to informal economy workers, unions must be able to deliver tangible benefits and increased protection.

6.1. Family and Local Solidarity Networks

The role of the family in providing income security is essential, irrespective of a country's level of development. Income-sharing within the nuclear family provides income security both for the young and for those (mainly women) who work at home as unpaid careers. The family also tends to be the major source of care for young children and, though to a lesser extent, for adults with disabilities and elderly persons.

The role of the extended family in providing income security for adult members who are elderly, sick or disabled varies considerably: in some countries of Africa and Asia it remains extremely important; elsewhere it has been eroded by recent social and demographic developments. Large families were often the best guarantee of income in old age, and for many people who are still not covered by any kind of social security system this continues to be the case. Of course, even if the family is large and income is shared fairly within it, the family income may simply not suffice. The poorest families are sometimes able to call on mechanisms of financial solidarity operating at the level of the local community.

6.2. Institutions of Civil Society

The institutions of civil society which help to maintain income security through social protection are of many kinds: self-help groups providing assistance in kind or in the form of labour, savings societies, associations, cooperatives, mutual benefit societies, religious bodies, charities, etc. Their role and their aims vary according to the national and local context. They may provide benefits in addition to those offered by public institutions, or they may be designed to afford a modicum of social protection for people who are not covered by any other system. Some of them may not have any legal status, as in the case of self-help groups providing assistance in kind or in the form of labour. In general, however, the activities of these groups are governed by law and monitored by the public authorities.

The range of benefits which these institutions can offer is very wide. Some are devoted to food security, others to health insurance or pension provision, others provide compensation for death or disability.

They are generally financed from the beneficiaries' contributions, sometimes with subsidies from elsewhere. Because they are so close to the beneficiaries, they are generally able to offer benefits which correspond to the recipients' main priorities.

Some social insurance systems had their roots in mutual benefit societies which became widely established and were ultimately converted into compulsory social security schemes. In certain countries they have continued to play an important role by supplementing the benefits of the compulsory system, for example, in health care or in retirement provision. In other countries their role is limited to certain marginal groups. Overall, their contribution at the global level has increased in recent years owing to spreading marginalisation and to the growing gaps in statutory social protection.

6.3. Enterprises and Commercial Market

Income security can be purchased on the commercial market, for instance, for old age, death and disability. Individual contracts involve high transaction costs and tend not to be very widespread, except in countries where they have been made compulsory or where they benefit from generous tax concessions. They can, however, be important for self-employed persons, for whom alternative opportunities to obtain income security may be quite limited.

Occupational or employer pension schemes are another form of income security provided by the private sector. They may be managed in the case of smaller enterprises by commercial providers, or be self-administered in the case of large companies. The transaction costs of these schemes are much lower than for individual arrangements. Typically, the scheme is not open to people not working in the enterprise concerned, so marketing costs are avoided and collecting the premiums or contributions is straightforward.

While occupational schemes were traditionally established at the initiative of the employer, many are now the subject of collective agreements or indeed in some countries have been made compulsory by law or by decree. Employers' organisations and trade unions have played an important role in the development of occupational pension schemes, not only at the level of the individual enterprise, but also at the industry or sector level. This role may be crucial not just for the negotiation of occupational schemes, but also for their subsequent management.

Some industry-wide schemes in such countries as the United States are wholly run by trade unions. As pension funds come to play an ever more important part on financial markets, there is an increasing demand from the primary stockholders to participate in decisions concerning pension fund investments. With billions of dollars of workers' capital circulating in the global markets, many national labour organisations have taken steps to try to control and redirect these funds in order to advance workers' broader interests.

6.4. Government and Social Security Institutions

In most countries the organisation and provision of social benefits are mainly the responsibility of the public authorities. In historical terms, the development of national social protection systems often reflected the desire of legislators to harmonise and make compulsory various schemes which had developed in individual companies or sectors. It was a question of gradually ensuring that everyone had access to the same social rights.

The structure of the social security scheme will often determine the arrangements for its administration. Thus, schemes which provide universal and means-tested benefits are more likely to be directly administered by the State. But there is a broad spectrum of institutional arrangements ranging from direct administration by a government department to reliance on private-sector management. Where the social insurance tradition (or the contributory principle) is the strongest, as in France and Germany and throughout most of Africa, Asia and still much of Latin America and the Caribbean, schemes are generally administered by a public institution which is supervised by a board of directors or trustees and which, invariably, is legally autonomous. The board is typically bipartite or tripartite, with representatives of employers, workers and government; sometimes other sections of the community and experts such as bankers or medical professionals may also participate. Day-to-day management of the scheme is in the hands of a chief executive who may be appointed by the board or by the minister.

Particularly in some developing countries, administrative segmentation has been a major cause of the lack of focus and thrust in social protection policies. Government policy-making is often concentrated in the ministry of finance, which tends to have a particular interest in pensions. Various other ministries, such as labour, health, social welfare and civil affairs, may be responsible for different social security schemes, often managed by separate agencies. Depending on the extent of fiscal decentralisation, local-level governments may also have some independent role, particularly with regard to social assistance.

6.5. The International Community

Since the end of the 1980s it has been increasingly acknowledged that the international community should develop its own responsibility for humanitarian and social affairs. Humanitarian actions have been accepted as a first area, because according to United Nations General Assembly resolution 43/131 of 8 December 1988 failure to assist the victims of natural disasters and emergency situations "constitutes a threat to human life and an offence to human dignity".

The core labour standards identified by the Social Summit in 1995 as the social floor of the emerging world economy are now the subject of the ILO Declaration on Fundamental Principles and Rights at Work adopted by the International Labour Conference in 1998. The concept of a global social floor can be extended to include the guarantee of basic entitlements with regard to education, health and social protection. With regard to education and health, these entitlements have been formulated as aims by the Social Summit in Copenhagen, i.e. the achievement of universal primary education and an under-five mortality rate below 45 per 1,000 by the year 2015.

The follow-up Special Session of the United Nations General Assembly in 2000 recommended the strengthening of "modulates of coverage of social protection systems to meet the needs of people engaged in flexible forms of employment", but did not formulate quantitative objectives or time frames.

6.6. Partnerships for Social Protection

In addition to strengthening the role of the various actors in social protection listed above, there are a number of ways in which partnerships can be formed among them in order to enhance the effectiveness of social security and extend social protection.

6.6.1. Enhancing the Effectiveness of Social Security

The State can shape social security systems and influence their effectiveness in a variety of ways:

— Organisation and provision of social benefits.

— Regulations imposing obligations on employers to provide benefits or obliging commercial insurance companies or private pension funds to maintain prescribed standards.

— Fiscal policy, including tax concessions for social security benefits or contributions.

— Ratification of ILO social security Conventions and participation in bi- and multilateral social security agreements.

Choices made as to the relative weight given to these different approaches have determined the overall structure of the social security system. This has provided the State with both the responsibility for and the opportunity of determining the extent of its own involvement, the range and level of protection to be provided by the market and by the community, etc., the financial arrangements and the organisation and management of schemes.

It has long been considered important that the social partners, particularly the representatives of the workers covered, be involved in designing and running social security schemes. The Income Security Recommendation, 1944, states that "the administration of social insurance should be unified or coordinated within a general system of social security services, and contributors should, through their organisations, be represented on the bodies which determine or advise upon administrative policy and propose legislation or frame regulations".

Under the terms of the Social Security (Minimum Standards) Convention, 1952, "where the administration is not entrusted to an institution regulated by the public authorities or to a government department responsible to a legislature, representatives of the persons protected shall participate in the management, or be associated therewith in a consultative capacity, under prescribed conditions; national laws or regulations may likewise decide as to the participation of representatives of employers and of the public authorities". Similar requirements are contained in later instruments, such as the Invalidity, Old-Age and Survivors' Benefits Convention, 1967, the Medical Care and Sickness Benefits Convention, 1969 , and the Employment Promotion and Protection against Unemployment Convention, 1988.

One reason for the participation of the social partners is the fact that the schemes are, at any rate in the case of social insurance, financed wholly or predominantly by the contributions which employers and workers pay on the basis of labour incomes. However, even in the case of schemes which are financed from general tax revenues and administered by a government department, tripartition can play an important role in improving policies and in making systems more responsive to workers' needs. Other forms of popular participation in these schemes can also serve to enhance them, for example patients' consultative committees in the case of public health services.

Convention No. 168 requires that where the administration of employment promotion and protection against unemployment is entrusted to a government department, representatives of the protected persons and of the employers shall be associated in the administration in an advisory capacity.

Within the framework of contributory social security systems, enterprises are almost in variably given important responsibilities with respect to the deduction and payment of contributions. In some countries, however, enterprises are obliged under labour legislation to provide certain benefits themselves or to make appropriate arrangements with an insurance company. This technique, known as employer liability, has been widely used in the past for employment injury benefits and maternity benefits. Owing to its numerous shortcomings, it has tended to be replaced by social insurance in these fields. However, in recent years, there has been an important trend towards making the employer liable for the payment of cash sickness benefit or sick pay for the first few days or weeks of absence.

This type of reform has been inspired by research findings which show that short-term sickness absence can be greatly reduced if employers have a financial incentive to take appropriate action to improve the quality of working life and to monitor absence from work. In many countries responsibilities for the provision of social protection, especially retirement pensions and health care, are ascribed to enterprises, not explicitly by employer liability legislation, but implicitly by the absence of satisfactory provision through statutory mechanisms.

The intentions of the State are usually indicated clearly by the fact that enterprises (and to a lesser extent employees) receive substantial tax concessions if they fulfil these responsibilities. Lower-paid workers in less secure jobs, especially women, tend to benefit less from voluntary employer schemes. Providing social protection in this way rather than through social security can mean much greater inequality in the distribution of benefits. Legislation or government decisions have in certain countries extended private or occupational pension schemes to cover all enterprises and workers in an industry or even entire sectors of the economy.

The resulting system falls somewhere between compulsory social insurance schemes and voluntary private schemes. It combines the advantages of broad coverage and pooling of risk with autonomy from any direct involvement of the State. The sound financial base of such schemes and the absolute requirement for them to be jointly managed by employer and worker representatives create favourable conditions for their functioning. Experience in countries such as Finland, France and the Netherlands suggests that these basic safeguards greatly facilitate the regulatory function of the State. By contrast, in countries which rely widely on individual company schemes, vast regulatory systems have developed, accompanied in some cases by the establishment of pension guarantee mechanisms. The regulations tend to be experienced as burdensome by employers and are difficult to police.

Some countries, particularly in Latin America, have indicated a number of reasons for the privatisation of their pension systems. To what extent is privatisation the answer for improved governance in social security? The debate is essentially on two levels: one relates to the responsibility for providing it, and thus to its structure, and the other to its management. At the structural level, those who argue against the principles of social insurance maintain that it overprotects individuals and removes their freedom of choice. It is argued that the State should withdraw to a position in which it provides a minimum level of social protection and then creates and encourages an environment under which private arrangements can be made.

At the administrative or institutional level, it is argued that the social insurance institutions are not subject to market competition (they are effectively monopolies) and they are not required to make a profit. Administrators, according to this view, consequently pay insufficient regard to the financial implications of the decisions they are obliged to make. There has been a tendency to assume that the competitive forces of the marketplace would have a generally beneficial effect.

However, experience has shown that it is much more costly to administer individual savings accounts than social security records, that pension fund management companies (for example the Administrators de Fondues de Pensions (AFP) in various countries of Latin America) have high marketing costs, that levels of concentration among pension funds are high, and that private management companies cannot be relied upon to enforce compliance.

On the other hand, many schemes have recognised the need for improved governance and have either reformed their institutional arrangement to achieve a greater level of real autonomy or involved the private sector in various aspects of their administration. The trend is therefore for public schemes to contract out some of their functions and for other private-sector management concepts and practices to be introduced to improve efficiency and accountability.

6.7. Towards Social Protection for All

The appropriate paths for extending coverage depend on a number of factors, such as the country's level of economic development, the state of the social security system and the degree of informations of employment. Certain industrialised countries have reached full personal coverage for some contingencies, but not for others. As a result, in these countries extension can be achieved within the context of existing systems.

For middle-income developing countries it may be possible, for some contingencies, to achieve universal coverage through existing systems. In other cases, it may be necessary to first develop and support schemes specifically designed to meet the needs of workers in the informal economy. Given the small size of the formal sector in low-income developing countries, it is imperative to give priority to schemes specially designed to meet the needs of informal economy workers.

6.7.1. Micro Insurance Schemes and Area based Schemes

Access to health care is one of the top priorities for workers in the informal economy, especially in low-income countries. The extent to which micro-insurance schemes have been successful has depended on the characteristics of the bodies that set up the schemes, on their design and on the context in which they operate. The organisation should be based on trust among its members, which is enhanced by factors such as strong and stable leadership, its economic base, the existence of participated structures and a reliable financial and administrative structure.

Scheme design should include measures to control fraud and abuse, to promote some form of mandatory participation, to contain costs and to foster preventive and promotive health services. Important context variables concern the availability of good-quality and affordable health-care services (public or private) and a favourable climate for the development of micro insurance schemes.

Most of these schemes remain fairly small, and it is therefore important to know with what mechanisms and under what forms of partnership their coverage can be expanded. One option is for such schemes to form organisations among themselves, which will enable them to achieve various objectives, such as a stronger negotiating power in relation to the government as well as (public and private) health providers, sharing of knowledge and greater financial stabilisation through re-insurance.

A second approach is to devote more effort to the marketing of micro insurance, as a large percentage of the target population is still not well informed of the benefits of being insured. Linked to this is the need to strengthen the credibility of micro insurance. Subsidisation of micro insurance is undoubtedly a promising way to expand its coverage, but this is entirely dependent on the capacity and will of the

State to redistribute income through the tax system from the rich to the poor.

However, with the growth of micro insurance schemes, other forms of partnerships may also be necessary. Such schemes may team up with, and/or receive support from, larger organisations in civil society (cooperatives and trade unions for instance). They may also seek to involve private companies and social security agencies that already have a well-functioning administration. Experience with successful scaling-up efforts shows that two sorts of changes are needed: in the culture and organisation of participating organisations as well as in linkages and forms of collaboration between organisations.

The role of the government is critical for the successful upscaling of these schemes. Local governments can play an important role in setting up area-based social protection schemes in partnership with local groups of civil society. At the national level, governments are in the best position to ensure that particular experiences can be replicated to embrace other occupations, sectors and areas. Moreover, governments can create an enabling environment for the development of micro insurance schemes. By means of regulation, they need to clarify the relationship between the role of micro insurance and that of the compulsory social insurance system, in order to prevent contribution evasion and to promote, in the longer term, closer links between the two. In the case of health insurance various functions can be distinguished:

- Promoting health insurance through recommendations on design (benefits package, affiliation and administration) and the setting-up of a management information system;
- Monitoring and regulating micro insurance, possibly within the context of legislation on the efficient and transparent administration of schemes;
- Improving and decentralising the public provision of health care, which is an essential prerequisite for the development of micro insurance in many countries;
- Undertaking and organising training, based inter alia on the promotion and monitoring activities mentioned under.

— Co-financing the access of low-income groups to health insurance, possibly through subsidies or matching contributions.

— Trade unions and employers could also play a major role in setting up new special funds at the state or provincial levels for example for construction workers.

— In experimenting with area-based social protection schemes. The trade unions would ensure that the benefits provided correspond to the priorities of workers, while employers' organisations could convince their members to comply with their contribution obligations.

6.7.2. Social Insurance

There are various ways in which social insurance programmes can be modified and reformed so as to achieve greater coverage. As the guarantor of such programmes, the government obviously plays a critical role here. However, the social partners can also help achieve the extension of social insurance benefits to regular workers not covered so far, as well as to casual and contract labour employed in formal-sector enterprises. The social partners, and in particular the trade unions, could press for measures to extend effective coverage to workers in small enterprises. Training and awareness-raising, followed by consultation and dialogue with the government, would be the ideal road to greater coverage.

6.7.3. Tax-Based Social Benefits

It is generally better for social assistance and universal benefits to be mainly financed by the central government, since the much greater needs of depressed regions and localities cannot be adequately met otherwise. This guarantees that people in all regions of the country have access to the same basic benefits, which need to be adjusted where necessary for cost-of-living differences. Local and regional governments can add benefits to this basic benefit, for example for housing, food or work. Moreover, local government in collaboration with local institutions can play an important role in the effective delivery of benefits.

Demand for temporary social assistance measures often financed by international sources has increased in countries affected by wars, disasters and crises. In the long run as well, the international community has promised to contribute to the achievement of social objectives such as the reduction of poverty and universal primary education. Within this context, international resources could be used to finance child benefits, which in particular reduce child labour and foster school attendance, as well as basic social assistance benefits, which in combination with other policies would make a significant contribution to the reduction of poverty.

References

Augusztinovics, M. 2002. "Issues in pension design", in *International Social Security Review* 55(1), pp. 21-35.

Baeza, C.; Montenegro, F.; and Nuñez, M. 2002. *Extending social protection in health through community based health organizations: Evidence and challenges.* Geneva,ILO-STEP.

Chaabane, M. 2002: *Towards the universalization of social security: The experience of Tunisia*. Geneva, ILO; Extension of Social Security, ESS - Paper No. 4.

Devereux, S. 2000. *Targeting social protection programmes: Case study examples of issues.* Easthampstead Park Conference Centre, Inter-Agency Workshop on Social Protection, 22-23 March.

Dror, D.M.; Jacquier, C. 1999: "Micro-insurance: Extending health insurance to the excluded", in *International Social Security Review.* Geneva, ISSA, Vol.52, No.1, pp. 71-97.

7

Democratic Governance for Social Security

Democracy is a system of government in which the principal positions of political power are filled through regular, free, and fair elections, then about three of every five independent states in the world are democracies today. There were only 39 democracies in 1974. Today, there are about three times as many. With the growth in the number of democracies has come a parallel, albeit more gradual, expansion of freedom in the world. The proportion of states rated as "free" by Freedom House increased from one-third in 1985 to over 40 percent in 1991, and today it stands at about 45 percent, nearly the highest level ever. The average freedom score improved from 4.29 in 1985 to 3.61 in 1992, and after a slight deterioration thereafter it has continued a modest pace of improvement. The current average of 3.47 is a full point lower than that in 1974, when the third wave began. In most years since 1990, the number of countries showing discernible improvement in political and civil liberty has out paced the number of countries in decline.

The global expansion of democracy was particularly rapid in the years immediately after the fall of the Berlin Wall in 1989 and the collapse of the Soviet Union in 1991. Within just a few years of the implosion of the Soviet communist empire, democracies increased, as a proportion of all the world's states, from about 40 to 60 percent. Since 1995, however, the overall number of democracies in the world has remained more or less constant . Transitions to democracy have been largely offset by reversions from democratic to authoritarian rule.

In the past few years, democracy has scored a number of strategically and symbolically important advances. In 1999, democracy was introduced in two of the largest and most influential developing countries, Indonesia and Nigeria, even while democracy was breaking down that year in Pakistan. In 2000, Mexico completed a transition to democracy with the peaceful electoral overthrow of seven decades of hegemony by a single party.

That same year, one-party hegemonic regimes were also brought down at the ballot box in Senegal, Serbia, and Ghana, while Taiwan experienced a historic breakthrough to a more competitive system with the defeat of the long-ruling KMT. In each of these countries, the victory of the opposition party signalled the arrival or deepening of democracy, with promising long-term implications for the regional status of democracy. The march of democratic progress has been one of the defining developments of the late twentieth century. By the mid-1990s, democracy was the only broadly legitimate form of government in the world, and many other regimes had liberalised their politics at least superficially. Indeed, today well over half of the remaining non-democracies of the world portray themselves as democratic by holding regular, multiparty elections.

Few regimes explicitly eschew and condemn the basic principles of democracy. And most of the non-democracies have significant socialite movements or critics seeking democratic political change. Internationally, there has also been a distinct trend toward the affirmation of democratic principles, which are increasingly being codified into international law through various international and regional treaties and resolutions.

However, beyond the levelling off of democratic expansion since the mid-1990s, there have been four other major caveats to the democratising trend. First, as democracy has spread rapidly in the world, it has become a more shallow phenomenon. The quality of governance and the rule of law have actually deteriorated in some existing democracies, and the more recently established democracies have tended to be less liberal and more corrupt.

Second, the spread of democracy has been far from uniform across regions and sub-regions. While some regions of the world are now overwhelmingly democratic, others have been only very partially touched by the democratic trend, while the Arab world remains without a single true democracy. Third, many of the regimes (particularly in Africa and the former Soviet Union) that once appeared to be "in transition" from authoritarian rule have settled into varying shades and forms of authoritarian rule that fall well short of democracy.

Finally and cause for perhaps the greatest concern many of the democracies that have come into being in the past two decades exhibit growing problems of governance that are eroding their legitimacy among the public and undermining their stability. With the breakdown of democracy in Pakistan in 1999, the recent economic and political crisis in Argentina, and mounting citizen disgust with corruption worldwide, the global democratic trend is at greater risk of reversal than at any time since the end of the Cold War.

7.1. Rise of Illiberal Democracy

The "third wave" of democratisation has seen a growing divergence between the form of electoral democracy and the deeper structure of liberal democracy. The latter entails not only regular, free, and fair elections but also a strong rule of law; buttressed by an independent judiciary and other institutions of accountability that check the abuse of power, protect civil and political freedom, and thereby help to foster a pluralistic and vigorous civil society. A rough indicator of "liberal democracy" is an average score of 2.0 or better (lower) on the Freedom House combined seven-point scale of political rights and civil liberties.

With the dramatic expansion in the number of democracies during the third wave, the phenomenon of "illiberal democracy" has markedly increased. In 1974, over 80 percent of the democracies of the world were "liberal", and all of them were rated "free" by Freedom House. Even in 1987, almost three-quarters of the democracies of the world had average freedom scores indicating liberal democracy. However, as democracy exploded with the demise of communism, liberal democracies declined markedly as a percentage of the overall number of democracies in the world. By 1991, less than 60 percent of the democracies in the world were "liberal," and that proportion continued to fall with the expansion of democracy through the mid-1990s.

The presence of democracy in the world today is broader but also thinner than a decade ago. There has been a striking rise of illiberal democracy. In fact, some of these regimes are only ambiguously democratic, and many of them function very poorly in protecting human rights, controlling corruption, and addressing economic and social problems. The shallow and illiberal nature of so many existing democracies in the world demands concern for several reasons.

First, human rights and the rule of law are ends in themselves, and a number of democracies (as well as all authoritarian regimes) fall seriously short of their obligations to foster and protect the basic rights of their citizens. Second, there is growing evidence of a strong association between the quality and the legitimacy of democracy in the minds of the public. Citizen support for democracy is more robust, and democracy is more stable, when there is greater civil liberty, restraint of power, justice, and accountability.

Third, underlying this relationship is the strong connection between the quality of governance and the stability of democracy. Where democracy is less liberal, governance is poorer more corrupt, wasteful, incompetent, and unresponsive. This entrenches poverty, obstructs economic development, disposes the country to recurrent crisis, and prevents poor countries from making effective use of international assistance. Liberal democracy is thus a major foundation of the architecture of good governance that fosters and sustains broad-based development.

7.1.1. Regional Disparities

In its reach around the globe, democratisation has been sweeping but far from universal. There remain significant regional disparities in the extent, depth, and stability of global democratisation. The United States and Canada, Australia, and New Zealand, together with the 24 states of Western Europe (some quite small), are all stable, liberal democracies. Stable means that they are consolidated: there is such widespread and deeply ingrained commitment to the legitimacy of democracy among all major elite groups and social strata, and major democratic institutions have such strength, depth, and predictability, that there is no prospect of a breakdown of democracy. These 28 advanced industrial democracies are also liberal (as defined above). Outside of Western Europe and the Anglophone states, liberal democracy is much more uneven and thinly rooted.

In Latin America and the Caribbean, Cuba remains the only country of significant size to resist completely the democratic trend. Haiti has competitive elections but, tragically, it has increasingly reverted to its long historical pattern of autocracy and violence. There have been important breakthroughs. As electoral administration became more neutral and fair, Mexico made a transition to democracy in the late 1990's, leading in 2000 to the defeat of the long-ruling party.

Peru returned to democracy in 2001 with the implosion of the autocratic, military-dominated regime of President Alberto Fujimori. Overall in Latin America and the Caribbean, about nine of every ten states are democratic, but only about half are liberal democracies. And a few, such as Argentina, Jamaica, and Trinidad and Tobago, have seen the quality of democracy deteriorate in recent years. As with other regions, there is significant variation among subsets of countries.

The most important liberal democracy in Africa is South Africa, which has so far sustained high levels of freedom despite political turbulence, economic hardship, and dominance by a single party. By contrast, Africa's other big states are all struggling politically. The effort to build democracy in Nigeria, the most populous African country, is besieged by corruption, religious and ethnic violence, and a weak and fractious party system. Sudan remains a highly repressive regime unable to resolve its 19-year-old civil war.

The Democratic Republic of the Congo (DRC) is struggling to overcome a profoundly debilitating legacy of predatory corruption, state failure, and civil war. While a few African countries, such as Ghana and Mali, seem to be functioning reasonably well as democracies, most of Africa's new democracies and quasi-democracies seem to be slipping backwards to less accountable, more abusive and personalists rule. Africa remains an arena of highly contested forms of governance, where both democratic and authoritarian institutions are weak and open to change. Of the principal regions of the world, the Middle East (including North Africa) is the one least hospitable to democracy at present. At most, only two of the 19 states in this broad region.

Israel and Turkey are democratic (and in Turkey, the military still exercises a veto on many important issues). None of the sixteen Arab states is a democracy, although several (Lebanon, Jordan, and

Morocco) have at least some degree of electoral competition and socialite pluralism. Bahrain is gradually exploring a possible democratic opening. Yet not a single Arab state affords its people true political sovereignty, and the very tentative movement toward greater political openness has largely been arrested and reversed by the growing fear of terrorism and radical Islamic mobilisation in the wake of the September 11 attacks on the United States. The only liberal democracy in the region is the only Western-oriented state, Israel, and there freedom has diminished in recent years under the stress of terrorism.

The prospects for democratic development appear especially dim in the Arab Middle East because of the likelihood in some countries that a sudden and immediate opening to free and fair elections would bring the victory of antidemocratic Islamist forces. The alienation and extremism of these radical Islamists have been stimulated by the mix of globalisation and the development failures of their own societies. Now, even the Islamists who pursue nonviolent political struggle and social mobilisation appear intent on using electoral competition merely as a vehicle to win power so that they can impose an Islamic fundamentalist order on society and thus in many respects, a more rigidly repressive regime.

Unfortunately, a number of Arab authoritarian regimes as in Egypt, Algeria, and Syria have deliberately played on this danger to delegitimise political opposition in general. This has created a more polarised political arena, and a kind of self-fulfilling prophecy, in which the radicalism Islamists constitute the only viable opposition in the eyes of a growing proportion of the population.

The Arab Middle East, then, is not only the region with the weakest prospects for democracy but also the one that harbours the greatest near-term dangers for U.S. National security. Many of the strategically important authoritarian regimes that have been friendly to the United States and Europe such as Egypt, Algeria, and Saudi Arabia have become more unstable. In these and other states in the region, the old "ruling bargain," in which society acquiesced to autocracy in exchange for economic and social resources, has broken down as resources have become scarcer and social problems and divisions have intensified. A growing number of observers believe that these regimes must begin now to construct a new ruling bargain based on better, more accountable governance, gradually increasing freedom and pluralism, and serious reform of the economy and state. Otherwise, they face the prospect of deepening political instability and possibly breakdown.

7.1.2. Electoral Authoritarian Regimes

After a decade of arrested and inverted political openings, it can no longer be said that countries like Kenya, Cameroun, Cambodia, Haiti, Morocco, Egypt, Kazakhstan and Azerbaijan are "in transition" to democracy. There were transitions from authoritarian rule and they imploded or went off course, leaving authoritarian regimes still largely intact. In most cases, however, these regimes did not completely close off political pluralism.

Rather they are electoral authoritarian: they allow multiple political parties to contest in elections that are held at regular, constitutional intervals, but they do not allow opposition parties and candidates full freedom to campaign and a fair chance to win. Formal democratic institutions, like multiparty elections and parliaments, exist precisely to obscure (and sometimes soften) the reality of authoritarian domination.

Rather than a true form of rule, they are a legitimating facade with which to purchase some acceptance from the international community and domestic constituencies (hence the term pseudodemocracy). Such regimes combine varying degrees of competition, pluralism, and repression. In the more hegemonic of these regimes, such as Cambodia, the ruling Cambodian Peoples Party, under the former communist autocrat, Hun Sen, thoroughly dominates power and political life, both through corruption and extensive violence and intimidation.

But the political opposition has a significant presence both in parliament and in the local government councils, and there is at least some space to question government policy and conduct. In the more competitive of these regimes, such as Russia, alternative voices in politics, government, and civil society are stronger and more numerous. Even though Russian President Putin has largely eviscerated the principal independent media, opposition parties and leaders still win elections in some of the regions and challenge government policy in the Duma (parliament), and the resulting competition and pluralism inject some uncertainty into political life.

With reform of the electoral process, mobilisation by civil society, and relative unity among opposition forces, this uncertainty can mutate into the surprising defeat of once hegemonic parties, as has happened in recent years in Mexico, Senegal, Serbia, and Ghana. But the mere fact of regular, multiparty elections does not put these regimes on a path to democracy. Unless, there are fundamental changes in the nature of the regime to permit free and fair elections and greater civic and political space, a transition to democracy is most unlikely.

7.1.3. Mounting Problems of Democratic Governance

Since the mid-1990s, two global trends have been colliding, making for a more turbulent and unpredictable world politically. One trend has been the surprisingly robust and resilient third wave of democratisation, producing a record number of electoral democracies. The other trend has been a spreading democratic malaise in many parts of the world. In most countries outside Western Europe and the four other Anglophone states, democracy (where it exists) is not functioning very well.

Serious deficiencies of governance are heightening public cynicism about parties and politicians in general, and diminishing public esteem for democracy. Three generic problems of governance underlie this malaise and obstruct the consolidation of democracy. The most urgent and pervasive problem is the weakness and frequently the decay of the rule of law. No problem more alienates citizens from their political leaders and institutions and undermines political stability and economic development than gross, endemic corruption on the part of government and political party leaders, judges, and officials up and down the bureaucratic hierarchy.

The more endemic the problem of corruption, the more likely it is to be accompanied by other serious deficiencies in the rule of law: smuggling, drug trafficking, criminal violence, personalisation of power, and human rights abuses. Even in the wealthy, established democracies of North America, Europe, and Japan, scandals involving political party and campaign finance have eroded public confidence in parties and politicians. In the less established democracies, where the legitimacy of democracy is not so deeply rooted, political corruption scandals are much more likely to erode public faith in democracy itself and thereby to destabilise the entire system.

This is particularly so where corruption is part of a more general syndrome involving the growing penetration of organised crime into politics and government, the misuse of executive and police powers to intimidate and punish political opposition, and the politicisation and inefficacy of key institutions of "horizontal accountability," such as the judiciary, the audit agency, and even the electoral commission. In many countries today, democracy is weak and insecure because political leaders lack sufficient democratic commitment "political will" to build or maintain institutions that constrain their own power. And civil society is too weak, or too divided, to compel them to do so.

The second broad source of malaise is economic. Economic reforms insofar as they have even been implemented have not yet generated rapid, sustainable economic growth in most of the developing and post-communist states. A few states have experienced rapid growth, and some others are at least growing modestly. However, in most new and troubled democracies, economic growth is not rapid enough, and is not broadly distributed enough, to lift large segments of the population out of poverty or a very tenuous economic existence.

In most of Latin America, in some parts of Africa (such as South Africa), and in some Asian countries (Pakistan, the Philippines), the problem is compounded by extreme levels of inequality in income and wealth (especially, in rural areas, land). Very little progress has been made in these countries in reducing poverty and tempering massive inequalities of income and wealth. It is inconceivable that democracy can be consolidated in these countries unless substantial progress is made toward reduction of poverty and inequality.

The third problem is the inability to manage ethnic, regional, and religious differences in a peaceful and inclusive way. Cultural diversity is not, in itself, an insurmountable obstacle to stable democracy. With all of its problems, India has learned how to manage this diversity through complex institutions of federalism. Spain largely contained its secessionist pressures with the adoption of a system of asymmetrical federalism, and, like the United States, Canada, and Australia, Europe is learning to adapt its democratic institutions to assimilate immigrants from a wide range of other countries and cultures.

The problem arises when one ethnic or religious group seeks hegemony over others, or when some minorities perceive that they are being permanently and completely excluded from power, including any meaningful control of their own affairs. These three problems indeed, crises of governance intensify and reinforce one another. Highly visible corruption accentuates the sense of injustice and grievance associated with poverty, unemployment, and economic hardship. Corruption has also been a major obstacle to the successful implementation of economic reforms, especially privatisation.

Poverty and economic stagnation reinforce the resentment of discrimination and political marginalisation felt by the indigenous peoples of the Andes (and many other parts of Latin America). The entrenchment of political corruption and clientelism as the principal means of economic advancement aggravates ethnic and regional conflict in Africa and Asia, by raising the premium on control of the state and rendering politics a more desperate, zero-sum struggle for control of economic opportunity.

The weakness of the rule of law makes it easier for leaders of different ethnic and sectarian groups to mobilise violence at the grassroots as part of their efforts to win power for themselves. It also facilitates electoral fraud and violence. Underlying all of this in many countries is a weak commitment to the public good and the rule of law. Citizens and elates have low levels of trust in one another and in the future. Thus, they strategies on how to take from a stagnant stock of resources, rather than on how to cooperate and produce to enlarge that stock. They focus on ends rather than means securing power and wealth by any means possible, rather than doing so with respect for the constitution and the law.

These interrelated crises of governance account for the main sources of democratic insecurity in the world today. All three crises contributed prominently to the breakdown of democracy in Pakistan in October 1999. The accumulation of poor governance and deferred economic reforms led to the implosion of the Argentine economy and the resignation of its president amid public rioting and looting in December 2001. Each of the three crises of governance is visible in the current travails of democratic performance in Nigeria and Indonesia, as well as in the Andean region and many other smaller countries.

The weakness of the rule of law and continued economic stagnation and decay now also threaten the prospects for building democracy in Russia, Ukraine, and other post-Soviet states. In these and other countries, not only are major political leaders ambivalent (at best) in their commitment to democracy, but democratic political parties and civil society groups lack the resources, the organisational strength, and the popular bases to promote successful democratic reforms.

The failure to govern effectively ultimately takes a toll on the legitimacy and stability of democracy. The democratic malaise is particularly visible in the trends in public opinion in Latin America. The 2001 Latinobarometro survey recorded significant drops in support for democracy among most of the countries it surveyed in Latin America. Between early 2000 and April-May 2001, support for democracy as "preferable to any other kind of government," declined from 60 percent to 48 percent in the entire Latin American region.

Support for democracy declined in a number of key countries in the region, from 71 to 58 percent in Argentina, from 50 to 36 percent in Colombia, and from 39 to 30 percent in Brazil. These decreases do not always give rise to parallel increases in support for authoritarian rule, but there is, at a minimum, growing apathy with and alienation from democracy. Even in Uruguay and Costa Rica, the most stable and clearly consolidated democracies in the region, support for democracy declined by five and twelve percentage points respectively.

Latin America's democratic malaise is driven by the accumulation of governance problems. Three in five Latin Americans overall rated their country's economic situation as "bad" or "very bad" in 2001. A growing proportion, now four in five, believe that crime and drug addiction have "increased a lot" in recent years, and the same proportion give the same response about corruption. Trust in major democratic institutions is very low and continuing to decline; only around one in five trust the national congress or political parties; trust in the judiciary has declined to under 30 percent.

While support for democracy appears greater in the post commissure countries of Central and Eastern Europe, those democracies also suffer high levels of disaffection, with only 22 percent trusting parliament and only 13 percent political parties in 1998.14 And in Korea, support for democracy declined sharply after corruption scandals and economic crisis in 1997, from 69 to 54 percent. The spread of democracy in the world today is thus impressively broad but worrisomely thin. With the demise of communism, and other one-party socialist regimes, and with the failure of the Islamic fundamentalist state in Iran to become an attractive and dynamic model, liberal democracy remains the only model of governance with any broad ideological and political attraction in the world.

Globally, democracy today is triumphant and dominant. However, it is also under severe and growing strain from the intersecting crises of governance. The next decade will thus be a time of great danger and opportunity for democracy in the world. If the crises of democracy are not addressed with lasting reforms to improve governance by reducing corruption, strengthening judicial, administrative, and political institutions, and professionalism the state bureaucracy, especially economic management, many more democracies are likely to disappear.

Breakdowns may come through a military coup, as in Pakistan, an executive coup, as in Peru in 1992, or often through the slow strangling of democratic pluralism and competition by an overbearing president. On the other hand, improvements in governance, even incrementally, could buy time for democracy to gradually sink deeper roots in political party life and diverse areas of civil society, as well as in the culture of a country.

7.2. Assisting Democratic Governance

The prospects for development, and the potential for development assistance to be effective, heavily depend on the quality of governance the way in which public power is exercised and public resources are managed and expended. Good, democratic governance is the key to development, and to aid effectiveness. Unless states can be made more responsible, competent, efficient, participatory, open, transparent, accountable, lawful, and legitimate in the way they govern, stagnating and poorly performing countries will not experience the kind of vigorous, sustained development that transforms levels of human development and permanently lifts large segments of the population out of poverty. And badly governed states will produce diffuse threats to global. How can we foster stable and effective democratic governance in the coming decade?

First, we must be clear about our objectives. The goal is not simply to advance democracy in the world. As was demonstrated by the collapse of democracy in Pakistan in 1999, a country can have vigorously competitive national elections with frequent alternation in power and still have rotten governance that fails to generate development and loses the confidence of the people. Neither is the goal simply better, more capable and transparent government.

Few are the leaders in the world who can deliver and sustain good governance with its overarching commitment to the public good and restraint of the abuse of power without the institutionalised means of accountability to other branches of government and to the people that democracy provides. Even when non-democratic leaders come into power with a manifest and sincere commitment to reform, the absence of any institutional mechanisms to restrain and monitor the exercise of power eventually degrades the quality and legitimacy of governance.

In almost every country, good responsible, accountable, public-spirited governance must ultimately go hand in hand with democracy. Of course, for peoples around the world, from every culture and religion, democracy and human rights are ends in themselves, independent of the material development progress that they facilitate. But democracy is an essential companion of good governance for several reasons. For one thing, democracy provides the people with an indispensable instrument of electoral accountability the opportunity to remove leaders who do not perform well. Second, when this opportunity is denied through impediments to fully free, fair, competitive, and neutrally administered elections the incentive of incumbents to restrain themselves and serve the public good withers.

Corruption seeps through the financial and political system, as in Indonesia. Rulers become not only venal and distant from public concerns, but also increasingly abusive of human rights, as in Zimbabwe. Rot and sclerosis set in, because there is no way of cleansing the system of bad leadership. Third, democracy provides publics with the freedom and institutional means, in between elections, to scrutinise the conduct and policy decisions of public officials and hold them accountable.

Thus, fourth, leaders in a democracy have more pressures, means, and incentives to explain and justify their decisions, and to consult a broad range of constituencies before passing laws and making decisions. Fifth, wider public dialogue and participation in the policy-making process produces decisions that are more legitimate and sustainable. Competitive, free and fair elections are the sine qua non of democracy. But other institutional components of good governance are also much more likely to be vibrant and effective in a democracy than a non-democracy.

These include an independent judiciary with a clear and predictable rule of law; an elected parliament that is autonomous and capable of checking and scrutinising the executive branch of government; and a civil society with the freedom and resources to monitor, evaluate, question, and participate in the making and implementation of policy. When governance is open to the scrutiny and involvement of a wide range of socialite actors (NGOs, interest groups, think tanks, and the mass media), it is more likely to be transparent, public-spirited, and thus legitimate. There is no guarantee that electoral democracy will bring such transparency and inclusion, but it is an illusion to imagine that "liberal autocracy" is a developmental option in the contemporary world.

Precious few are the examples of a well-governed autocracy, and the few that exist (Singapore, for example) have sustained good governance for highly idiosyncratic reasons that are not broadly transferable. The typical recipient of US foreign assistance is a country that needs the openness, competition, and broad and free public participation of democracy in order to develop truly good governance. The pursuit of stable and effective democratic governance will entail different sequences of political reform and development in different countries.

In some cases, the basic framework of multiparty democracy is in place, but it needs to be deepened and made more effective and accountable in a variety of ways. Some emerging democracies suffer from more particular obstacles to consolidation such as the institutionalisation of the rule of law. In some repressive, corrupt, and closed regimes, multiparty competition, if it exists at all, is largely a facade, but the reform of the economy and the strengthening of moderate forces in civil society might be more viable near-term steps than an immediate transition to electoral democracy.

It is impossible to offer a general strategy or sequence of political reforms to fit such widely varying cases. That is why careful assessment must be done of the current state of democracy and governance in each country. There is no one sector that provides the key to fostering democracy and good governance. There is no one "answer." And there are no short-cuts. In most countries that lack stable and effective governance today, we must be prepared to work on a number of fronts over a prolonged period of time. Nevertheless, a few characteristic priorities do emerge with striking regularity.

These priorities involve making democracy work better to advance development and respond to the needs of society. They would generate the capacity for and commitment to using the public resources of a country to advance the public good. Most of these themes and approaches are not new. The foreign assistance community has worked in and with most of them, particularly over the past decade. What is needed now is not wholesale invention but innovation, adaptation, refinement, elaboration, a deepening of commitment, and an expansion of activity in some areas. Strategic priorities for democratic development include:

— Controlling corruption and improving the entire apparatus of horizontal accountability.

— Strengthening the rule of law and the way it affects the lives of individual citizens, not only through judicial functioning but through more professional, vigorous and democratic policing.

— Strengthening and democratising political parties, and deepening their roots in society.

— Helping pro-democracy and good-governance NGOs to widen their domestic constituencies while also using more traditional interest groups to strengthen democracy.

— Developing stronger, more professional and capable states that are better able to respond to rising socialite demands for better governance.

7.2.1. Comprehensive Approach to Difficult Cases

International democracy and governance assistance is difficult and uncertain work. The countries that most need such assistance are precisely the ones most resistant to positive change. These are the countries with chronically poor governance. In these countries, rulers who have typically been in power without accountability for a long period (sometimes decades) have little commitment to the public good, and the distinction between public and private is scarcely recognised by those with access to political power and public resources. In these countries, political power bestows enormous wealth and privilege, and incumbents do not wish to give it up or have it checked.

Lacking voluntary and sincere support, autocrats must accumulate vast fortunes to purchase it, in chains of patron-client relations that cascade throughout the decrepit system. In this context so common in Africa, the Middle East, and the former Soviet Union democracy assistance fails because it is "disconnected from the structures of power, authority, interests, hierarchies, loyalties, and traditions that make up the dense weave of sociopolitical life."

In countries like Nigeria, Kenya, Egypt, Morocco, Georgia, Azerbaijan, Haiti, Paraguay, and Cambodia, the odds are stacked against democratic progress in part because a number of unfavourable factors reinforce one another. Endemic corruption drains away resources, energy, and purpose from development. Poverty usually goes hand in hand with illiteracy and ignorance. Society is fragmented and organised mainly on hierarchical, clientelistic lines. People in growing numbers may have come to recognise the importance of freedom and responsible, accountable government, but they understand only vaguely the norms and practices necessary to sustain democracy, and they lack the skills, resources, and organisational strength to hold their rulers accountable.

The scope for political and economic reform therefore heavily depends on "political will" within the state and the ruling party especially at the highest levels of leadership. But it is precisely leadership commitment to serious reform that is lacking. At its most intractable and egregious, bad governance constitutes a vicious cycle that is very difficult to penetrate. Corruption and rent-seeking have seeped so deeply into the culture that everyone expects public officials will use their power for private gain, and there is great pressure on them from clients and kin to do so.

Corruption tilts investment decisions toward contracts that yield large kickbacks rather than public goods. State rules and regulations proliferate in deliberate pursuit of ever more opportunities to collect rents. Businesses cannot get licenses to operate, and farmers can't get title to their land. These distortions stifle private enterprise and generate chronic deficits and resource scarcity, making society even more dependent on corruption and clientelism to survive. All of this reproduces the culture of corruption: diffuse distrust and lack of commitment to the public good.

People lack confidence in their fellow citizens and in all of their public institutions the executive, parliament, parties, the judiciary, the civil service, local government, the military, and the police. Ethnic and religious communities vie intensely for state power, resources, and favour, and often clash violently. State institutions lack any real sense of public purpose or discipline, as they mainly function to loot and extract rather than generate or protect. The state as a complex of institutions of power because so hollowed it and dysfunctional it is at risk of collapse.

The more a country approaches this model of bad governance, the more formidably difficult is the challenge of improving governance, and the more international engagement must be coherent and cumulative to be effective. The strategy proposed here thus relies heavily on a comprehensive and integrated approach to intractable cases of development failure" poorly performing states." To turn around a poor performer, every source of influence must work toward a common end. Every point of leverage must reflect a clear and common purpose: fundamental reform of governance. If different international actors work at cross-purposes, or if the different elements of an aid program do not cumulate and interact, foreign assistance will fail, and the country will remain mired in poverty and oppression.

In instances of protracted development failure, foreign assistance must pursue dense linkages and a asynergy of investments if it is to have a significant and lasting impact. But ultimately, governance cannot improve and development cannot happen without political will for reform. In fact, one reason why linkage and asynergy is so crucially important is precisely to help generate, deepen, and amplify this will.

7.3. Generating Political Will

In most countries where development has failed or stalled, the most important missing ingredient is the political will of the nation's leaders to improve the quality of governance. "Political will" is the commitment of a country's rulers to undertake and see through to implementation a particular policy course. At its most resilient, political will here involves a broad consensus among ruling elates, across parties and sectors of government, in favour of democratic and good governance reforms. But consensus is always imperfect, and will is most important at the top levels of government (among major political leaders and senior civil servants).

There, political will must be robust and sincere. That is, reform leaders must be committed not only to undertake actions to achieve reform objectives, but also "to sustain the costs of those actions over time." Without a robust commitment to fundamental reforms to control corruption, open up the economy, enhance the rule of law, respect basic civil and political rights, and allow independent centres of power both within and outside the government foreign assistance will fail to ignite sustainable development.

Children may be inoculated, only to find that they have no access to education, and then no jobs that lift families out of poverty. Schools may be built and then destroyed in civil war. Clinics may be constructed and then not be sustained because there is no access to medication. Participation may be stimulated at the local level, but improvements in local governance may be overwhelmed and vitiated by a national context of predatory government. Opposition political parties may be strengthened organisationally only to be marginalised by massive electoral fraud. Judiciaries may be assisted technically and then corrupted and intimidated by the national leadership.

Political will is not an either/or phenomenon. In the typical recipient country, the will to reform is mixed and ambiguous in several respects. Within the state and ruling party, there are some elements who favour reform (or would favour it if it gained any momentum) and a number of obstructionists. Different officials may favour different kinds of reform; some may favour economic reform to the extent it can be accomplished without surrendering political power or favoured monopolies. Others may favour democracy but only of the "neopatrimonial" kind, driven by the lavish dispensation of corrupt patronage.

A president or prime minister may promise international donors a package of governance reforms, but then grow cold when he realises the political risks. Or he may promise anything to get aid, with no serious intention of ever delivering In the worst cases (often countries of some strategic importance to one or more donors), international development assistance takes on the appearance of a mutual con game: intractable countries pretend to be developing, and international donors pretend to be helping them. No one is facing up to the reality that development is not happening because governance is rotten. Over time, it is this rotten governance that most often drags a society down into violent conflict and a state into decay and collapse.

The most urgent challenge for international assistance in the coming years is to determine how to engage such "poor performers" regimes with grossly inadequate political will. How can the will to bring about basic, systemic reform be generated? Such political will is generated from three directions: from below, from within, and from outside. Organised pressure from below, in civil society, plays an essential role in persuading ruling elates of the need for institutional reforms to improve the quality of governance. There may also be some reform-minded elements within the government and the ruling party or coalition who, whether for pragmatic or normative reasons, have come to see the need for reform (but are reluctant to act in isolation). Finally, external actors in the international community often tip the balance through persuasive engagement with the rulers and the society and by extending tangible benefits for improved governance and penalties for recalcitrance.

International assistance can help to develop the first two forms of pressure, and in fact has done so in a number of countries in the past decade. When political will for systemic reform is clearly lacking, the principal thing that foreign assistance can do to help governance is to strengthen constituencies for reform in civil society, including NGOs, interest groups, think tanks, and the mass media. Assistance can enhance these actors' understanding of key reform issues, their knowledge of other country experiences, their coordination with one another, their capacity to analyse and advocate specific institutional and policy reforms, and their mobilisation of support and understanding in society. Often political will appears more patchy and ambiguous. In that case, the best strategy is to work with those elements of the government in particular agencies or ministries that seem serious about improving governance, while seeking to enhance demand for reform within the society.

A key lesson from international efforts to stimulate governance reform is that fundamental reform is only sustainable when there is a "home-grown" initiative for it. If changes in policies and institutions are promised merely in response to international pressures, they will not be seriously and consistently implemented. "Imported or imposed initiative confronts the perennial problem of needing to build commitment and ownership; and there is always the question of whether espousals of willingness to pursue reform are genuine or not."

International engagement, therefore, does not succeed if it simply compels a government to sign on the dotted line of some package of dictated reforms, as has frequently been the case with IMF assistance packages. Its goal must be deeper and more procedural democratic: to generate public awareness and debate, and to induce government leaders to sit down with opposition and socialite forces to fashion a package of reforms that is unique to the country and owned by the country.

The vigour and depth of the political will to reform can then be assessed by several additional criteria. First, to what extent have (self-proclaimed) reformers undertaken a rigorous analysis of the problem and used it "to design a technically adequate and politically feasible reform program" that rises to the scale of the challenge? Second, to what extent have reformers mobilised political and socialite support for their initiatives broad enough to overcome the resistance of threatened interests (and how sustained are these efforts to rally support)? Third, to what extent are reformers seeking changes in laws and institutions and allocations of human and financial resources that hold promise of effecting real change?

In the case of controlling corruption, this would include, for example, laws to monitor and punish corrupt conduct and an anti-corruption agency with the authority and staff to enforce them. Another key lesson of democracy and governance (DG) assistance is the need to periodically use the above criteria "to track the evolution of political will over time" and to feed that assessment back into the reform implementation process. Successful international engagement must shift from conditionally to selectivity in foreign assistance. Traditionally in international lending, for example, conditionally has been "ex ante in the sense that governments promise to change policies in return for aid."

As a result, "reforms are 'owned' by the donors." A better approach is to dispense aid selectively to reward and deepen, and thus preserve and consolidate, reforms that have already begun to be implemented by the country, according to its own design. Selectivity focuses aid on good performers countries that have reasonably good policies and institutions and on assisting reform movements that are seriously underway, by governments and societies that have taken responsibility for the design of their own policies and institutions.

7.4. Demand for Political Reform

Across a number of sub-sectors, one of the major lessons to emerge from DG assistance over the past decade has been the need to balance the demand and supply sides of the political reform equation. DG assistance cannot be successful if it only works on one side or the other. Even if state elates propose institutional reforms for example, to privatise state industries, reform the tax system, or crack down on smuggling and bribery these reforms may not be sustainable unless society is educated about the need for them and mobilised to support them.

Urgently needed reforms are often vitiated in implementation because of the failure to generate broader pro-reform constituencies among logical "stockholders." State officials who want to promulgate reforms need technical assistance within their ministries or agencies to accomplish the changes and to train and equip the new institutions. But sustainable reform also requires complementary programs targeted at interest groups (such as chambers of commerce and trade unions), advocacy NGOs, think tanks, and the mass media.

And often, the momentum for systemic governance reform begins with the articulation and mobilisation of these kinds of groups. By the same token, reform cannot be accomplished only with a strategy of pressure from below, in civil society. In the absence of genuine political will, that is a necessary place to begin, and in some countries at some historical junctures, it may be the only arena in which a DG program can work. But ultimately, it is the leaders of various governmental and political institutions who must enact and implement reform.

And once new, more democratic and accountable institutions are constructed, they must be enabled to work and to respond. When DG programs focus too heavily for too long on civil society, to the neglect of political parties and formally democratic state structures, they may help to generate a level of demands and expectations with which the state and political system simply cannot cope. The resulting overload of political participation and consciousness can generate not better and more stable governance but heightened cynicism and frustration, a growing rupture between the people and their government. Development assistance must pay more attention to the supply side of reform, in programs to strengthen the capacities of the state and political parties to respond to citizen expectations and complaints and to deliver development and good governance.

7.5. Strategic Priorities for Assistance

Given the difficulties of democratic governance and the intractable nature of corruption and autocracy in much of the world, what should be the substantive, thematic priorities for international assistance to advance democracy and improve governance in the coming decade? When results are disappointing and conditions frustrating, there is always a temptation to search for something new a new method, a new set of tactics, new strategic priorities. There is always the hope that a new approach will catapult us over the muck of the deeply embedded norms and structures that perpetuate venal, sloppy, abusive, exploitative governance. There is always the search for the miracle cure.

Unfortunately, there are no miracle cures for what ails the politics of badly governed countries. We can and must periodically re-evaluate our strategic priorities, both globally and within each country. We must give more attention, as indeed we have begun to do in recent years, to some of the key bottlenecks to democratic progress: political corruption, feckless political parties, and weak states. But obstacles that rise into sharper focus may coexist with more long-standing targets of concern, and each country represents a distinctive mix of problems, possibilities, and currents of progress or sclerosis. The overarching lesson is that DG assistance priorities must fit the particular political conditions of the country, and this requires periodically an authoritative, shrewdly perceptive, and well-focused strategic assessment.

7.5.1. Assessing and Classifying Countries

Fortunately, countries are not entirely unique. Their political regimes can be roughly grouped into categories according to the extent and nature of democratic development. Strategic priorities overlap across categories, but a country's place in a typology of regimes begins to tell us something about what needs to be done. At the extremes are two types of regimes. One type is the consolidated democracy, which by its level of economic and political development has "graduated" from assistance.

Botswana, Mauritius, Costa Rica, Chile, Poland, Hungary, and the Czech Republic fall into this group. These countries can play an important role in democracy assistance to their neighbours in the region, by providing institutional lessons and human resources for cross border linkages. But they no longer need significant external assistance. The second extreme is occupied by repressive, closed regimes where there is very little space for democratic development at present.

In between these extremes (more or less) are some 75 or more countries where democracy is not consolidated but where there is scope for democratic progress, and for international assistance for this purpose. This includes almost the entire former Soviet Union, the politically lagging countries of Eastern Europe, 25 African countries, and most of Latin America. These countries can be roughly grouped into the following four categories of regime:

— Electoral democracies with problems of democratic performance. These regimes such as Ghana, Mali, Senegal, Benin, South Africa, Namibia, the Philippines, Bangladesh, Brazil, Mexico, and most of Central and South America have more or less institutionalised competitive, relatively free and fair elections. In some of these countries, not even that basic element of democracy is secure, but in most, the threats to democracy derive from other shortcomings: corruption, judicial inefficacy, party weakness, human rights abuses, state incapacity, and in a few cases one-party dominance. This also includes very new democracies, such as Kenya.

— Ambiguous (quasi-democratic) regimes. In these cases most prominently Ukraine, Nigeria, and Venezuela it is just not clear (and independent experts disagree) as to whether elections are really free and fair, or elected authorities have full power to govern. These countries have competitive, multiparty elections, but there is significant fraud and manipulation or insecurity surrounding the contest. There are all the formal institutions of democracy, but most of them function poorly or with constraints. To the extent that their elections are not democratic, the regimes in this category are instances of "competitive authoritarianism," a sub-type of the category below.

— Electoral authoritarian regimes. These regimes have multiparty elections, and they may even be quite competitive, but elections are so tainted with fraud and tilted with advantages for the ruling party (and typically the incumbent president) that they cannot be considered free and fair. This category encompasses wide variation. To the extent these regimes allow for serious competition and pluralism (as in Russia, Jordan, Lebanon, Morocco, Uganda, Tanzania, and Georgia), this is evident not only in the electoral arena but also in the actions of legislative and judicial systems that may take prudent steps to break free of executive domination. The mass media may be another sector that seeks to erode constraints and exercise some accountability. At the lower boundary are regimes that maintain the facade of multiparty elections while in fact allowing little real pluralism or freedom, as in Egypt, Azerbaijan, Belarus, and most of the Central Asian republics. To the extent these regimes become seriously challenged (as in Zimbabwe) they can also become quite brutally repressive.

— Closed authoritarian regimes. These regimes do not conduct multiparty elections and generally exhibit the highest levels of political repression and closure. There is precious little space for opposition or dissent in civil society or the political system. The state executive and the security apparatus are thoroughly dominant, at least within the territory they control.

A scheme of categorisation such as that above is not an arid, academic exercise. It helps to organise thinking about strategic priorities. Within these four categories, different countries will need different strategies for democratic progress. But generically, the following strategies and priorities are likely to be most suitable for each group of countries.

— Electoral democracies face one overriding challenge: to improve the quality of governance and political representation. Securing the freedom and fairness of elections may be important in some of these countries. However, in the majority of them, it is either no longer a major problem or it is one that domestic political actors have learned to manage through their own organisation and resources (or which domestic actors can be assisted to manage with modest further investments of aid). In these countries, where democracy is not consolidated and major problems of governance persist, a nearly universal priority is corruption control and the rule of law. Nearly all of these countries need significant help in strengthening and professionalism their judiciaries, their other institutions of horizontal accountability, such as counter-corruption commissions, and their political parties. The overriding goal must be to make politics more transparent, accountable, and responsive. In all of these countries, civil society has an important role to play in educating and mobilising for systemic reform and deepening democracy.

— Ambiguous, quasi-democratic regimes share the programmatic priorities of the first group, but with one major addition: electoral assistance. In these countries, there is often still considerable need for several dimensions of electoral assistance: to develop the technical capacity, independence, neutrality, and professionalism of electoral administration; to educate and inform voters; and to empower domestic monitoring efforts in civil society. In a few cases, particularly Indonesia, civilian authorities need help developing their capacity to manage the military and subordinate it to their constitutional authority.

— Electoral Authoritarian Regimes encompass wide variation. Some of these regimes have considerable competition and pluralism, and could become democratic if elections became free and fair. For these more competitive regimes, electoral assistance is a major priority, as is assistance to civil society to intensify demand for reform. Without the uncertainty and incentives generated by truly democratic competition, the political will for reform is unlikely to emerge.

— Closed authoritarian regimes fall into two categories: failed states, struggling to reconstruct a viable political order, and very repressive regimes in which political opposition is banned. In failed states, rebuilding state capacity is essential for improving governance. Yet even in these cases, unless some means of political accountability, participation, consultation, and power sharing emerge, the state is unlikely to garner the minimum level of legitimacy necessary to consolidate peace and establish effective governance. That is true as well for states still plagued by civil war or violent conflict, such as Angola, Sudan, and Congo.

The problem with the typical, repressive closed regime is that there is little political will for liberalisation, since that means surrendering some political power and resources (or risking control altogether). In these circumstances, probably the most that international assistance can do is to work with civil society to keep hope alive: to improve the demand and potential for democratic governance, to defend citizen rights by fighting the worst abuses of power, and to promote peaceful resolution of conflict and even reconciliation among warring parties.

Raising citizen awareness and access to information, and empowering citizens to organise peacefully for political change, are particular imperatives. In some cases, it may also be possible to help courts and representative bodies to become more independent and effective. However, it makes little sense to train or work with state agencies or actors in closed regimes unless there is evidence of some commitment to improving governance and opening up political life, even if that will only happen incrementally.

In thinking about prospects and priorities for DG assistance, it is important to be realistic about where a country stands. As Thomas

Carthorse has recently noted, most electoral authoritarian (or what he calls "gray-zone") regimes are not "in transition" or "stuck in transition." The way they combine authoritarian and (often quite limited and superficial) democratic elements constitutes a distinct and possibly persistent regime form. This recognition underscores two points. One is that for these regimes (particularly the less competitive, more repressive ones) to become democracies they must actually initiate a transition, not complete one that is still "underway." This necessitates a whole series of institutional reforms to allow a more level and neutrally administered field of electoral competition, and to allow more space for independent civil society and political actors. And second, this returns analysis to the crucial matter of the political will to reform.

7.5.2. Promoting Transparency and Accountability

No problem is more broadly shared across all four classes of regimes than corruption in government and party politics. And no problem has more seriously eroded public confidence in democratic institutions and the stability of electoral democracies. Across Central and Eastern Europe (including Russia, Ukraine, and Belarus), surveys find that over 70 percent of the public, on average, believe that their new regime is more corrupt than its predecessor, and in every post commissure country surveyed a majority of the public believes the national government is corrupt.

The Latinobarometer, surveying public opinion in 17 Latin American democracies since 1995, has consistently found similarly high levels of cynicism. When asked whether corruption has increased a little or a lot, remained the same, or decreased a little or a lot in the last 12 months, an astonishing 75 percent of Latin Americans said in 2000 that corruption has increased a lot. Another 10 percent said corruption has increased a little and less than five percent perceived any decline. Even in countries with strong support for democracy, such as Costa Rica, Uruguay, and Argentina, most people think corruption has increased a lot.

These figures reflect a pervasive perception that parties and politicians of all stripes are corrupt and self-interested, rather than serving the public good, and this perception is alienating many citizens from the democratic process. Tenuous democracies cannot become consolidated and regimes of all kinds cannot improve the quality of their governance and their capacity for sustainable economic development unless corruption is significantly diminished. For this reason, assisting counter-corruption institutions and programs must become one of the major priorities of international political and development assistance in the next decade.

International donors have learned a great deal in the past decade about what is necessary to control corruption. To repeat a general lesson, nothing is more important than political will to reform on the part of top leaders. The global struggle against corruption should thus continue on two tracks: to mobilise public demand and support for reform, and to change the institutional environment in which the public and private sectors interact. To become more effective, these efforts need more forceful and coordinated diplomatic engagement to back them up.

On the demand side, assistance should raise public awareness of the costs of corruption, changes expectations about ethical behaviour, and empowers the public with information. Citizens must come to see that corruption obstructs development, heightens inequity, and damages the entire country. Linkages of all kinds are important here:

— Between advocacy NGOs and the mass media.

— Between NGOs and sectorial interest groups (such as business chambers, trade unions, and professional associations); between local actors and international business.

— Between national movements and international networks and conventions.

Where state actors are themselves pushing reforms, there is also a need to foster public-private partnerships to deepen and accelerate the process. Advocacy NGOs need not be focused on the corruption issue per se in order to have an impact. In many countries, environmental groups have galvanised public action by exposing the links between environmental abuses and political corruption.

In Nigeria and other African countries, human rights organisations are making the link between corruption (as a major motive for obtaining and retaining power) and repression, and they have campaigned eloquently for serious institutional reforms. In many countries, chambers of commerce, business associations, and other advocates for economic reform chip away at the enabling environment for bribery and corruption by seeking to streamline state regulations, eliminate unnecessary controls, and make government more transparent.

For example, Ecuador's National Association of Entrepreneurs (ANDE) has enlisted the support of business leaders, government officials, NGOs, and even the Catholic Church in its effort to mobilise public concern and institutional reforms to address corruption. The mass media have a crucial role to play in the campaign against corruption. We need to enhance the skill—but also the professional responsibility of the media in investigating and reporting on acts of corruption.

This can be done in part through assistance to journalism training centres and to national media associations to strengthen professional skills and norms and to advocate for legislative and administrative reforms to improve transparency and media openness. NGOs can also be assisted in their efforts to use the mass media to educate and mobilise the public against corruption. Argentina's Proud Ciudadano has developed imaginative television and radio spots as part of its public education campaign.

Regional and international initiatives are also vital in changing the normative climate of tolerance for corruption and pressing for national-level changes. One hopeful step was the OECD adoption of the Convention on Combating Bribery of Foreign Officials in International Business Transactions. One of the most important international civil society initiatives is Transparency International (TI), is one of the truly great success stories of international civil society mobilisation and public-private partnerships to improve governance over the past decade. Its practical methods for promoting public debate, making government more transparent, forging reform coalitions, and assembling comprehensive national systems of integrity have put it on the conceptual and political cutting edge of the campaign against corruption. On the supply side, there are many things that can be done to help change the environment in which the public and private sectors interact. These include:

— Supporting legal and regulatory reform to reduce government's involvement in areas more efficiently handled by the private sector. Here economic reform and anti-corruption efforts converge.
— Streamlining and making more transparent government procedures (including budgeting and procurement) to reduce the opportunities for corruption.
— Elaborating and improving governmental institutions of accountability.
— Introducing incentives for officials to act in the public interest.

Reforms need to establish independent government oversight and auditing institutions, streamline regulations, standardise and computerise government financial management, improve contracting procedures, train in fraud investigation, and reform and strengthen judiciaries.

The problem is that where political will is lacking, new laws and institutions amount to a Potemkin village: the facade is impressive, but there is nothing behind it. When political leaders want to frustrate anti-corruption reforms, they staff oversight agencies with cronies or timid timeservers, or they starve the bodies of funding and authority. (This has repeatedly undermined the quest for accountability in Nigeria, for example). They file false assets declarations and forbid their public disclosure. They open up new avenues of corruption just as old ones are closed. They intimidate and stonewall auditors and investigators. They may even murder them if they come too close to the truth. They transfer corrupt practices to levels and arenas that reforms have not yet penetrated. And they routinely use the privatisation process itself as a major vehicle of corrupt accumulation.

Anti-corruption initiatives therefore do not succeed unless demand proceeds apace to stimulate and sustain political will for reform. Institutional reforms must include some kind of independent, authoritative, and resourceful counter-corruption commission, designed in conjunction with reform advocates in civil society, and clearly empowered to investigate, expose, and prosecute corrupt conduct. The entire structure of horizontal accountability including the courts, public auditors, ombudsman's office, and human rights commission must have similar autonomy, energy, and resources.

International pressure is crucial, not in dictating the precise shape of institutions but in demanding that government officials take seriously socialite demands for reform and allow home-grown institutions the authority, autonomy, leadership, and resources to function effectively.

7.5.3. Political Party Assistance

In most of the electoral democracies and competitive authoritarian regimes, political parties are a major problem. Quite often they are corrupt, insular, internally undemocratic, detached from socialite interests, and ineffective in addressing the country's problems. When one weighs their performance against high citizen expectations for performance and accountability after authoritarian rule, it is perhaps no surprise that they are held in astonishingly low repute.

It is tempting in these circumstances to write off political parties; they are not very serious about governing, not very democratic, and so we should focus on strengthening "purer" actors in the state or civil society. Such a blanket dismissal would be a grave mistake. In a modern society, democracy cannot function without political parties. It is political parties that structure electoral competition, organise government, and recruit leaders. And even if parties are only one among many vehicles for stimulating political participation and representing interests, they remain essential to the overall functioning of democracy. To the extent that they are feckless and corrupt, so is democracy itself.

Democratic political parties must become more capable and mature as organisations, more internally competitive and transparent, and more externally responsive and accountable. At the same time, international assistance and cooperation efforts must serve the larger goal of creating a representative and competitive multiparty system, which offers citizens choices of leaders and policies, responsiveness to their concerns, and a means for exercising vertical accountability. For both of these broad strategic aims, work with political parties must be ongoing, not just a temporary program a few months in advance of an election. Party assistance programs should continue to focus on three traditional objectives while intensifying work in two more innovative arenas. The three established themes are:

— *Organisational development*: helping parties to research issues, assess public opinion, develop policies and platforms, craft long-term strategies, build professional staffs, recruit members, raise funds, and manage resources.

— *Electoral mobilisation:* helping parties to select and train candidates, craft campaign messages, manage campaign organisations, improve communication skills, contact voters, identify and mobilise supporters, and activate women and youth.

— *Governance:* helping parties to function effectively as a legislative caucus, to constitute a government or opposition (including at the regional and local levels), to forge coalitions, to reform electoral laws, and to monitor elections through poll-watching.

Two more recent foci that merit much more emphasis in the coming years are:

— *Internal Democratisation*: helping parties to develop more democratic and transparent means of selecting candidates (e.g., through primaries and caucuses), choosing leaders, making decisions, formulating policies, and eliciting member participation.

— *Reforming party and campaign finance*: helping party, legislative, governmental, and civil society actors to identify alternative rules and systems for reporting and monitoring financial donations to parties and campaigns, auditing party accounts, providing public funding to parties and campaigns, and widening the access of all political parties to the electronic mass media. Also: helping parties to promote higher standards of ethical conduct among their leaders, candidates, and members; and helping civil society actors and electoral administrations to develop better technical means to monitor party and campaign finance.

The traditional and newer objectives are intimately related. Many parties cannot develop organisationally because they are personal vehicles of the party leader. Unless they become more broad-based and democratic in their internal governance, their institutional development will be stifled. If parties are going to be effective in deepening their organisation, mobilising support, and structuring governance, they must improve their image among the people. Such improvements will only be possible (and certainly, only sustainable) if parties become more open to grassroots participation, more internally democratic, more transparent in their financing and decision-making, and less corrupt.

The challenge of reforming party and campaign finance is a particularly vexing one, because campaign costs are continually rising (especially as countries become more reliant on television and other modern technology), and no democracy in the world has a very satisfactory system. Nevertheless, the problem is central, because in most electoral regimes, a good portion of the corruption in a country goes to fund the ruling party at various levels. To the extent that countries adopt systems of partial public funding for parties and guaranteed media access for campaigns, it will also help to level the electoral playing field.

What is the incentive for a party that is personalistic and corrupt to become more internally democratic and externally responsive and accountable? One overriding incentive may become more apparent over time. Parties that do modernise and reform themselves may gradually develop wider appeals and competitive advantages over those that do not. Moreover, if momentum gathers behind other efforts at institutional reform to rein in bribery, kickbacks, vote buying, and electoral fraud, and to raise citizen intolerance for these practices parties will come under growing pressure to reform, and will be at significant risk if they do not Political parties will not be strengthened by party assistance alone.

If one of the problems is that parties are detached from socialite interests, democratic development strategies may also find value in approaching the party issue from the civil society angle. Interest groups and NGOs can be supported in efforts to forge channels of communication and working relations with political parties. Civil society activists can be given training if they opt to enter the arena of party and electoral politics. One of the crucial challenges of improving party politics is recruiting better-educated and more public-spirited actors into the process.

Strengthening Judicial Capacity and Autonomy and the Rule of Law Democracy cannot be consolidated and governance cannot be improved without broad enhancement (and in some cases sweeping transformation) of all the institutional components of the rule of law: legal codes, constitutional frameworks, judiciaries, prosecuting authorities, police, and the entire legal profession, including legal education. In most emerging democracies and virtually all non-democracies, judges need better, more up-to-date training, greater resources (technical and financial), and greater autonomy from political pressure.

Typically also, the courts need to streamline their administrative management and their capacity to track and process cases, both criminal and civil. Both bilateral and multilateral donors have made substantial investments over the past two decades in court administration and facilities, including computerisation of case administration procedures and legal codes and precedents, as well as the physical infrastructure of the courts, legal information systems, and public law libraries. In many countries, these needs remain huge and will for many years to come.

Rule of law strategies must also continue to advise and support law schools and judicial training academies, and the drafting of strategies for judicial reform including the insulation of judges and prosecutors from political control. Bar associations must also be strengthened, not only to advocate for rule-of-law reforms, but also to work among legal practitioners to elevate professional norms and monitor the conduct of the legal community.

Fundamental reform usually requires legal and constitutional reform. Transitional systems and tentative democracies need to draft well-conceived constitutions that learn from the institutional experience of other countries. They also need new, better, fairer, and clearer legal frameworks that protect civil liberties, property rights, and the rule of law. International assistance and cooperation can help with these efforts. However, technical and infrastructure assistance to the judicial sector will not in itself strengthen the rule of law.

If corrupt political leaders appoint pliant judges who are politically obligated to the politicians, if the judges, prosecutors, and court administrators are themselves corrupt, if the broader context of bad governance is not addressed, millions of dollars in assistance to the judicial sector may have only a marginal impact, producing judges that are more knowledgeable and better equipped but no less corrupt or politically dependent. A major lesson of rule-of-law assistance to strengthen and modernise formal institutions is that it must be accompanied by socialite demand for more capable, neutral, professional, and accessible systems of justice, and by socialite capacity to monitor and make use of these systems.

Deepening democracy and improving governance thus requires strengthening the rule of law from below as well as above. Citizens must be educated to know their rights under national law and international covenants. Society must be organised effectively to demand protection for these rights and specific reforms in the judiciary and police to secure individual rights. A major pillar of rule of law assistance thus involves aid to human rights, good governance, and civic education groups. Assistance in this realm helps NGOs and networks to engage in public advocacy and media campaigns on such issues as human rights, official and police impunity, judicial independence, and corruption. Public interest law groups also have a major role to play in creating a fairer legal system.

Donors can help marginalised groups gain access to justice through support for the public interest law movement among civil society groups and grassroots organisations, and through help to establish or expand legal aid centres and public defenders offices, and to train criminal defence attorneys and public defenders representing poor people. Police assistance and reform is also a vital dimension of improving the rule of law and of the related goals of mitigating conflict and enhancing citizen security for several reasons.

The police are one of the institutions of the state with which the ordinary citizen is most likely to have contact, and from which citizens most often suffer abuse. Rampant violence and crime diminish social trust and public faith in democracy. They are two of the pervasive concerns of poor people in particular and major obstacles to development, deterring investment and generating huge costs in health, productivity, and distorted investment (for example, in private security measures). Security of persons and property is essential to lowering transaction costs and generating productive investment. Policing is thus a realm in which international assistance must be more active in the coming decade, particularly in countries that have been devastated by internal conflict or face rising levels of violent conflict and crime.

To be effective, police assistance must be part of a broader program of rule-of-law assistance that includes not only the police and the judicial system but also neighbourhood crime prevention groups and projects and human rights NGOs. In this context, international assistance programs have helped to improve the professional competence of the police—their criminal investigative capabilities, police academy training programs, forensics, management, community relations, and coordination with prosecutors and judicial agents. More must be done to develop competent, professional policing that is also more respectful of human rights.

Because the rule of law touches on virtually every other aspect of democracy and governance, and so many dimensions of development, there is great scope for cross suctorial linkages. A stronger rule of law requires an effective counter-corruption apparatus, and a national legislature that is competent and autonomous in its lawmaking functions. In helping poor people and marginalised groups get access to justice, legal aid programs also help them address the environmental problems of their communities, the obstacles to registering a business, obtaining credit, and getting title to land, and other issues that are fundamental to the development process. Strengthening policing, if done in the appropriate way, can also enhance human rights and accountability, and can proceed well in tandem with community human rights programs.

7.5.4. Strengthening Civil Society

In recent years, international donor assistance to civil society has become a subject of growing controversy. The gathering critique of Western civil society assistance indicts it on several counts:

— That it has focused too heavily, if not exclusively in many countries, on assistance to NGOs (particularly public advocacy or democracy NGOs), which are only one type of actor in civil society.

— That the kinds of NGOs supported are "top down," elitist, often internally undemocratic, and based in the capital city, with weak roots in society and faint connection to real socialite interests.

— That Western donors, particularly USAID, have imposed their own goals and agendas on civil society recipients of aid, robbing them of ownership and initiative and orienting them away from their own societies.

— That the organisations and efforts funded are unsustainable without continued international aid, particularly given the salaries they pay and the technology they use.

— That the relatively generous international funding is drawing human talent and energy away from other, more authentic institutions and activities into these structures born in the image of the West. These criticisms are overly generalised and often lacking in a balanced recognition of the contributions that many NGO recipients have made to democratic development around the world. Nevertheless, strategies of DG assistance in the coming decade must begin from a frank recognition of the validity of much of this criticism.

There has been too much emphasis on aiding a certain kind of civil society actor, which explicitly (and perhaps exclusively) targets issues of democratic governance reform, and which speaks the stylised language of Western donors. There has been too little consultation with the broad social forces of these societies, and too little readiness to respond to what existing civil society actors see to be their organisational and developmental needs. Assisted NGOs are sometimes lacking in accountability to anyone but the donors, while floating in an ethereal and largely internationalised space above their own societies. And even the most effective organisations are likely to remain dependent on international funding for many years, if not decades, to come.

The challenge for international assistance in the coming decade is not one of wholesale redesign but rather to adapt strategies and programs to address the real problems of past approaches. One need for adaptation is in the time horizons that shape strategy. Building effective and stable democratic governance is going to require protracted engagement over at least another decade, and probably several. In any country with deeply entrenched structures of power and privilege, a serious strategy to foster democratic and accountable governance must aim for the long haul, undertaking efforts that may only exhibit an impact on the quality of national governance gradually over a long period of time.

Viewed in this way, one promising strategic priority lies in increased assistance to civil society organisations that have as their ostensible purpose economic or social development but that are taking on DG objectives as well. The battle against corruption requires the involvement not only of explicit democracy or good-governance NGOs, but of groups with an environmental, gender, or agrarian focus as well. The struggle to raise citizen awareness and mobilise civic participation can only reach an enduring critical mass when it seeps into the deep structures and concrete interests of daily life. As Stephen Golub has observed:

> Battered women, subsistence farmers, street vendors, and urban squatters usually respond far better to appeals to their legitimate self-expression than to their democratic spirit. They may well care about important concepts like democracy, and may be moved to action in times of dramatic national transition. But once the smoke has cleared, they act on 'felt need.' International assistance in the coming decade must therefore do much more to get programs addressing "felt needs" such as family planning, (women's) literacy and health, potable water, rural livelihood, and ending domestic violence to also serve DG objectives, such as extending legal services, rights education, and civic participation.

Such integration accelerates momentum for DG reforms by rooting them more broadly in society, especially in organisations that have built up credibility dealing with issues that are more functional and (often) less controversial. It is important to emphasise that such a cross-sectorial approach need not and must not entail a wholesale shift away from NGOs that advocate more explicitly for democracy and systemic governance reforms. "Professionally run NGOs and watchdog groups are indispensable to sustaining democratic change because they are typically more 'civic-minded' and are relatively resistant to governmental corruption and repression."

The campaign for more accountable and responsive governance may lose its energy, dynamism, and strategic focus if it lacks the articulate involvement of NGOs and think tanks that are pushing an explicit agenda of democratic reform. In fact, one recent assessment of

USAID civil society assistance programs in seven countries suggests that fundamental improvement of democratic governance is unlikely to occur without sustained support of civil society initiatives for system change.

However, more must be done to encourage these reformist organisations to reach out to the mass public, to establish links and alliances (as some of them have been doing) with interest groups and other organisations, to develop regional offices and programs, and even to recruit displaying members (however nominal the sums raised). It is a mistake to conclude that because these organisations are run by Western-educated elates who are paid comfortable, middle-class salaries, and because they begin with a narrow organisation and focus, they are fundamentally incapable of sinking broader roots in the society.

Many of them will not sink such roots, because they are poorly led, opportunistic, or half-hearted. But given time and incentives, some (perhaps many) of them will do so. In fact, many of these NGO leaders are capable, serious, sensitive to their own cultures, and working at some sacrifice (given the professional opportunities they forego in their own private sectors or in the West). In some countries where the legal environment for civil society is relatively benign (if not positively facilitating) and where professional competence, breadth, and integrity have been demonstrated among civil society leaders, it may be time for international donors to consider endowing indigenous foundations to assist civil society.

These foundations would have to establish some scope of purpose and priorities. They might initially have foreign representation on their boards, but they would be locally "owned" and governed, and would make judgements about funding and priorities that would respond to local demands and needs rather than to US or other external assessments. With less demanding and expensive requirements for auditing and reporting, they could make grants to a wider variety of civil society organisations, including smaller and more informal groups. International donors could periodically evaluate the work of the foundation, and increase its endowment if it performs well.

More also needs to be done to build up the enabling environment for civil society. At a minimum, laws and regulations that put barriers in the way of registering and legally protecting independent organisations need to be removed. Where necessary, diplomacy needs to weigh in with state elates who are not inclined to want a vigorous and independent civil society. In countries that are more advanced economically and politically an important reform frontier lies in changes to laws and tax regimes that permit and encourage private philanthropic grants to civil society organisations.

Some NGOs may be assisted to develop services, such as public opinion polling, policy analysis, or development activities, which can earn significant consulting or user fees. Beyond this, a strong note of realism is warranted on the part of international donors. The plain truth is that many of the best public interest organisations are not really self-sustaining even in the United States or Western Europe.The difference, of course, is that in the U.S. Or Europe, public advocacy NGOs can turn to a vast array of foundations; in poor countries, they have only their own corrupt governments or the outside world. Golub therefore suggests that a better test for continued support than the prospect of sustainable domestic funding would be whether the NGO is generating sustainable impact because it is doing "quality work." If it is, and it is gradually building indigenous constituencies for that work, there is no reason why external donors should not be prepared to support it until that time well into the future when the society becomes rich enough to assume the burden.

References

Andreas Schedler, Larry Diamond, and Marc F. Plattner, eds., 1999. *The Self-Restraining State: Power and Accountability in New Democracies* Boulder, CO: Lynne Rienner Publishers.

Derick W. Brinkerhoff, 1999. "Identifying and Assessing Political Will for Anti-Corruption Efforts," Working Papers no. 13, *Implementing Policy Change* project, USAID, January.

Thomas Carothers, 1999. *Aiding Democracy Abroad: The Learning Curve* Washington, D.C.: The Carnegie Endowment for International Peace, , p. 101.

Marta Lagos, 2001. "How People View Democracy: Between Stability and Crisis In Latin America," *Journal of Democracy* 12 January.

Yun-han Chu, Larry Diamond, and Doh Chull Shin, 2001. "How People View Democracy: Halting Progress in Korea and Taiwan," *Journal of Democracy* 12. January.

8

Terrorism vs. Political Freedom

The subject of "terrorism" seized the world's attention in late 2001 as a result of one fairly brief, yet highly dramatic and destructive, attack on two of the core symbols of the world's most powerful political actor, the United States of America. The targeting of the World Trade Centre in New York City, the symbol of the United States' enormous global economic power, and the Pentagon Building in Washington, DC, the symbol of the United States' overarching military superiority, was well planned, coordinated, and executed. The attack itself attained symbolic stature as an affront to the established global order, a challenge to the world's dominant power, and an announcement that the prevailing US-led global order was not viewed, or valued, equally by all those whose daily lives are increasingly caught in the vortex of post-Cold War change.

Of course, the problem of terrorism was already well-known when the planes struck their targets in full view of a vast, global, tele-connected audience and created their indelible psychic images of sophisticated savagery. The politics of terror, and the overpowering fear that terror produces in its wake, lay at the very foundation of the evolution of social order. And it is the ultimate irony of socialite development that modern acts of savagery have attained such high levels of sophistication. In its most simple terms, terror has stood as the stark alternative to civility in social relations from the time of humankind's earliest recorded reflections.

As Hobbes explained in his 17th century treatise, "Out of civil states, there is always war of every one against every one the nature of war, consists not in actual fighting; but in the known disposition there to and which is worst of all, continual fear and danger of violent death; the life of man sic, solitary, poor, nasty, brutish, and short." At their roots, terror, force; and violence are integral and, as such, terrorism as a course of action is hardly distinguishable from coercion as a strategy or violence as a tactic.

Contemporary analyses of the problem of terrorism have usually foundered between the perceptual extremes that are inherent in the amorphous ideas of terror: conceptualistic of terrorism are either too broad to be analytically useful, too narrow to be analytically meaningful, or too complex to be applied systematically. The conceptualisations themselves are all too often politically motivated as the analyst attempts to rationalise a distinction between civil and uncivil applications of violence: (useless) terror and (useful) enforcement, (undisciplined) terrorism and (disciplined) war, and (dishonourable) terrorists and (honourable) "freedom fighters."

Conceptual confusion is further exacerbated by the often cavalier usage of the pejorative term "terrorist" to refer to any political opponent, much as "communist" was used for political effect in the West during the Cold War. Hoffman offers an example of a broad definition, "Terrorism is] the deliberate creation and exploitation of fear through violence or the threat of violence in the pursuit of political change." Hoffman attempts to differentiate his definition of terrorism from criminal and lunatic violence by emphasising the "altruistic" and "intellectual" qualities of terrorist motivation.

However, it seems clear that all acts of terrorism are criminalist acts that are made particularly effective because they are unconventional (extralegal or non-rational) applications of violent or coercive behavioural. The parallels between terrorism, state repression, organised crime, and war are too great to be discounted. The use of arbitrary and indiscriminate violence in wartime has become increasingly criminalistic since the establishment of the Nuremberg trials at the end of the Second World War in 1945. State repression, or "state terror," which finds its most extreme form in totalitarianism has become increasingly scrutinised and criminalist by the international community.

In a similarly broad definition, Carr goes so far as to equate terrorism with conventional warfare, with one very important distinction: "Terrorism is warfare deliberately waged against civilians with the purpose of destroying their will to support either leaders or policies that the agents of such violence find objectionable." For Carr, terror is established through the unrestrained demonstration of violence; it is an induced emotional state intended to disable the will in individuals to resist, or seek rectification for, a perceived injustice through the credible threat (fear) of unspecified, unbearable consequences. While both Hoffman and Carr concentrate on the serious psychosocial affects of terror, their perspectives are separated widely by the perquisites of power:

Hoffman's low-power, non-state terrorists using terror to challenge authority and facilitate change, Carr's high-power, state terrorists using terror to establish authority and facilitate conquest. Schmid and Jongman provide an example of a definition of terrorism which, due ironically to their attempt to increase definition specificality, is far too complex (and, at once, too broad) to be applied systematically in research. For them, terrorism is an anxiety-inspiring method of repeated violent action, employed by (semi) clandestine individual, group, or state actors, for idiosyncratic, criminal or political reasons, whereby in contrast to assassination the direct targets of violence are not the main targets.

The immediate human victims of violence are generally chosen randomly (targets of opportunity) or selectively (representative or symbolic targets) from a target population, and serve as message generators. Threat and violence-based communication processes between terrorist (organisations), (imperilled) victims, and main targets are used to manipulate the main target (audiences), turning it into a target of terror, a target of demands, or a target of attention, depending on whether intimidation, coercion, or propaganda is primarily used.

The core qualities of Schmid and Jongman's definition are its inclusion of state actors, as well as non-state actors, as potential agents; its inclusion of wide ranges of power and political intent, and its recognition that acts of violence must be reiterative and somewhat arbitrary in order to induce widespread terror (rather than the more immediate response of revulsion to acts of brutality). Pillar emphasises this later point in his definition of terrorism, that terror gains its greatest strength from its focus on the possible future rather than the knowable present.

A variant of the "narrow" approach to defining the problem of terrorism has been to identify a special class of terrorist activity, that is, "international," or "transnational," terrorism. This conceptualisation has gained currency among policy-makers, particularly in "global powers" of the West, as it appears, on surface, to focus on a particular subset of terrorist actions with "global scope," thereby inferring that this subset of terrorism stands as a direct threat to the "global social order."

The concept is based on two important, implicit, a priori assumptions: first, the West, and particularly the US, is the recognised authority leading the establishment of an emerging global order and, second, the actions taken by the leading authorities in establishing and maintaining the emerging global order are either legitimate by definition (an extended form of the classic reason detect) or that the interests of population affected by the global order are adequately represented within the emerging global political system.

This narrow form of terrorism, then, is conducted by those, usually non-state actors who may or may not receive support from dissident states or population, who are intent on challenging, and changing, the terms of the prevailing social order. The essential qualities of this conceptualisation relate to issues of distance and jurisdiction. The first quality, distance or "reach," may be best viewed as simply a spatial artifact, often made salient by asymmetric of power between contending groups and established authorities. That is, challengers to a particular form of social order take advantage of available technologies and the prevailing vulnerability associated with distance by using, or seeking to exploit, available advantages in communication, information, and mobility to identify and attack relatively distant (and comparatively weak) outposts of authority. This spatial component of international terrorism is not unique, however.

Opposition always collective consciousness as it is shaped by central authorities. Most acts of non-international terrorism have similar qualities of combining local, proximate, and distant action. In a strategic interaction between distanced groups, what is considered local to one is necessarily considered distant by the other. Agents of violence find it logistically easier to conduct local attacks but strategically important to demonstrate their capability to mount attacks on relational distant targets located in their opponent's heartland.

The perceived value, and therefore the terror potential, of targets increase with proximity to the heartland (and breach of the security perimeter). Two contending groups rarely occupy the exact same political space and, even when they do share competing claims to authority over the same political space, their "heartland" remain spatially distinct and separated even when their territorial or jurisdictional interests contend and overlap. So, for instance, the Irish Republican Army has operated mainly in the British province of Northern Ireland but has conducted operations in London at the centre of the British heartland; the Tamils of Sri Lanka have struck targets both in Colombo (the Sinhalese heartland) and in India, including the May 1991 assassination of Indian Prime Minister Rajiv Gandhi; and Chechen militants have allegedly struck targets as "remote" as Moscow.

The relatively recent "internationalisation" of anti-authority terrorism may be simply a function of increased popular access to distance or technological reach. Friedman has referred to this phenomenon as the "super-empowered individual." Such strategic behaviour is not confined to asymmetric power relationships or non-state actors. The US air raids against Tokyo in April 1942 and NATO air raids against Belgrade during the 1999 Kosovo war are similar demonstrations of the capability to mount "distant" attacks in the opposition's heartland.

The second essential quality of international terrorism, jurisdiction, is particularly important in defining potential remedies to a contestation between groups or individuals. Operating outside of, or across, an established juridical boundary complicates remedial action (ameliorative or coercive) and limits the range and/or effectiveness of institutional options. With the lack of definitive and effective instruments for addressing the problem of terrorist action in international law and institutions, ambiguities and uncertainties of juridical responsibility provide special opportunities and vulnerabilities for exploitation both by terrorist agents and affected authorities.

In the absence of established institutional mechanisms, it can be expected that those entities that are most greatly affected and who enjoy the greatest capacity for direct action will act within such a "political vacuum" in terms of their own perspectives and according to their own interests, that is, unilaterally. The unregulated strategic interactions of the most directly affected parties played out in the greater communal space will undoubtedly serve to terrorise the entire system, creating a global imperative to act.

But the ability to respond rationally and effectively will be limited by selection biases inherent in our understanding of the problem. Again, selection biases often reflect asymmetric of power. Powerful actors have recourse to a wide array of instrumentalities to promote their parochial interests, whereas weak actors may feel they have very few options to demonstrate their position and the strength of their resolve other than violence. Diffuse and indirect actions often have very direct consequences, as Galtung has argued with his concept of "structural violence." Such structural violence, that is, violence embedded in the underlying structures of social relationships, is necessarily biased toward power and established authority and, thus, makes it particularly difficult to identify the interactive, reciprocal, and alternating qualities of "terrorist" and "terrorised."

The problems of distance and jurisdiction act within a context of immediacy and imperative created by the violent attack and, as such, treatments of the problem of international terrorism tend to favour emotive and reactive responses, focusing on the symptoms and rarely considering the nature of the problems that might have stimulated such extreme or radical actions. While studies of international terrorism usually contain the recognition of the political intent of terrorist acts, the convention of non-negotiation with terrorists often obviates the identification of possible motives and, thus, stifles our ability to avoid or preclude the resort to terrorism (which would, of course, obviate the need to negotiate with terrorists).

In addition to ignoring the structural foundations of terrorism, the literature on international terrorism does not usually include reference to comparable attacks on agents and institutions of international organisations such as the UN, international NGOs, and international journalists, thus confounding that concept with "anti-internationalist" or "anti-US" resistance This is especially confusing in a global environment where the vestiges of "anti-colonialism" often intertwine with emerging strands of "anti-globalism."

In systematic studies of international terrorism, the US, Israel, and the former colonial powers of Western Europe account for the vast majority of the targets of international terrorist acts. The fact that the US, especially, enjoys an unprecedented extent of "international reach" in global affairs and, therefore, runs an unprecedented level of risk from engendered international contention should not be conflicted with, and used as, a measure of the general security of the global system. In this sense, both the United States' pro-active policies and reactions to those policies must be included in any objective measure of the affects of such strategic interaction on global security.

Perhaps the most difficult aspect to reconcile in our various attempts to define terrorism has been the almost universal claim that terrorism is necessarily political. Beyond the broadest sense of what is political, that is, the sense in which all actions taken in a social context are inherently political, the idea that an action is political implies that the action is instrumental in pursuing or achieving some commonly understood goal.

This rationality conundrum presents terrorism as an unsolved problem. The conundrum can only be reconciled by examining the emotive qualities of terrorism: that terrorism is borne of an emotive or psychic impulse in search of a political expression. Perhaps the most powerful emotive impulse is vengeance, whether as a result of a perceived injustice or indignity or an act of humiliation. Such powerful emotive impulses are often individuality, internalised, and personalised by affected individuals leading to acts of self-destruction where the unworthy self becomes the target for retribution of perceived wrongs.

The act of externalising these emotive impulses may be facilitated by political rhetoric that emphasises the congeniality of the aggrieved and a common source of grievances. In this politicisation of vengeance and other, lesser forms grievance, the rationalisation of externalisation and the identification of targets for retribution find expression in a common political perspective and agenda for action. Common emotional impulses provide the impetus for overcoming collective action problems among politically dis empowered individuals.

The immediate and direct goal of such emotive action is to establish the capacity to "strike back." Although the impetus to "strike back" implies grievance and, thus, a desire for political change, the immediate and realisable goal is to inflict hurt, not to effect change. The politics of terror, in this instance, are imposed from the outside, recast on the inside, and redirected toward an external target. This emotive, relational quality makes (non-repressive) terrorist action less amenable to rational deterrent strategies. Deterrent actions can be viewed as consistent with, and therefore validation of, the structures of perceived injustice and very often widen the scope of persons directly affected by the actions of authorities and, so, can actually stimulate rather than deter further acts of terrorism.

It can be seen that it is the political quality of common experience, the common attribution of causal agent or target, and the collective coordination, or mobilisation, of emotive response that differentiates (non-repressive) organised terrorist action from lesser forms of terror, such as psychotic, sociopolitical, or criminal violence. Even these lesser (less-politicised) forms of terror can create a climate of terrorism that has serious effects on social relations, especially when those ostensibly random non-organised acts of disturbed individuals attain a sense of regularity and arbitrariness.

For example, psychotic and sociopolitical terror have become more extreme and regularised in US society such that hardly a week goes by without news of another attack on a school or a multiple murder-suicide. This form of terror is much closer to most Americans and is likely to have produced more diffuse effects than the more dramatic but far less frequent form of political terrorism that has culminated in the September 11, 2001, events and the subsequent "war on terrorism" in Afghanistan. Similarly, terror does not need to be premeditated as is evidenced in the regularity of "spontaneous" Hindu-Muslim riots in India.

Such communal pogroms are not unique to this context but have been, and continue to be, a fairly common method used to maintain power asymmetric in situations of communal competition. Purely sociopolitical terrorism, such as the anarchist groups that have operated in Western democracies, are particularly difficult to sustain as they lack sufficient emotive strength (they are steeped mainly in malaise, disaffection, and indignation) and, by nature of their ideological perspective, can not define a common political agenda other than the destruction of the existing order. Organised terror, while it can be orchestrated to a certain extent among "violence sycophants" (i.e., those individuals who are predisposed to value and commit violence), is most problematic when it achieves a broad network of popular support.

Even the "super-empowered individual" who ultimately "pulls the trigger" requires a relatively broad base of support in order to ensure secrecy long enough to realise their full capacity for technological empowerment. Although greater and more accessible technologies of destruction make possible greater power to the individual actor, the preparation of such technologies for actual implementation draw greater aversion, publicity, and attention. Terror requires secrecy and secrecy demands silence not only by those who are integral to the conspiracy but, also, all potential witnesses (i.e., the "sea" in which the "fish" must swim).

Silence is sometimes a function of ignorance (particularly in the first instance of a new form of terrorist action) but is most often achieved through popular, supportive, and cooperative behaviour. As such, most terrorist cells operate in close association with larger, more conventional political associations that are sympathetic with the terrorists' political rhetoric and agenda but uncomfortable with the terrorists' methods. Equally important to the instrumental and operational aspects of broad, popular support is the creation of a supportive rhetorical environment in which extremist rhetoric may reverberate, amplify, and escalate over time. Terrorism, as a political act, stands at once at the nexus between individual and collective action, the emotional and rational, the conventional and the unconventional. It is can be the strongest form of protest or the weakest form of rebellion or a specialised tactic in warfare. Above all else, it is the most personal form of violence.

The nature and quality of the association between the tactical terrorist organisation and the larger support network are crucial in defining the scope, efficacy, resilience, and persistence of terrorist activity. Carr makes a particularly strong argument regarding the "galvanising" effects of terrorist tactics on the strategic interactions between contending groups. Rather than undermining, intimidating, or disabling the will to support contention, the intentional targeting of noncombatant population, that is the actual, potential, or imagined opposition support base, further polarises the contending groups and strengthens and fortifies the affected group's collective resolve to resist and/or strike back. Carr claims this as compelling evidence of the inevitable failure of terror.

Like the myth of the Hydra, terrorist organisation tends to recreate and regenerate itself in direct response to the strength of coercive attempts to thwart its activities and remove its leaders or operatives: as one head is removed, several others appear to take its place. Even when the organisational structure is broken completely in a mass sweep of operatives, if there is no attendant change in the underlying conditions that gave rise to the original terrorist psyche, the organisation of affected individuals will most likely be recreated over a period of time and such activity will re-emerge.

This is surely the general experience of brutal dictatorships and a large part of the reason why these forms of governance are inherently unstable, giving way eventually to more open and less coercive forms of governance. This is also the lesson of the use of "right-wing death squads" in places such as El Salvador, Colombia, and Algeria that create great death, injury, and mayhem but are ineffective in quelling dissent, even when great care is taken to identify and target the leadership cadres of the opposition. It is surely the lesson of the Israeli-Palestinian terrorist conflict which has continued in various forms for seventy years or more.

The strong emotive quality of terrorism is at once a powerful motivating and an inherently limiting factor. Terror is a dynamic, transitional quality that rarely exists for long periods of time without transforming to or integrating with more complex forms of instrumental conflict behaviour. The strength of our emotional responses tends to wane over time unless transferred to hate. More often, strong emotional responses stimulate the search for rationality; in this application repeated, or re-stimulated, emotional responses can be very important in sustaining levels of activity. The greatest threat of terrorism lay not in its capacity to threaten, and deliver, personalised violence but, rather, in its relation to the more institutionalised forms of violence. Terrorist activity is commonly associated, as Carr argues, with all forms of warfare. It is a common instrument in separatist violence, used both by government authorities and separatist agents.

Terrorism's greatest strategic value may lay in its demonstration effects, that is, its capacity for signalling both the group's strength and resolve and the target's complicities and vulnerabilities. Terrorism may not be successful in achieving tangible political goals, but, through its capacity to galvanise public opinion, it may be instrumental in polarising contending groups and stimulating group members to increase their support for more conventional tactics such as protest or the transformation of protest to open, armed rebellion.

These conventional conflict strategies are generally more acceptable alternatives to terrorist activities. Where terrorism exists without ties to these more collective forms of conflict, it is generally due to one of two reasons:

— Terrorism, as a limited form of engagement, more quickly and effectively overcomes collective action problems that may retard or thwart the mobilisation of mass conventional action.
— State repression may prevent the formation of mass movements, in which case terrorism may be the only available avenue for demonstrations of dissent. Terrorist activity is often the prelude to the transformation of nonviolent protest movements to armed rebellion. The transformation of protest to armed conflict provides a tactical niche for acts of terrorism.

The emotive content of terrorist motivation makes it compatible with both political, as argued above, and spiritual rationalisation or justifications. Terrorist activity can be doubly emotive as the moral and ethical dimensions of terrorist action have to be reconciled in the mind. The contemporary predominance of secular government also contributes to the utility of sectarian rationalisation of dissent as accentuating the moral divide between an unjust temporal authority and aspirations for an ideal and just society in its place. This separation of "state and church" may also help to explain the recent claims of analysts, like Hoffman, that "terrorist incidents perpetrated for religious motives result in so many more deaths than those with purely political motives" terrorist.

Spiritual rationalisation can be particularly effective, and threatening, as they better match the absolution of personal responsibility, legitimising authority, and community of cause and perspective. After all, what greater authority exists in the mind of the believer than the "will of God?" What has come to be known as "Islamic fundamentalism" is especially emblematic of the utility of spiritual or theocratic rationalisation and mobilisation of dissent as it purports a convergence between the spiritual, political, and economic aspects of human social relations. Judicium is very similar in this regard.

The sole redeeming quality, so to speak, of the theocratic rationalisation is that it is at once empowering and restraining. The appeal to cosmic authorisation implies recognition that the contemplated deed is wrong and regretted and that the course of remedial action must be "fit" within the theological parameters of spiritual beliefs in divine benevolence. Purely secular (political) rationalisation of terror may not provide either of these inhibiting qualities: the recognition of transgression and the need for redemption.

The recent examples of Nazism and Communism verify this apprehension regarding the qualities of purely human rationalisation of "social engineering." Such claims are based on statistical artifacts generated by selection biases in data collection (i.e., evidence of state terrorism not included; only non-state terrorism is considered).

From this brief discussion of the various conceptualisations of terrorism, a common thread seems to emerge from which the core elements of an operational definition of the terrorist action may be identified. The essential defining quality of terrorism is that it is a direct and intentional violation of the intrinsic vulnerability of the human condition; in the context of the modern state and its structures of collective security this translates into the intentional targeting of civilian, noncombatant population. As McKeogh explains, "It is because it is a breach of the [principle of noncombatant immunity] that terrorism is forthrightly condemned: its wrongness consists primarily in the fact that it targets, not military installations and personnel, but civilian ones."

This essential quality has two fundamental political forms which derive from the prevailing structures of authority in socialite systems and are part of the same strategic interaction process: repressive (state) and expressive (non-state) terrorism. The underlying assumption of terrorism is that it is a primarily emotive, rather than rational, action in direct pursuit of psychic, rather than, material goals. Factors that contribute to determining the strength and persistence of the "terror" produced by violence against noncombatant population include the dramatic, shocking (i.e., extraordinary) impact of the attacks; the intensity of media coverage; the frequency, lithology, and arbitrariness of the attacks; the perceived potential for future attacks, and the recognised connections between individualised acts of contention and collective action.

The historical record of terrorism seems to indicate that it is becoming less ordinary, that there is a strong negative relationship between the scope and frequency of terrorism and the pace of socialite development in specific locations and that the general trend has been a gradual decrease in the scope and frequency of terrorism over the course of evolution of human societies. An important caveat is the positive relationship between the destructive capabilities of terrorism and the general extent and pace of technological development: the "super-empowered terrorist." Think, for example, of the very powerful, subliminal terrorism produced by the growing availability of the technologies of mass destruction and the fear that these weapons may fall into the hands of ill intent.

8.1. Political Economy of Terrorism

Many key intuitions about how government policy might relate to terrorism (and political violence more broadly) concerns terrorism's relationship to the economy. In discussions of the root causes of terror, it is frequently argued that poverty and lack of access to opportunity are likely critical determinants of terrorist mobilization. Moreover, our concern with terrorism as a policy issue flows as much from the number of people killed by terrorists (which, compared to other types of political violence, is very low) as from concerns that the persistent fear of attack might damage both our politics and our economies. Political economy scholarship has attempted to address both of these relationships and, in some cases, have come to surprising conclusions.

A central question in trying to understand the root causes of terror is whether economic depravation leads to radical mobilization. Among recent political economy work, the first wave of studies to address this question attempted to do so by exploiting both cross-country and over-time variation in the state of the economy and in the level of terrorism. These studies report different findings, depending on choices regarding model specification, covariates, and the operationalization of the level of terrorism. Both Blomberg, Hess and Weerapana and Drakos and Gofas report a statistically significant negative correlation between measures of economic performance and the level of terrorist violence. Krueger and Laitin study both the country in which an attack occured and the home country of the terrorists who carried out the attack. They find that wealthy countries are more likely to suffer terrorist attacks and that economic performance is not a statistically significant predictor of which countries terrorists emerge from. Li and Schaub find no relationship between terrorism and foreign direct investment (FDI) or portfolio investment, but do find that economic development in a country, or in its top trading partners, reducess terrorism in that country.

Concerns have been expressed about the reliability of the studies discussed above on two dimensions:the quality of the data and the persuasiveness of the causal identification. The literature has gone about addressing these concerns in two ways. Abadie attempts to address both of these issues within a cross-country setting. On the data side, rather than using the standard data sources that provide counts of terrorist attacks or fatalites, Abadie bases his dependent variable on the World Market Research Center's Global Terrorism Index, which he writes, "encompasses five factors forecasting motivation, presence, scale, efficacy, and prefention of terrorism." More importantly, Abadie uses an instrumental variables approach to address the potential endogeneity between economic performance and the level of terrorism risk—i.e., poor economic performance may cause terrorism but terrorism (or the anticipation of terrorism) may also depress economic performance. Abadie's instrument for national GDP is whether or not a country is landlocked.

The identification assumption is that landlocked status directly affects GDP but does not affect the risk of terrorism through any mechanism other than its effect on GDP. Abadie finds that, controlling for other factors (including level of political freedom), there is no statistically significant relationship between per capita GDP and terrorism risk in the instrumental variables estimates. The other approach that has been taken to trying to shore up our empirical understanding of the links between the economy and terrorism is to abandon cross-country studies, focusing on micro-level details in important terrorist conflicts. For instance, Krueger and Maleckova and Berrebi study the individual characteristics of terrorist operatives from Hezbollah and Hamas, respectively. They find that that terrorist operatives are, themselves, neither poor nor poorly educated. Rather, their economic and educational statuses tend to lie around, or even slightly exceed, the averages in their societies.

Krueger and Maleckova argue that, since terrorists are neither poor nor poorly educated, the economy and education must not be important determinants of terrorism. Indeed, in a recent book, Krueger argues, based on this evidence, "there is not much question that poverty has little to do with terrorism" (Krueger 2007). Bueno de Mesquita presents a formal model to argue that, although the evidence regarding the socio-economic status of individual terrorists is of considerable interest, it does not entail the conclusion that poverty is not an important determinant of terrorist mobilization. The key assumption in Bueno de Mesquita's model is that terrorist organizations screen potential recruits on a "terrorist ability" dimension that is positively correlated with socio-economic status (i.e., better educated people make better terrorists). Benmelech and Berrebi present empirical evidence showing that better educated terrorist are indeed more effective in carrying out difficult tasks.

To see the problem this creates for the argument that the relatively high socioeconomic status of terrorist operatives implies that the economy is not an important determinant of terrorism, suppose that terrorist organizations accept recruits only over some competence threshold and that, as suggested by the data, competence is positively correlated with income or education. Suppose, further, that economic downturns increase mobilization (perhaps by decreasing opportunity costs). In such a world, because of screening, the terrorist operatives actually observed will be neither poor nor poorly educated, just as in the data described above. Yet, the conclusion will not be true: the supply of acceptable operatives and, therefore, the expected level of violence will be affected by economic factors. Of course, this theoretical argument does not establish that poverty causes terrorism. But it does suggest that the data presented thus far do not settle the question. Berman and Iannaccone and Berman take a somewhat different approach, embedding a model of terrorism and mobilization within a club model inspired by the literature on the economics of religion.

They argue that religions are likely to succeed at creating violent factions because their organizational structure is well suited to solving the fundamental problem that terrorists face—mobilizing supporters while weeding out low-commitment types. Successful religions do this by providing public goods to their members while imposing significant barriers to entry that exclude all but the most committed. Berman and Laitin provide empirical evidence that terrorist groups organized along these lines are more deadly and effective. Thus, the argument goes, the economy matters to the extent that a failed economy and failed government produce demand for social services not provided by the government, creating a niche for extremist factions to fill. In these models, governments can curtail religious extremists by increasing religious competition and by providing public goods to substitute for those offered by violent groups.

8.2. Counterterrorism

The key political economy insight into the problem of optimal counterterrorism comes from Enders and Sandler's (argument that terrorists respond strategically to counterterrorism measures, thereby generating "substitution effects." That is, terrorists, on observing an increase in a particular government counterterrorism program, can switch tactics, pursuing attacks less affected by the government's efforts. A variety of empirical studies find that counterterrorism generates such effects. For instance, Enders and Sandler (demonstrate that when the United States installed metal detectors in airports in the 1970s, hijackings decreased but other forms of terrorism increased. Both Bueno de Mesquita and Powell build on this insight in order to characterize the optimal division of counterterrorism resources in game theoretic models. Bueno de Mesquita's analysis (which is primarily focused on why we observe suboptimal counterterrorism) is restricted to a zero-sum games between the terrorists and the government where the government allocates resources prior to the terrorists attacking.

Powell and Powell allow for more generality, encompassing games that are simultaneous or sequential move (respectively) and that need not be zero sum. Interestingly, as the Powell papers demonstrate, the optimal allocation of counterterror resources is not sensitive to dynamics nor is it sensitive to being zero sum. In all three papers, the optimal counterterrorism strategy involves minimizing the expected value of attacking the targets that are most valuable to the terrorists. Powell describes the following algorithim for achieving this goal. The government first allocates resources to defending the target with highest expected value to the terrorists (where expected value is a function of underlying value to the terrorists and vulnerability to attack). Doing so decreases that target's vulnerability and, therefore, its expected value to the terrorists. The government does this until that target has the same expected value to the terrorists as the target with the next highest expected value. It then spends counterterror resources on these two targets until they have the same expected value as the target with the next highest expected value. It continues this procedure until it runs out counterterror resources.

Bueno de Mesquita and Powell also both consider the possibility that the govern-ment can invest in counterterrorism that is not target-specific (e.g., border security or intelligence). One advantage of such counterterror tactics is that it is more difficult for terrorists to substitute away from them. Thus, as the number of targets that need to be defended increases, counterterrorism that is not target specific becomes more attractive. Powell argues that another advantage of some such measures is that they may provide protection against events other than terrorist attacks. For instance, increased investment in emergency response is of value when there are natural disasters as well as when there are terrorist attacks. Of course, while understanding the optimal counterterrorism policy is critical, a variety of political and strategic considerations may lead to equilibrium counterterrorism strategies that are far from optimal.

One impediment to implementing an optimal counterterrorism policy is that counterterrorism may impose externalities across countries. For instance, Sandler and Siqueira draw a distinction between proactive and defensive counterterrorism. They argue that proactive counterterrorism (such as driving terrorists out of safe havens or investing in intelligence prior to attacks) is a public good among countries and, consequently, may be undersupplied. Sandler and Lapan and Rosendorff and Sandler suggest that one country's proactive counterterrorism may impose negative externalities on other countries by diverting attacks toward foreign targets. Thus, they argue, in some circumstances proactive measures may be oversupplied from the global perspective. Siqueira and Sandler embed these concerns in a model of domestic politics. They argue that voters will demand that politicians under-invest in proactive counterterrorism for two reasons: to free ride on other countries' counterterrorism investments and to avoid reprisal attacks from terrorists.

In a related argument, Azam and Delacroix find a positive correlation between the level of foreign aid a country receives and the number of terrorist attacks originating from that country. They argue that this relationship is caused by donors delegating counterterrorism responsibilities to government's whose countries are hosts to terrorist groups. Bueno de Mesquita also embeds the choice of counterterrorism policy in a model of electoral accountability. He divides counterterrorism policy into those measures that are tactic-specific and observable by voters and terrorists (e.g., hardening targets) and those measures that are neither tactic-specific nor observable by voters and terrorists (e.g., intelligence). The analysis suggests that strategic substitution among different modes of attack by terrorists and agency problems between the voters and government create a situation in which the politically optimal counterterrorism strategy pursued by the government in response to electoral and institutional incentives is quite different from the security maximizing counterterrorism strategy. In particular, the government allocates resources to observable counterterror in excess of the social optimum. This problem is particularly severe when terrorists have a large set of tactics from which to choose. Powell considers a different source of inefficiency in counterterrorism policy: informational asymmetries.

In Powell's model, governments have private information about the vulnerability of various targets that the terrorists might like to attack. Consequently, if the government follows the optimal policy described above—defending those targets where the expected value of an attack (i.e., vulnerability times value) is highest for the terrorists—it will reveal information about which sites the terrorists ought to attack. The government, then, has competing interests. On the one hand, it wants to defend vulnerable targets. On the other hand, it wants to maintain secrecy. Powell shows that if, independent of these signalling concerns, the marginal security return to resources devoted to defending more vulnerable targets is smaller than the marginal return to resources devoted to defending less vulnerable targets (i.e., if, on the margin, vulnerable targets are harder to defend), then secrecy dominates security. The government allocates resources by "pooling" on a common allocation for all targets (thereby revealing no information to the terrorists). The allocation chosen is the one that is optimal against the average level of target vulnerability—thus, it devotes too little to highly vulnerable targets and too much to safe targets, relative to the complete information optimal allocation. It is worth noting, however, that the existence of private information benefits the government .

8.3. Political Freedom, Security, and Mobilization

A major problem for governments, in setting counterterrorism policy, is not where to allocate of resources, but how to use those resources without creating adverse indirect effects. The dilemma is that counterterrorism tactics that increase short-run security may diminish long-run security by fanning the flames of conflict (e.g., border closings, bombings that kill innocent bystanders and destroy infrastructure, curfews, etc.). Both empirical and theoretical political economists have made efforts to understand this problem and its implications for the politics of terrorism.

Several game theoretic models study this problem under the assumption that counterterrorism measures always radicalize terrorist supporter. Rosendorff and Sandler argue that, because harsh government crackdowns increase support for terrorists, they also increase the risk that the terrorists will have the capacity to engage in large scale attacks that do significant damage. Of course, they argue, such crackdowns also increase the probability that the government prevents terrorist attacks more generally, creating a trade-off for the government. de Figueiredo and Weingast also assume that counterterrorism radicalizes moderates, making negotiation more difficult. They then show how this assumption can give rise to cycles of violence between terrorists and a government in equilibrium.

Other theoretical models attempt to endogenize the effects of counterterrorism on terrorist mobilization, allowing for competing effects. Lichbach focuses on the consistency of government policies over time to explain variance in mobilization responses. When government policies are inconsistent, he claims, government counterterror increases violence. Bueno de Mesquita also argues that government crackdowns can lead to an increase or decrease in support for terrorism. In his model, counterterrorism can increase terrorism by diminishing economic opportunities for potential terrorists (e.g., by destroying infrastructure) and thereby lowering the opportunity costs of mobilization and by ideologically inflaming the population of terrorist supporters. It can decreases terrorism by decreasing the likelihood that the terrorist organization succeeds at achieving its goals (conditional on a level of mobilization), thereby making mobilization less attractive. In the model, whether crackdowns increases or decrease terrorist violence depends on their relative impact on these competing margins.

Empirical scholars have also invested considerable effort into assessing the relationship between political freedom, counterterrorism policy, and terrorist violence. The foundational studies in this literature investigate whether democracy increases or decreases terrorism. In an attempt to reconcile competing claims in this literature, Li , using two different measures of democracy, finds two competing effects of democratic governance on terrorism. On the one hand, he argues, democratic participation seems to reduce the number of terrorist incidents in a country. On the other hand, increased constraints on the government increase terrorism.

8.4. Government-Terrorist Negotiations

The reason that political terrorists engage in violence in the first place is to extract concessions from the government or to change the political order. This brings us to the question of the nature of government-terrorist negotiations. Here, political economists have studied questions such as the following: When should or will governments negotiate with terrorist groups? What are the strategic issues associated with attempting to conciliate a militant adversary? How do the internal politics of terrorist organizations affect the dynamics of peace making? With whom should a government negotiate if it wants to end a terrorist conflict?

A standard intuition, and a policy to which many governments claim to subscribe, is that governments should never negotiate with terrorists. If governments make such a commitment, the argument goes, potential terrorists will be deterred because they will believe that violence will be unlikely to further their goals. Lapan and Sandler, however, argue that such a policy is not credible—once, for example, terrorists have taken hostages, governments will want to negotiate, as long as the benefits of gaining the hostages release outweigh the costs in terms of concessions made as well as any signal of government irresoluteness that increases incentives for future terrorism. Atkinson, Sandler and Tschirhart present empirical results on how various features of the strategic environment (e.g., terrorist demands, bluff attempts, types of hostages taken) affect the ultimate willingness of governments to make concessions in hostage-taking environments. As an empirical matter, governments do negotiate with terrorists. The question thus becomes what happens in such negotiations.

Higher levels of violence may lead to greater concessions by signaling information about expected future violence. Arce and Sandler consider a model where the government faces a trade-off between target-specific counterterrorism and gathering intelligence, where intelligence does not prevent attacks, but informs the government about the terrorists' type so the government can more accurately choose when conciliation is likely to be an effective counterterrorism strategy. Kydd and Walter and Bueno de Mesquita also both focus on government uncertainty about the type of terrorist group they are facing. But they do so in the context of a terrorist movement made up of competing factions: one moderate and one extremist. In both of these models, the government is uncertain whether the moderate terrorists with whom they are negotiating are willing and able to curtail extremist violence following concessions.

In Kydd and Walter's framework, this gives rise to equilibria in which there is "spoiler violence"—the extremist faction attempts to derail peace negotiations by increasing violence in order to convince the government that the moderates are not valuable negotiating partners. Bueno de Mesquita attempts to identify situations in which the negotiating process is best able to provide incentives for moderates to crackdown on extremists. He finds that both promised future concessions and the threat of replacement with a substitute negotiating partner provide incentives for moderates to exert effort in order to decrease extremist violence. This is particularly true when the potential substitute negotiating partner's expected capacity to curtail violence is moderate (i.e., neither to high nor too low) because in such a circumstance extra effort by the current negotiating partner can actually swing the government's decision about whether to continue with negotiations. Bueno de Mesquita also studies a case where the terrorist organization is made up of heterogeneous factions, but focuses on issues other than government uncertainty. In his model, terrorist organizations become more militant following government concessions because only moderate terrorist factions accept concessions, leaving extremist factions in control of the residual terrorist group.

Governments nonetheless are willing to make concessions because their counterterror capabilities improve because of the collusion of former terrorists. The model also allows the government to choose its level of investment in counterterrorism endogenously and explores how both the expected level of violence and the aid of former terrorists affects this investment decision. The model yields additional hypotheses regarding the terms of negotiated settlements between governments and terrorists, when moderates accept concessions, the effect of concessions on the duration of terrorist conflicts, the incentives for moderate terrorists to radicalize their followers, reasons for governments to encourage radicals within a terrorist organization to challenge the moderate leadership, and changes in moderate control over extremists before and after negotiated settlement. Berrebi and Klor present a model in which the public is uncertain whether terrorism is being produced by a moderate or an extremist faction. Hence, the public is uncertain whether or not concessions are likely to be effective at curtailing violence because they are uncertain, after granting concessions, whether the terrorists are likely to keep the peace. Their model yields two key predictions: First, the relative support for concessions is expected to decrease after periods with high levels of terrorism because the population concludes that the terrorists are extremists. Second, the expected level of terrorism is higher when a government inclined to make concessions is in office because the terrorists want to signal that not making concessions will be costly in the long run. Interestingly, Kydd and Walter, Bueno de Mesquita, and Berrebi and Klor all argue that evidence from the Israeli-Palestinian conflict supports the causal mechanisms identified in their models.

Both Bueno de Mesquita and Bapat are concerned with the question of how governments and terrorists can credibly commit to honor the terms of a negotiated settlement. In Bueno de Mesquita, negotiation is credible because terrorists who accept concessions use their knowledge of the inner workings of the remaining terrorist factions as bargaining leverage by withholding valuable counterterrorism aid if the government reneges on concessions. Similarly, the government can withhold concessions if former terrorists do not aid in counterterror. One implication of this approach is that, since concessions may not be credible in the absence of ongoing violence, it may be difficult for a government to end a conflict by reaching a negotiated settlement with all terrorist factions. In Bapat, concessions are made credible through the efforts of a host country. In particular, if target governments are able to credibly threaten sanctions against hosts of international terror groups that they cannot threaten against the terrorists themselves, the host governments may have an incentive to force the terrorists to honor negotiated settlements. Bapat presents empirical data to explore several hypotheses regarding the relationship between the international context and government-terrorist negotiations that flow from his model.

8.5. Internal Politics of Terrorist Organizations

In order to understand government-terrorist negotiations and the strategic use of violence, it is critical to understand the inner workings of terrorist organizations. The political economy literature on the internal politics of terrorist groups was pioneered by Chai, who applied some of the basic insights of the new institutional economics to terrorist organizations and teased out a variety of implications for terrorist strategies. A recent literature has begun to refocus on these questions.

Shapiro and Siegel argue that it is common for terrorist organizations to underfund operatives relative to available resources. This phenomenon, they suggest, is a consequence of principal-agent relationships within terrorist organizations. Terrorist leaders in their model delegate financial and logistical tasks to middlemen, but because security concerns require weak linkages, the leaders cannot perfectly monitor these agents. The middlemen's interests sometimes diverge from the leaders, leading to rent-seeking. Given this, terrorist leaders will sometimes not fund (or will underfund) attacks that they otherwise would have been willing to support. One implication of their model is that the relationship between resources and the level of violence may not be continuous. When an organization is flush with resources, these agency problems do not loom large and small decreases in resources do not dramatically diminish the quality of funding for attacks. However, if resources become sufficiently scarce, cooperation within the terrorist organization begins to break down and suboptimal funding becomes an issue (i.e., funding for attacks diminishes even beyond just the direct effect of having fewer resources). Thus, they argue, restricting terrorists' funds may be an ineffective counterterrorism tactic until a critical threshold is reached, at which point it becomes highly effective.

A literature linking terrorism to the economics of religion addresses similar concerns. This literature argues that religious organizations, with their strong barriers to entry, are well designed to reduce agency problems, by selecting for members who are likely to be highly committed and willing to contribute to the group's mission without having ulterior motives.

Instead of agency relationships within a terrorist organization, Siqueira and Bueno de Mesquita focus on the relationship among terrorist factions. Siqueira studies the interaction of militant and political wings of a terrorist organization. He shows that the actions of one of these factions can have spillovers on the other, whether or not the factions coordinate with one another. As a result, the existence of competing factions can increase or decrease the overall level of violence. The precise relationship between factionalization and violence depends on how internal divisions affect public support for the terrorist movement and the complementarities or substitutabilities between attacks by the various factions. The model, thus, adds nuance to the argument in Bloom that factional competition is a key force behind escalation in terrorist conflicts.

Bueno de Mesquita studies the formation of a splinter faction in a model that endogenizes affiliation and mobilization as well as the strategic selection of ideological positions by terrorist leaders. The model highlights that, for strategic reasons, changes in the structural environment (e.g., the economy, the ability of terrorist leaders to provide public goods) often entail important trade-offs: many factors that decrease terrorist mobilization do so at the cost of increasing ideological extremism. For instance, a strong economy is found to decrease terrorist mobilization, increase the extremism of terrorist factions, and decrease the likelihood of a splinter faction forming. He argues that this suggests that economic shocks have competing micro-level effects on the expected level of violence that might not be observed in the type of macro-level data employed in many of the studies of relationship between terrorism and the economy described above. Thus, understanding the internal politics of terrorist organizations is critical, not only for understanding government-terrorist negotiations, but also for assessing the root causes of terror.

References

Eyerman, Joe. 1998. "Terrorism and democratic states: Soft targets or accessible systems." *International Interactions* 24(2):151–170.

Fearon, James D. 1998. Commitment Problems and the Spread of Ethnic Conflict. In *The International Spread of Ethnic Conflict*, ed. David Lake and Donald Rothchild. Princeton: Princeton University Press pp. 107–126.

Iannaccone, Lawrence R. 1992. "Sacrifice and Stigman: Reducing Free-Riding in Cults, Communes, and Other Collectives." *Journal of Political Economy* 100(2):271–292.

Krueger, Aland B. 2007. *What Makes a Terrorist: Economics and the Roots of Terrorism*. Princeton: Princeton University Press.

9

Social Security: Context and Effectiveness

One of the key global problems facing social security today is the fact that more than half of the world's population are excluded from any type of statutory social security protection. They tend to be part of the informal economy, and are outside the scope of contribution-based social insurance schemes or tax-financed social benefits. In low-income countries, such as in sub-Saharan Africa and South Asia, more than 90 per cent of the population is generally not covered, while in middle-income countries this percentage tends to range between 20 and 60 per cent. It is estimated that worldwide only 20 per cent of population enjoy adequate social security.

The large majority of the non-covered and poor workers are employed in the informal economy, which includes both urban-based and rural-based activities. This term has been used widely to refer to that segment of the economy and labour market that has absorbed significant numbers of job seekers and unemployed workers, mostly in self-employment and in very small production units. For the most part these units have a number of features in common: low levels of capital, skills, access to organized markets and technology; low and unstable incomes and poor working conditions; outside the scope of official statistical enumeration and government regulations; and, almost invariably, beyond statutory systems of labour and social protection.

There is growing awareness that social security should be understood within the context of the development process. Classical development theory had traditionally anticipated that as a result of economic growth all workers would sooner or later end up in secure formal sector employment. However, experience in developing countries and more recently also in the transition and developed countries has shown quite the contrary. Even in countries with high economic growth, more and more workers are in less secure employment, such as the self-employed, the casual and home workers.

9.1. Social Security Coverage

Globalization, either alone or in combination with technological change, often exposes societies to greater income insecurity. A cross-section analysis covering OECD countries investigated the relationship between social protection expenditure and two explanatory variables: the openness of the national economy (measured by the ratio of trade to Gross Domestic Product) and the level of external risks a country faces. The results suggest that income transfers tend to be largest in economies that are simultaneously very open and subject to a substantial price risk in world markets. Other observers claim that governments increasingly have to compete with each other, in order to promote competitiveness and attract direct foreign investment. This competition influences in turn the social policy formation towards a "business-friendly social policy", possibly leading to reduced taxation on capital incomes, lower shares of employers' contributions in social security revenues, more limited income security programmes, and an increased allocation of resources for active labour market programmes.

The world today also faces a large number of complex crises, often with global repercussions. One of the most visible recent examples has been the Asian financial crisis, which led to massive job losses in the formal sector of the economy, rapidly rising unemployment, and an expansion of employment in the informal economy. Another example are the numerous armed conflicts in recent years, particularly in sub-Saharan Africa (Angola, Congo, Liberia and Rwanda) but also in Europe (Bosnia, Kosovo).

Several countries around the world continue to be afflicted by health disasters, such as the HIV/AIDS crisis, leaving many children as orphans. Natural disasters, such as recurrent droughts and floods (in Africa and Asia), earthquakes and hurricanes (for example, in Central America, India and Turkey) have left many communities not only without homes and sources of income but have also wiped away decades of their countries' developmental efforts. Finally, some countries are facing the difficult process of making economic as well as political transitions, such as from a centrally planned economy to a market-oriented system, or from a politically restricted regime to a democratic society.

The transition in Central and Eastern European countries led to unprecedented unemployment, which still continues in some of these countries. Together with globalisation and crises, the structural adjustment policies pursued consistently in many developing countries have contributed to a decline in the small percentage of the working population in the formal economy. The successive waves of structural adjustment programmes have also led to wage cuts in the public and private sectors, thereby eroding the financial base of statutory social insurance schemes.

Simultaneously, some of these schemes have suffered from bad management and bad governance, both factors that have often seriously reduced the trust of members. In addition, structural adjustment programmes have often resulted in severe cuts in social budgets. While in some Asian countries such as the Republic of Korea there is universal health insurance coverage, in most (low-income) developing countries governments cannot guarantee access to free health and education. As a result, there is greater demand for community arrangements to finance and organise these social services. It is often more efficient to be part of a community-based insurance or financing scheme than to have to face health and, possibly education, expenditures individually.

Structural adjustment, socioeconomic changes and low levels of economic development have also produced large vulnerable groups that cannot contribute to social insurance schemes. The most vulnerable groups outside the labour force are the disabled and old people who cannot count on family support, and who have not been able to make provisions for their own pensions. The fundamental reason for exclusion from statutory social security coverage is that many workers outside the formal economy are unable or unwilling to contribute a relatively high percentage of their incomes to financing social security benefits that do not meet their priority needs.

In general, they priorities more immediate needs, such as health and education, in particular because structural adjustment measures have reduced or eliminated access to free health care and primary education. Within the range of pension benefits, they seek protection in case of death and disability, rather than for old age. In addition, they may not be familiar with, and/or distrust, the way the statutory social security scheme is managed. As a result, various groups of workers outside the formal sector have setup schemes that better meet their priority needs and contributory capacity. Moreover, there are also a host of factors that restrict access to the statutory social security schemes, such as legal restrictions, administrative bottlenecks and problems with compliance.

9.2. Social Security: Concept and Linkages

The ILO's research on the informal sector has demonstrated that a wider concept of social security is needed in order to respond to the realities faced by informal economy workers, who constitute the majority of the world labour force. The traditional concept of social security is included in various ILO standards. According to the Income Security Recommendation, 1944, income security schemes should relieve want and prevent destitution by restoring, up to a reasonable level, income which is lost due to the inability to work (including old age) or to obtain remunerative work, or by reason of the death of the breadwinner.

Income security should be organised as far as possible on the basis of compulsory social insurance, and provision for needs not covered by compulsory social insurance should be made by social assistance. In the same vein, the Medical Care Recommendation, 1944, suggests that medical care should be provided either through a social insurance medical care service with supplementary provision by way of social assistance, or through a public medical service. The Social Security (Minimum Standards) Convention, 1952, identifies nine areas for social insurance, i.e. medical care as well as benefits in case of sickness, unemployment, old age, employment injury, family circumstances, maternity, invalidity and widowed.

Various authors have considered that this definition is too narrow for the problems faced by developing countries. Guhan claims that social security in poor countries will have to be viewed as part of, and fully integrated into, anti-poverty policies, providing access to productive assets, employment guarantees, minimum wages and food security. Dress and Sen as well as Burgess and Stern distinguish two aspects of social security, which they define as the use of social means to prevent deprivation (promote living standards) and vulnerability to deprivation (protect against falling living standards). The definition provided by Eurostat also includes housing and rent subsidies in the definition of social protection. The Eurostat statistical definition of social protection which is increasingly accepted internationally also makes a distinction between social protection in cash and in kind.

There is quite a bit of confusion about what social security means, and also about the concept of social protection. The very broad definition of social security, such as developed by Sen, makes it equivalent to all policies that promote and protect living standards. Social protection, according to the European Union, is defined as all policies in the field of health, education and what used to be defined as social security. The World Bank considers all activities linked to "Social Risk Management" as part of social protection. The International Financing Institutions normally include employment policies and micro-finance in the concept of social protection, even though health insurance is normally considered to be part of health-care financing. The ILO has an administrative concept of social protection, which basically includes social security and labour protection.

The goal and concept of Decent work matches this broader concept of social security. In his first report to the ILC , the ILO Director-General, Mr. Juan Somavia, introduced the "Decent work for all" strategy, which established as the primary goal of the ILO "to promote opportunities for women and men to obtain decent and productive work, in conditions of freedom, equity, security and human dignity". The Decent work strategy adopts a broad perspective on work, which includes not only (paid) employment, households through public and collective measures to guarantee them a minimum standard of living and to protect them against low or declining living standards arising out of a number of basic risks and needs". The first element in this definition establishes that people derive individual rights and entitlements from social security. The second element defines the social element of social security, i.e. that it is provided within the context of public or collective and often voluntary not-for-profit arrangements. The third element makes it clear that social security aims at protection, and that its role should not be confused with policies for the promotion of employment and the economy. Finally, it makes the point that social security is not only concerned with cash benefits and benefits in kind for a limited range of contingencies, but also with reducing the impact on the household budget of the cost for basic needs and capabilities, such as medical care, education, housing and nutrition.

The two main components of social security are social insurance and tax-financed social benefits. Tax-financed social benefits are usually targeted on the needy, and are often awarded on the basis of an income and/or asset test. Social insurance is financed by contributions, and its benefits are awarded when a specific risk or contingency occurs.

Statutory social insurance is compulsory for the whole population or for a particular group, because non-insurance would create external costs (such as adverse selection and moral hazard) and because it permits maximum opportunities for risk pooling. In most statutory health and unemployment insurance schemes, contributions are income-related, which implies breaking the link between contributions and individual risks and some cross-subsidisation of the poor by the better off. In statutory pension insurance schemes there is usually a closer link between contributions and benefits. Most voluntary social insurance schemes, such as micro-insurance and community-based schemes, are relatively small and tend to be characterised by flat-rate contributions.

People cannot contribute to society and their own well-being, unless they have the capacity to do so and can satisfy their basic needs. This fact justifies government intervention and financing in health and education services, as well as in food and housing. Social security mechanisms can play an important role in the financing and the provision of access to these services. Social insurance often plays an important part in the financing of health care, and government subsidies can improve access to food, education and housing. The main (contingencies), to avoid indebtedness, and to make household expenditure more predictable. The main functions of tax-based social benefits are to support low incomes and to reduce household expenditure on basic items.

People can be functionally deprived when they cannot exercise their employment capacity and do not benefit from family cohesion. The risks related to these functional capability deprivations are those that have been traditionally covered by social security, i.e. old-age, death, disability, employment injury, sickness, maternity and unemployment. Finally, when government action on basic and functional capabilities does not reach everyone, the final resort for tax-financed social benefits is to focus on low personal incomes or neediness.

Social security and other public policies can interact with each other in different ways. For example, among social security policies, tax-financed social benefits may for certain groups or in certain circumstances be a more effective mechanism to provide basic income security than an employment guarantee or a food subsidy scheme. However, unemployment insurance and employment guarantee schemes are generally complementary, because they target different groups in the labour force. It is therefore important to assess what are the main linkages between and among social security and other public policies, since they can have a significant impact on the effectiveness of efforts to extend social security.

9.3. Concept of Effectiveness

The constitutive elements of a social security scheme consist of coverage, benefits, financing and administration. For each of these elements there are some principal. The concept of effectiveness is first of all related to that of coverage, i.e. the number of persons covered and the scope of coverage (in terms of contingencies), as well as to the level of benefits. The effectiveness of a social security scheme depends on the design and choice of benefits as well as on its financing structure and the quality of its administration. As a result, indirect measures of effectiveness are related to the design, financing and administration of social security systems, such as the delivery of benefits and the question of compliance.

Effectiveness of efforts to extend the personal coverage of social security can be measured in various ways. In the case of social insurance, the most common way of measuring is the number of actually contributing and insured persons as a percentage of the legally targeted population. For most social insurance benefits, it is also possible to measure their effectiveness in terms of beneficiaries. The so-called beneficiary rate can be defined as the percentage of the legally entitled target group that actually receives benefits. In the case of tax-financed social benefits, effectiveness can be defined as the number of actual beneficiaries as a percentage of those that in principle fulfil the criteria for obtaining benefits (the take-up rate). In a wider sense, it would also be good to assess which percentage of the poor population does not receive tax-financed social benefits (poverty incidence) as well as the amount of money needed to lift everybody, within a The level of benefits can be measured with some of the following indicators:

- Legal replacement rates (legal benefits levels related to average or last-earned incomes).
- (Tax-financed) benefit levels as a percentage of the poverty line; poverty incidence and the poverty gap.
- Actual benefit levels relative to average earnings or incomes.
- Patients' co-payments as a percentage of private or total expenditure.
- Shares of income from different social transfers in cash or in kind in total household income.
- Medical services available relative to some "normative basket" of medical services.

9.4. Social Health Insurance

Under social health insurance schemes, members pay a premium to a social security or other non-profit agency in exchange for an agreed entitlement to a defined package. Health insurance allows payments for services to be spread across time and between those insured, and implies cross subsidisation between the healthy and the sick. Social health insurance provides a secure and cost-effective protection against the financial consequences of medical treatment and it greatly increases the predictability of household expenditure. Both advantages have a direct and positive impact on the income earning capacity of the household. This insurance focuses on personal (curative) health services, which in the case of a national health service could also be financed by public revenue.

"Public" health services, such as prevention and promotion, are generally publicly financed, and they can significantly reduce the cost of (curative) health care. In the low-income countries, promotion and prevention should concentrate on the main causes of avoidable deaths, which are HIV/AIDS, malaria, tuberculosis (TB), childhood infectious diseases, maternal and perinatal conditions, micronutrient deficiencies and tobacco-related illnesses. For many middle-income countries, mortality from communicable diseases has already been significantly reduced, so public action should focus on non-communicable diseases. Many of them, including cardiovascular disease, diabetes, mental illness and cancers, can be effectively addressed by relatively low-cost interventions, especially using preventative actions relating to diet, smoking and lifestyle.

Historically speaking, various important factors have been at play in establishing statutory social health insurance in developing countries. Dissatisfaction with the quality and quantity of curative services provided by public systems, along with a growing inability of a substantial proportion of the population to pay for private medical services, often One option that countries then have is to set up a national health service which provides health care as a right of all (or groups of) citizens, and which is financed and organised by the government.

The other option is statutory social health insurance, mainly financed by (employers' and employees') contributions, supervised and often co-financed by the government, and managed by semi-public or private institutions. Initially, statutory social health insurance institutions tended to build physical facilities for both hospital and ambulatory care of insured persons. Afterwards, there has been a process of diversification of delivery patterns, as other public and private facilities and health services have become available. This process has included the purchase of services from public and private hospitals, clinics, dispensaries or individual doctors. As purchasing increased, so have various options for provider payment mechanisms.

In extending statutory social health insurance, most developing countries have followed the strategy of "gradual implementation". This meant that compulsory coverage was limited according to various criteria, such as geographical area, size of undertaking, category of dependant and type of medical benefit. This approach towards "gradual implementation" was inspired, first of all, by the realisation that compulsory coverage could not be extended indefinitely, because of major political, financial and material constraints.

In addition, there were various practical reasons why it was logical to start with covering the large enterprises, where registration, deduction and monitoring of contributions is much easier. This procedure would allow the administrators of compulsory health insurance to gain experience in both collecting contributions and paying benefits without having to cope with the identification and control of small and often unstable employers.

9.4.1. Universal Health Insurance Coverage

Among the countries that achieved health insurance coverage for the whole population, the Republic of Korea is a striking example. Their goal was attained in 1989, within about 12 years of the commencement of compulsory medical insurance in 1977. The main strategy of extending health insurance in Korea was to mandate the insurance to employees first, and extend the population coverage to the self-employed after wards. Employees of large corporations with more than 500 workers were the first group to be covered by the compulsory health insurance in 1977.

Health insurance was further extended to government employees and teachers as well as to industrial workers in progressively smaller workplaces. For the purpose of extending health insurance to the self-employed, 17 areas in 1981, and in one urban area and two additional rural areas in 1982. In January 1988, the self-employed in rural areas joined the health insurance programme. In 1989 the self-employed in urban areas were the last remaining group that was covered. The introduction and extension of social insurance for health care had a lot to do with political legitimacy of the military and authoritarian regime. When the military government first gained political power in the early 1960s, it wanted to introduce the social security system for political legitimacy. In addition, it decided to keep the existing approach of pluralistic health insurance societies, so as to minimise long-term public financing commitment for health care and maximise public resources for economic development. Moreover, reports in the early 1970s indicating that the South Korean health care system was inferior to that of North Korea pushed the South Korean government into introducing the national health insurance scheme.

Both economic and political factors contributed to the rapid extension of health insurance to the self-employed. First of all, the booming economy in the late 1980s substantially improved labour incomes and therefore people's ability to pay for social insurance. The government also had the fiscal capacity to subsidise health insurance for the self-employed. As a political factor, the presidential election in 1987 drove the ruling party and the Government to expand social welfare programmes as a major campaign agenda. In 1986, the Government announced the plans to cover the self-employed in the national health insurance, to introduce the national pension scheme and to implement the minimum wage system.

Contrary to the rather smooth extension of health insurance to industrial workers and employees, its extension to the self-employed faced tough resistance. Farmers refused to pay contributions and requested major reforms in the health insurance scheme such as the discount or exemption of the contribution, a change in the method of setting contribution, an increase in government subsidy, and the expansion of health care facilities in rural areas for a better accessibility to medical care. Farmers' organisations led the protests and had coalitions with progressive civic groups on health insurance reform. Consequently, the Government responded to the farmers' protests by increasing its subsidy to the health insurance for the self-employed.

Since the public regarded the social health insurance scheme more as a welfare benefit, the Government was forced to design a system with low levels of contributions and a limited benefit package. At the end of the 1990s, the average contribution rate for industrial workers was 3.75 per cent, while 5.6 per cent for government and school employees. In addition to the co-payment for insured medical services, which can vary from 20 per cent for inpatient care to 55 per cent for outpatient care, people have to pay in full for uninsured services, such as meals at inpatient care, home care and traditional medication. For example in 1997, patients' total out-of-pocket payment accounted for about 40 per cent of expenditure on inpatient care and more than 60 per cent of that on outpatient care.

In October 1998, the health insurance societies for the self-employed merged with the single insurance society for government and school employees. In July 2000, the 142 health insurance societies for industrial workers merged into the National Health Insurance Corporation, which became the single insurer. As a result, all covered people were entitled to the same statutory benefit package, and all health care providers were reimbursed according to a standard schedule. The insurance funds of workers and government and school personnel were merged in 2001.

At the same time contribution schedules were changed, both for employees and self-employed, with drops for low-income and substantial increases for high-income workers. The merger with the fund of the self-employed was foreseen for 2002, but has now been deferred to 2004. The financing of the two systems is still separated, with the result that the merger achieved horizontal equity (paying the same contribution for the same level of income) among the self-employed and among the employees, but not between them.

So, the lack of horizontal equity as well as the chronic financial distress of the health insurance societies for the self-employed in rural areas have been the driving forces towards a unified health insurance scheme. Politically speaking, the representatives from rural areas, regardless of their party affiliation, have been most supportive of the merger. Moreover, the ideology of incoming President Kim Dae-Joong was based on a belief in social solidarity and on the idea that a single-insurer system is more equitable.

According to Kwon, the success of the future unified system will depend on two factors: (i) a fair income assessment for the self-employed as a basis for their contributions; and (ii) the development of the single-insurer system that acts as a prudent purchaser of medical care and that uses effective-provider payment systems, such as capitation, global budgeting and a Diagnosis Related Group (DRG)-based prospective payment system.

Taiwan, China's path to national health insurance took place in the period between 1950 and 1995. It started with the progressive extension of coverage of private sector wage earners through Labour Insurance (LI), which was enacted in 1950. It was followed by the enactment of the Government Employees' Insurance in 1958. The

Farmers' Health Insurance (FHI) was enacted in 1989, based on two experimental stages in 1985 and 1987. Through the setting up of a national planning commission in 1987, the Government gave a decisive push towards universal coverage. It did so, partly in response to demands from parliamentary members within the governing Nationalist Party, and partly in a bid to compete with the rising opposition.

Between 1988 and 1994 the proportion of the population enjoying health insurance rose from 33.5 to 57.5 per cent, but a large part of the population, mostly elderly as well as children of the insured under LI and FHI, was still not covered. The planning committee had recommended the launch of the national scheme in 2000, but the Government adopted the scheme in 1995, in anticipation of the first-ever presidential elections in 1996. The Government accepted to finance part of the extension, amongst others, through a 10 percent contribution to Labour Insurance and a 100 per cent contribution for low-income households. All insured are entitled to uniform and comprehensive medical care benefits, comparable to those in other advanced countries, even though contribution rates vary considerably depending on the insured's occupational and income status.

There are considerable differences between the health insurance systems in Taiwan, China and the Republic of Korea. Taiwan, China started off its national health insurance system with a much more extensive benefit coverage. Its contribution rate is at least 4.25 per cent of national income, while it is less than 3 per cent in the Republic of Korea. In Taiwan, China, the government subsidy amounts to 28 per cent of financing, while only 14 per cent in the Republic of Korea, mainly directed to the insurance societies for the self-employed.

In the future, Taiwan, China is likely to adopt a managed-care approach with multiple carriers, while the Republic of Korea is integrating its health insurance societies form a single insurance society. The toughest question for Taiwan, China is how to manage competition among carriers, because they have incentives to select the risk that they prefer. If such "creaming off" is prevalent, the national health insurance will fail to function as a social insurance mechanism.

The national health insurance system in the Republic of Korea has shown a deficit since 1996 and in Taiwan, China since 1998, mainly because of medical cost inflation (increased cost and/or intensity of treatment) and the gradual increase of people over 65 years among the population. Another similarity is that the majority of hospitals in both countries are for-profit. They have normally grown from a clinic or physician office, and are usually managed by owner-physicians.

The medical profession, and in particular the hospitals, are well organised and have usually strongly resisted payment system reforms. To what extent are the examples of the Republic of Korea and Taiwan, China applicable to other middle- and low-income developing countries? Indeed, both countries have achieved successful universal health insurance coverage, only when they were at relatively high levels of income, were largely urbanised, and had large wage sectors relative to informal sectors. Moreover, social health insurance was introduced when the national economy grew at very high rates. This enabled them to deal with the medical cost inflation, resulting from the facts that insurance lowers the amount the patient has to pay directly for medical care at the time of purchase and that mainly private sector providers supply the medical services.

The threat of medical cost inflation means that governments need to adopt cost-control measures, such as co-payments and provider payment mechanisms, as part of any social insurance plan. As noted earlier, both countries will also have to deal with the changing needs of an ageing membership. In Latin America and the Caribbean, there are 15 countries with a unified and standardised national health system, usually managed by the Ministry of Health, and which covers in principle all residents. Those legally entitled to protection by the public health system managed by the Ministry of Health usually do not have effective access to care, or the quality of services they receive is very poor.

All non-Latin Caribbean countries as well as Brazil and Cuba have such a system. In the other 18 countries there is a dual health care system: one provided by the social insurance scheme, which mainly covers the salaried labour force, and another by the Ministry of Health, which offers public health care to the non-insured poor and low-income population. Among the latter group of countries, two (Chile and Costa Rica) have achieved virtually universal coverage. It is not clear to what extent global health care coverage has been affected by the recent crises in Argentina and Uruguay. In the remaining 14 countries total population coverage ranges between 35 and 75 per cent and, therefore, leaves out most or all the poor and low-income strata. In some countries, such as Peru, coverage under statutory health insurance has gone down over the past 10 years.

Chile's health insurance coverage is largely dominated by the public sector. Insured workers and their dependants may channel their mandatory 7 per cent health care payroll contributions to either the publicly managed National Health Fund (FONASA) or to one of the private prepaid health insurance plans called ISAPREs. Individuals covered by FONASA may receive health services from either public facilities or from a preferred provider private system. Public facilities are organised as a national public health system or SNSS, which is decentralised at the regional and municipal level.

Alternatively, offer subscribers both outpatient and inpatient care on a cost-sharing basis via their own facilities or under contract with private and public providers. Basic health care is provided to the population as a whole. More comprehensive curative care is provided to 62 per cent of the population through FONASA and to 22 percent through ISAPREs. The remaining 16 per cent is covered through other systems, such as those for the Armed Forces and universities, or is not covered. People who are insufficiently covered by ISAPREs can fall back on services provided under the SNSS.

Costa Rica has the most extensive and equal coverage under the social health insurance scheme, with compulsory coverage for domestic servants, rural workers, employees of micro-enterprises and the unemployed (for a period after dismissal). The self-employed have voluntary coverage, but are subsidised, and virtually all of them are covered. Furthermore, all the dispossessed ("indignities") are covered by the social assistance (noncontributory) programme. The social insurance institute (and not the Ministry of Health as elsewhere in Latin America) administers this noncontributory programme through an integrated system that unifies all preventive and curative care. The Ministry of Health sets policy, oversees the system, and provides some minor services. The advantages of this approach are that health services are integrated, and that the poor tend to receive care similar to that received by the rest of the population.

The process of extending health (insurance) coverage has taken various decades. During the mid-1990s social health insurance coverage stood at more that 85 per cent of the population, while privately and publicly financed health programmes covered another 10 per cent of the population. Social health insurance coverage stood at about 15 per cent in 1960 and rose to almost 85 per cent at the end of the 1970s. Due to the financial crises in the early 1980s, coverage went down to less than 70 percent in 1982-83, to bounce back to 85 per cent at the end of the 1980s.

Costa Rica's good social performance is explained by a combination of factors, such as its favourable geographic position, a homogeneous society, the relatively early development of the wage sector and entry into world markets, combined with political stability and low defence expenditure. In 1961 a strong push towards universal coverage was given by a modification in the Constitution, which stipulated that mandatory coverage had to be extended progressively to manual and intellectual workers, as well as to the self-employed and the poor. The National Health Plan further supported this process by developing in the early 1970s which aimed at the creation of an integrated national health system managed jointly by the Ministry of Health and the Social Security Fund.

Costa Rica has been much more successful in providing health insurance coverage to self-employed workers than other countries in the region. Elsewhere, a self-employed worker must pay the typical 15 per cent contribution normally paid by both the worker and employer.

In Costa Rica the average contribution effectively paid by the self-employed is 5.8 per cent; a majority among them only contribute the minimum 5 per cent, which is smaller than the employees' contribution. Many self-employed pay low contributions, as they tend to under declare their income. Salaried workers in micro-enterprises often register themselves as self-employed or indigent to have access to cheaper or free coverage.

If the self-employed worker's (or seasonal worker's) earnings are lower than the minimum wage, the State is promoted special agreements with associations of self-employed, peasants, co-operatives, and unions, which are responsible for collecting their members' contributions and transferring them to the Fund. All these rules and practices have created large financial commitments for the central government, which since the early 1980s has devoted about one-third of its expenditure to social security.

9.4.2. Countries Striving for Universal Coverage

When countries wish to follow the path towards universal coverage, they have to consider the context and initial conditions, within which the extension of health care coverage is taking place. The first set of context variables concerns socioeconomic and the political situation of the country. Important indicators are the proportion of workers in the informal economy and in rural areas as well as the relative importance of the economically non-active population, such as the old, the disabled and children.

The second set of context variables concerns the state of—human, socialite and physical—health institutions in the country. The human infrastructure has to do with the quality of civil servants in the Government and social security institutions as well as with the competence of health care and management personnel. The socialite infrastructure refers to the social partners and other civil society groups who are able and/or committed to make a contribution towards universal coverage. The physical infrastructure consists of hospitals, clinics, water supply and sanitation works that have a key impact on the health status of the population.

There is a large variety of middle-income countries that are striving for universal coverage. In Latin America, Colombia and Mexico are such countries; in South-East Asia, the Philippines, Thailand and Vietnam; while in West-Asia and North Africa such countries are Iran and Tunisia. Some of them prefer a fast-track implementation, such as Colombia, while others, such as Tunisia, have followed a more gradual approach. Colombia is a country that has made important steps towards the goal of universal health insurance coverage in a relatively short time.

Health sector reform started in 1990 with the passage of Law 10, mandating the devolution of management and provision of health and medical services to 32 departments and 1,029 municipalities. Intergovernmental transfers to finance health care and other social services proposed by these entities—are described in Law 60 of

August 1993. The final element of the reform is mandated in Law 100 of December 1993, which introduces two innovations, because it reorients how health care is organised (demand-driven) and how providers are paid (capitation). This model is based on the belief that demand-side subsidies are preferable to supply-side financing of direct delivery mechanisms that eventually end up with enormous wastage, low-quality services, and no advancements in coverage. The social security reform law introduces three new institutional features:

— A health insurance fund, the "Fondo de Solidarity Garantía" (FSG).

— Public and private health management organisations, "Entidades Promotoras de Salud" (EPS).

— Provider organisations, "Institutiones Proveedoras de Servicios de Salud" (IPSS).

The EPSs are the institutions and organisations through which beneficiaries from the contributive regime (salaried workers) select benefits and providers. Under this regime workers and employers together pay 12 percent payroll taxes for financing the Contributory Mandatory Health Plan regime consists of two mechanisms for financing the demand for health care by non-salaried workers and low-income groups traditionally excluded from social insurance.

The first involves directing public funds through the FSG that will partially subsidise the "subsidised contribution" for low-income participants, who depending on a means test will also be required to make out-of-pocket contributions. The second feature involves the formation of "Impresses Solidarities de Salad" (ESSs), which organises the delivery of health services by health providers financed by the "subsidised contribution".

Another part of the reform is that hospitals and provider networks owned and operated by the health ministry, social security institutions and decentralised entities are to be converted into State Social Enterprises (ESEs), i.e. self-managed, autonomous public enterprises that are comparable with private sector IPSSs. Together with private health providers, these ESEs can conclude contracts with EPSs and ESSs.

Between 1990 and 1997 coverage climbed from 20.6 to 57.2 per cent, but dropped to 52.4 per cent in 2000. The level of health expenditure exploded from 4 per cent of GDP in 1990 to nearly 11 per cent in 1998. This is probably explained by the fact that the introduction of demand subsidies did not remove the supply subsidies, with the result that hospitals continued to receive budgetary funds while they could also additionally charge EPSs and ESSs for services provided. According to Jack , there are two potential problems with using consumer demand to discipline insurance providers. First, demand may not be elastic in response to quality changes, in which case incentives to control costs may outweigh incentives to improve or maintain quality. Secondly, quality competition can naturally induce active selection efforts on the part of EPS/ESS managers to attract inexpensive clients and charge an additional premium for extra services.

With regard to distributional consequences, a recent study shows that the quality and quantity of health services under the "subsidised regime" is much lower than under the "contributory regime". The study also suggests that the means test for the "subsidised regime" does not perform well in the rural areas, for various reasons. The education level seems too important a factor, income is very hard to measure, and the possession of certain assets, such as cows, is not included in the definition of the means test.

Vietnam is one of the Southeast Asian countries that strive for universal coverage. One of the 9th Party Congress resolutions states that universal coverage should be reached by the year 2010. In 2000 about 10.5 million people were covered out of a total population of more that 75 million. They mainly consist of workers and retires from the public and the formal private sector, as well as of school children covered under voluntary health insurance. The Vietnamese social health insurance system (managed by the Viet Insurance Company (VIC)) covers salaried workers in the private sector, and it targets only enterprises with at least ten workers. However, according to the new social security law, compulsory coverage will be extended to all workers with a contract of at least three months. Dependants can be covered through voluntary insurance; children below six are entitled to free care; schoolchildren and students are in principle covered by the VIC. The future strategy will be based on adopting family coverage, so that the voluntary arrangements for children and students can gradually be phased out.

Informal sector workers, part of the economically not active population and the poor still have to pay direct user charges whenever they seek medical care. One new idea for health insurance schemes". Communes and other mass organisations widespread in rural areas could be used as carriers for such schemes, and pilot projects financed by ADB are now underway. According to Ergo the benefit package of proposed schemes for rural areas should be comprehensive, including both preventive as well as curative, out and inpatient, care. In addition, premiums should be flat-rate and subsidised by the State. According to Akal, flat-rate premiums although regressive constitute the most cost-effective way of raising funds from the informal economy, since it makes enforcement of compliance so much easier. The subsidy by the State could be provided on the basis of risk-adjusted capitation fees.

According to the latest estimates, there are about 14 million people living in poverty. Ill health, which often leads to loss of revenues and high expenditures, is one of the prominent causes of poverty. According to Dahlgren, around 3 million individuals are forced into poverty every year due to high medical expenses the so-called "medical poverty trap". Some of the poor already receive the "Free Health Card for the Poor" (FHCP). Such a system could be viable in the long run, if it is funded by the central government (possibly initially supported by external donors), if it targets the whole household and if its level is based on a riskadjusted capitation fee.

According to Ron, the compliance problem is probably the key challenge, in particular with regard to statutory social health insurance. There are already private for-profit health insurance initiatives trying to garner the high-wage salaried sector, which would limit the chances to strengthen the financial base of the compulsory insurance system. This issue is linked to the following more fundamental question: at what stages should legislation to achieve universal health insurance be prepared and implemented?

The present health system is governed by a decree, which is appropriate during a period of experimentation, and which ensures that the design of the health insurance scheme is flexible and suits local factors. The basic problem, however, is the lack of sanctions, either because parts of the scheme are voluntary, or because the sanctions require the backing of legislation rather than decrees. Thailand has taken important steps towards extending health care coverage to its entire population. In 2001, the general the Thai Rak Thai Party won the elections (The Thai take care of the Thai). This result expressed a general feeling that national solidarity was the only answer to the uncertainties created by globalisation, and in particular by the Asian financial crisis in 1997. One of the electoral promises was the introduction of the Universal Coverage scheme (UC), the so-called 30 Baht scheme, through which all uninsured persons would pay this marginal user charge for every episode of medical care.

The UC will replace the former Social Welfare Scheme and the Health Card Scheme and will also cover all other uninsured persons. The Civil Servants' Medical Benefit Scheme (CSMBS) provides health care for public sector workers (both active and retired) and their dependants (spouse, children and parents) on a noncontributory basis. The Social Security Organisation (SSO) provides health insurance for private sector workers with ten or more workers. In 2001 these two schemes covered more than 20 per cent of the population, including a small group of privately insured people.

In 2002 the SSO extended its mandatory coverage to establishments with one to nine workers; in addition, it is planning to cover dependent year per non-covered person could be carried by the budget of the Ministry of Health. The introduction of the UC system would require a number of other reforms, such as prior registration of all uninsured people with approved primary care services, the payment of capitation fees to care providers (with additional provisions for certain high cost cares), the definition of a basic medical care package, a rigorous quality control of care, and the split between purchaser and provider, with independent regulators and participation of all stockholders.

Tunisia is a country that has followed the gradual way to extension, and it provides a wide range of social security benefits to its workers, i.e. health insurance, pensions, as well as maternity and employment injury benefits. For the time being, there are separate schemes for employees in the public and private non-agricultural sector, plus smaller schemes for employees and self-employed in agriculture, students and emigrated workers. Workers can be reimbursed for certain health services, and they may have free access to public hospitals and/or social security clinics. There is also a radical reform underway, that will create a unified health insurance system for all socially insured persons. Voluntary, complementary health insurance can be organised through enterprise group contracts or through mutual benefit societies (mainly in the public sector).

In 1999 personal coverage for health insurance, pensions, maternity and employment injury benefits stood at more than 84 per cent, up from 60 per cent in 1989. The main excluded groups are: casual and seasonal agricultural workers, (unemployed) construction workers on labour-intensive public works, domestic workers and the unemployed. There are three factors that have led to this fast extension of social security coverage:

— A change in mentality, in the sense that a large majority of workers seeks protection against rapidly rising health care costs.

— The improved benefits provided by the social security system brought about a change of mentality, supported by the sensitisation campaigns and educational role of the trade unions.

— The compliance monitoring system both at the work place and through accounting controls of large enterprises. These control mechanisms are all the more effective, since noncompliance can be punished with heavy financial sanctions. For middle-income countries striving at universal coverage, the key policy question is at what level of compulsory insurance coverage does it become feasible to extend a standard level of benefits to the whole population. A related question is whether progress is inevitably dependent on the growth of formal sector employment, and to what extent community (voluntary) schemes for workers in the informal economy can play a role. Under all circumstances, the Government will have to finance part of the extension, in particular for the self-employed and other low-income workers.

9.4.3. Potential of Community- and Area-Based Schemes

The recently published report Macroeconomics and health shows that challenges they face. The Commission estimates the minimum financing needs to be around US$30 to US$40 per person per year to cover essential interventions, including those for TB, malaria, HIV/AIDS, childhood diseases, maternal/perinatal diseases and smoking.

The least developed countries average approximately US$13 per person per year in total health expenditures, of which budgetary outlays are just US$7. The other low-income countries average approximately US$24 per capita per year, of which budgetary outlays are US$13. Even with more efficient allocation and greater domestic resource mobilisation, the levels of funding necessary to cover essential services are far beyond the financial means of many low-income countries.

Particularly in the low-income countries, much of the domestic health expenditure is out-of-pocket expenditure. In India, for example, the rural poor pay out of pocket for around 85 per cent of the total health services that they receive. Again on India, Jain reports that many workers even those with incomes under the poverty line spend between 5 and 10 per cent of their income on health services. Much of out-of-pocket expenditure goes for unnecessary or inappropriate drugs foisted on them by clinics that fund themselves through sales of pharmaceutical products, or to unlicensed and unqualified practitioners.

High and rising health costs exclude a significant proportion of the poor from essential services, and a very large number of families are thrown into poverty each year by health outlays. In Africa, many households spend enormous sums for informal and traditional forms of care with dire health consequences. There are, in fact, two other problems with the current health financing arrangements of low-income countries, in addition to the insufficient overall levels of spending. First, the proportion of total health outlays coming through the budget is relatively low, much lower that in high-income countries. Second, the private spending tends to be out of pocket, rather than prepaid, so that there is very little insurance element (i.e. risk pooling) built into private spending, again in contrast to the much higher rate of insurance coverage in high-income countries.

The Commission recommends that out-of-pocket expenditures in poor communities should increasingly be channelled into "community financing" schemes to help cover the costs of community-based health delivery. The characteristics of these community-based financing arrangements are that they involve collective action, that membership is voluntary, and that people covered by such arrangements generally have no other financial protection to pay for their health care. The basic idea of such arrangements is to offer local communities an incentive scheme, in which each US$1 that the community raises for prepaid health coverage would be augmented, by some rate of co-financing, by the national government (backed by donor assistance). These pre-payments by the community would mainly cover basic curative health services other than the package of essential interventions (TB, Malaria, HIV/AIDS, etc.), which are to be paid for by budgetary funds, with donor support.

Prepayment should not be confused with financing through user fees. As conventionally defined, user fees are payments for health services at the time of illness (that is, out-of-pocket expenditures), often levied on essential interventions. Experience has taught repeatedly that user fees end up excluding the poor from essential health services, while at the same time recovering only a fraction of costs. Thus, the community-financing approach differs from user fees in two key respects: first, the involves pre-payments rather that out-of-pocket expenditures, and second, contributions need not to be used to cover essential services as these services would be covered by public funding that would be entirely additional to community contributions.

9.4.4. Emergence of Community-Based Schemes

There is ample evidence for sub-Saharan Africa and for South Asian countries that new community-based schemes have emerged, as a result of the inaccessibility of health care services. Many of such schemes are based on insurance and risk-pooling, which has led to the term "micro-insurance" a concept coined by Door and Jacquier. Micro-insurance schemes are independent, non-profit organisations based on reciprocity and democratic management. Their aim is to improve access, mainly through their members' contributions, to quality health care for members and their families. These micro-insurance organisations have the advantages of cohesion, direct participation and low administrative costs. The concept of community-based schemes is wider, since it includes all collective action in raising, pooling, allocating, purchasing and/or supervising the management of health-financing arrangements.

Hospital-based micro-insurance schemes have emerged in countries, such as Tanzania and the Democratic Republic of Congo, which have the advantage that the insurance administration can be based on an already well-functioning infrastructure. In both countries, these schemes are also often based on religious communities, which do not exclude people from other faiths, which benefit from external support, which are also involved in complementary development activities, and which are usually characterised by strong social cohesion between people with different levels of income.

Alternatively, when hospital-based schemes provide primary and secondary health care services, their prices tend to be higher than those charged by smaller and specialised providers. Other, more "demand-driven" insurance schemes have emerged in countries such as Senegal and Tanzania, whose administrations are run by communities that make independent contract with health care providers. In some South-Asian countries, community-based schemes have sometimes also emerged as an offshoot to organisations dealing with income-generating activities, such as the Self-Employed Women's Association (SEWA) in India and the Kalyan Grameen scheme in Bangladesh.

The most recent reviews indicate that community financing improves access by rural and informal sector workers to needed health care and provides them with some protection against the cost of illness. One important new finding of a survey by Baeza et al is that most community-based health organisations provide a comprehensive coverage, including medicines as well as in- and outpatient care. They also find that most of such organisations function as an "entry-point" to mainly public

9.4.5. Impact of Community and Area-Based Schemes

The main advantage of community-based schemes is that they improve health expenditure efficiency or the relation between quality and cost of health services. There are basically three reasons why participants in such schemes would prefer community schemes to individual spending and financing :

— By regular contributions, the problem of indebtedness brought about by high medical bills can be alleviated.
— The financial power of the group may enable administrators to negotiate services of better quality or better value for money from health care providers.

— The group may be willing to spend on preventive and health promotion activities so as to keep down the cost of medical services.

The extent to which community-based schemes have been successful has depended on the characteristics of the organisations that set up the scheme, on their design and on the context in which they operate. The association should be based on trust among it members, which is enhanced by factors, such as strong and stable leadership, its economic base, the existence of participated structures and a reliable financial and administrative structure.

Good design features include measures to control fraud and abuse, to promote some form of mandatory participation, to contain costs and to foster preventive and promotive health services. Important context variables concern the availability of quality and affordable health care services (public or private) and a favourable climate for the development of community-based schemes. In their review of rural risk-sharing strategies in health, Bennett, Crease and Monash note that there are several threats to the scope for raising revenues through community health insurance schemes. The threats include:

— The small scale of the majority of schemes examined.

— Adverse selection leading to progressively smaller risk pools and higher costs.

— Heavy administrative structures and costs in some schemes.

These three threats are clearly interrelated, because the heavy administrative structure and costs are often the result of the scheme's small scale. In addition, the small scale of most of the schemes is reinforced by the problem of adverse selection. So one key issue is to define under what conditions community health insurance schemes can be sustainable and/or replicable.

There are various characteristics on the basis of which work and residence-based groups can organise themselves for the provision of health care. People can organise themselves because they share the same occupation, live in the same area or belong to the same gender, cultural or religious group, for example. Each of these characteristics has its own advantages and disadvantages with regard to community factors such as trust, leadership, as well as financial and organisational capacity. These characteristics also have a major impact on the extent and speed with which self-financed community health insurance

In most (developed) countries, work-based organisations have been at the origin of statutory social insurance programmes. Informal sector workers to the extent that they are organised at all are principally organised in occupation- or sector-based associations and cooperatives. Their first priority is to improve their economic base in terms of credit, marketing and production technology. Once that is ensured, their organisations can often constitute a foundation for the establishment of contributory social and health protection schemes. This is also frequently true for women's organisations, whose purpose often includes raising consciousness with regard to the position of women in the family, work and society. Some of these organisations have set up savings and/or credit organisations, which significantly improve the chances of successfully organising social and health protection schemes.

Organisations based on the place of residence are usually less cohesive, since they may reject the participation of poor people, given their weak financial base. This may be different in the case of rural areas, where communities are often close-knit, and people have similar financial resources. At the area (district) level the social cohesion is likely to be even lower, but the quality of local government strongly influences whether some form of consensus, incentives and accountability can be established.

The area based approach is very suitable for social health care financing, since it can take into account the provision of not only curative but also preventive and promotional activities. In addition, participation by local government can also increase the extent and speed of replication of pilot experiences. Moreover, local health insurance schemes can help to relieve some of the pressures on the budget of the Ministry of Health. Hsiao and Sen conceived this idea for India; they proposed that local communities manage and finance some primary and secondary health care services, particularly in the rural areas. Recent ILO experience in Nepal and ADB pilot projects on "commune-based health insurance" in Vietnam show that this approach may have durable practical relevance.

Commenting on the situation in Tanzania, Steinwachs examines the potential of health insurance schemes, based on religious organisations, such as churches, mosques and hospitals. The general advantages of such schemes are that their affiliated members come from different income classes and that they dispose of "trans local" structures that permit them to link up schemes between different parts of the country. Her analysis of the Lutheran hospital-based schemes shows that members of all faiths or convictions are affiliated.

9.4.6. Scope of Community and Area-Based Schemes

Since most of these schemes remain fairly small, it is important to know under what forms of partnership the coverage of these schemes can be expanded. One option is that such schemes form organisations among themselves, which will enable them to achieve various objectives, such as a stronger negotiating power towards the government as well as (public and private) health providers, sharing of knowledge and greater financial stabilisation through mechanisms, such as re-insurance. Such inter-group associations could grow into a professional organisation with a "beehive" structure. In other words, for a small fee the professional organisation would provide advice to individual associations on how to set up and manage their schemes.

Experience has shown that it takes at least ten years to build community-based health insurance schemes on occupational, geographical or gender groups. One idea is therefore to set up so-called "provisional" mutual health insurance schemes for those whose occupational associations do not yet have any specific mutual health insurance schemes as well as for individual micro entrepreneurs and any persons who are able to contribute but who have not yet been able to choose an appropriate micro-insurance scheme. Such provisional schemes would belong to and be supervised by the State, but the State would not interfere in the conducting of their day-to-day activities. The creation of these provisional schemes could be a first step towards the compulsory health care coverage of workers all over the country.

The heterogeneous nature of the persons to be covered by the provisional mutual insurance arrangements necessarily calls for harmonisation as regards the periodicity of recovery and the level of contributions. Thus with a view to generating solidarity everyone has to contribute equally for the same types of benefits. As regards periodicity, a certain degree of flexibility is recommended so that wage and salary earners and other workers whose activities are not subject to climatic hazards can contribute on a monthly basis, whereas a system of prepayment during the high season is recommended for categories of seasonal workers (such as market gardeners).

Steinwachs also proposes a new way to deal with the compulsory affiliation of workers under statutory national health insurance schemes. Commenting on the situation in Tanzania, she is in favour of the State accepting that under the general umbrella of compulsory affiliation people can choose and become a member of either State-initiated schemes, the National Social Security Fund or the National Health Insurance System, or of a certified health insurance scheme. This would have various advantages, such as:

— Formal sector employees could provide greater income stability to certified health insurance schemes.

— There would be greater competition on quality and costs between various schemes.

— A larger network of health insurance schemes would provide an opportunity for greater use of different health providers all over the country.

Such an approach would of course require that the State could keep track of the active affiliation of all workers concerned and that it puts in motion a rigorous process of certification and quality control. In addition to the expansion of community-based schemes, the impact of such schemes can also be enhanced through multiplication and mainstreaming. This means that small schemes can be seen as catalysts of innovations, the creators of strategic and programmatic knowledge that can be spun off and/or integrated into the three mainstream of society: governments, civil society and markets. The success of such experiments can then be judged, not only in terms of their size, but also in terms of the spin-offs they created, the number of projects that have been taken over by other actors, and the degree to which it contributed to the social and intellectual diversity of civil society.

However, with the growth of community-based schemes, other forms of partnerships may also be necessary. Experience with successful scaling-up efforts shows that two sorts of themselves, as well as in linkages and forms of collaboration with other organisations. Community-based schemes may team up with, and/or receive support from, larger organisations in civil society (cooperatives and trade unions for instance). They may also seek to involve private companies and social security agencies, which already have a well-functioning administration.

The role of the government is critical for the successful up-scaling of these schemes. Local governments must play an important role in setting up area-based social security schemes in partnership local groups of civil society. At the national level, governments are in the best position to ensure that isolated experiences can be replicated to other occupations, sectors and areas. Moreover, it can create an enabling environment for the development of community-based schemes. Four possible forms of government support can be distinguished here:

— Promote health insurance through recommendations on design (benefits package, affiliation and administration) and the setting up of a management information system.

— Monitoring the performance of community-based schemes, possibly within the context of legislation on the efficient and transparent administration of schemes.

— Undertake and organise training, based amongst others on the promotion and monitoring activities mentioned under the above first two points.

— Co-finance the access of low-income groups to health insurance, possibly through subsidies or matching contributions.

9.4.7. Policy Issues

In extending social health insurance, most developing countries have followed the strategy of "gradual implementation" due to major political, financial and material constraints. This meant that compulsory coverage was limited according to various criteria, such as geographical area, size of undertaking, category of dependant and type of medical benefit. Countries, such as the Republic of Korea and Taiwan, China, reached universal coverage through the extension of social health insurance, while some Latin American countries, such as Chile and Costa Rica, have virtually achieved universal coverage through a combination of social insurance and access to government (public) facilities. The most striking example is probably the Republic of Korea, which achieved universal health coverage within 12 years, between 1977 and 1989.

The success of these countries is, first of all, due to their political commitment, but could only be achieved when they were at relatively high levels of economic development, were largely urbanised and had large wage sectors relative to informal sectors. Still, there is considerable variety in the choices that these countries made. Compared with Taiwan, China, the Republic of Korea, for example, opted for a relatively limited benefit package, fairly low contribution rates and relatively high co-payments. The examples of the Republic of Korea and Costa Rica also show the complex balance of participation between wage earners and the self-employed who tend to pay relatively low contributions and have greater opportunities to under-declare their incomes. Finally, it is also noteworthy that the march towards universal coverage in Costa Rica started with a change in the Constitution at the beginning of the 1960s.

There is a large variety of middle-income countries that are striving for universal others, such as Tunisia, have followed the gradualist approach. Colombia's rise in social health insurance coverage seems to have come to a halt, as a result of exploding public health expenditure, probably explained by the fact that the introduction of "demand subsidies" did not remove the "supply subsidies" to public hospitals. The achievement of universal coverage in Tunisia will probably depend on continuing application of effective compliance mechanisms. To achieve universal coverage, Thailand and Vietnam are experimenting with health care systems that provide access to care and that are backed up by government financed risk-adjusted capitation fees.

For middle-income countries striving at universal coverage, the key policy question is at what level of compulsory insurance coverage does it become feasible to extend a standard level of benefits to the whole population. A related question is whether progress is inevitably dependent on the growth of formal sector employment, and/or whether voluntary schemes for workers in the informal economy could play a role. Vietnam's experience with commune based health insurance schemes may provide an interesting example for other countries.

Under all circumstances, the government will have to finance part of the extension, in particular for the self-employed and other low-income workers.

In low-income countries usually not more than 5 percent of the labour force is covered by statutory social health insurance. Notable exceptions are Cuba and Mongolia who have achieved universal coverage through respectively a national health system and a statutory social health insurance scheme. Governments in most other low-income countries do not provide free or subsidised access to basic health care, and this has contributed to the emergence of the community- and area-based health insurance schemes.

The main advantage of these schemes is that they improve health expenditure efficiency or the relation between quality and costs of health services. The extent to which these schemes have been successful has depended on the characteristics of the bodies, on the design of the scheme and on the context in which they operate. Since most of these schemes remain fairly small, it is important to know under what forms and partnerships the coverage of these schemes can be expanded. One option is to form organisations among themselves. Another is to look for partnerships with larger institutions, such as local government, social security institutions or private sector insurance companies, if they can be trusted.

A relatively new idea is for the government to set up so-called "provisional" mutual health insurance schemes, i.e. for individual micro-entrepreneurs and any persons who are able to contribute but who have not yet been able to choose an appropriate micro-insurance scheme. Another new idea is for the government to accept that people have the choice under the umbrella of compulsory affiliation to become a member of certified micro-health insurance schemes. This would imply that the national statutory social health insurance schemes would loose their monopoly on the affiliation of workers in the formal sector. This could have the advantages of greater income stability for community-based schemes, of more competition, and of an opportunity for greater use of different health care providers all over the country.

This would, however, require the State to keep track of active affiliation and to put in motion a rigorous process of certification and quality control. In order to support the development of micro-insurance schemes, the State would also provide technical assistance on design and administration, monitor the performance of these schemes and possibly co-finance the access of low-income groups to micro health insurance. It would be worthwhile to test out both ideas. Beyond these trends and experiences, there are still a number of general policy issues and questions that need to be clarified. The first and most important issue concerns the role of the State.

There is general agreement that the governments fulfils the role of "steward" in health policy, i.e. it should conceive the system as a whole, monitor its development, and steer all partners into the direction of better health outcomes. Apart from the direct provision of services, the government can provide incentives, set standards, and enforce compliance. There is also agreement on the fact that the State should finance access to health care for the poor, and co-finance that of the self-employed. International financial support is needed, in particular for the low-income countries.

The second question concerns the conception of universal health care coverage. Most developing countries turn away from the "national health service" model, because of the lack of public finance and of deficient public sector management. The choice for statutory social health insurance relieves the State of some of its financial commitments, but the issue of deficient governance remains unsolved. Moreover, given the heterogeneity of the labour force, statutory social insurance schemes may not have an inherent tendency towards universal coverage. There is agreement on the fact that social insurance is a more equitable health care financing solution than the system of user fees.

The third question concerns the ways in which public and private health care providers can be used most effectively. The classical way is to adopt various provider payment systems, but there is also a need to define public-private partnerships in the health sector. These partnerships can increase competition, because the government enables other actors to participate in the financing, provision and management of health services. According to Jutting, this has a positive effect on efficiency, equity and quality of health care provision.

Finally, more thought has to be given and experiments carried out with community and area-based schemes, particularly in the low-income countries. For the time being, such schemes have proven to be cost-efficient, but they have not been shown to be replicable at a large scale. One of the most promising avenues would the experimentation with area-based social health insurance schemes, which aim at full coverage within an area and are mainly run by the (local) government in collaboration with a wide variety of possible social security partners. In comparison with sector or occupation-based schemes, area-based schemes have the advantage that administration costs are low, and that local participation and control can be included in the design of the project. In addition, most importantly, coverage could be extended to other areas relatively quickly, because governments would be able to replicate the schemes on the same conditions.

9.5. Contributory Pensions

Many of the recent discussions on social security, particularly in the developed countries, have focused on the great changes in retirement policy. A large number of developing countries are planning or implementing major changes in their national pension schemes. Some are moving from pay-as-you-go (PAYG) to Fully Funded (FF) individual payments at retirement to a social security scheme providing periodical benefits. This worldwide process of change is being fuelled by multiple factors, such as the ageing of the population, the recognised weakness in the administrative and political management of some public pension schemes, the worldwide growth of informal sector employment and a consequent loss of pension coverage, and the transition towards a greater influence of the market economy.

One of the greatest challenges facing pension schemes is the extent to which contributory pensions should be funded or financed on a PAYG basis. The ILO reference book on social security pensions observes that the traditional PAYG form of financing basically links pension benefits to the outcomes of the labour market, and in particular to wage growth. The funded form of financing links pension benefits to the capital market, and in particular to the rate of return on stocks and bonds. Both forms of financing have their advantages and disadvantages, both in theory and in practice. The book recommends that PAYG is generally more appropriate for financing mandatory systems providing minimum pension benefits. It admits both PAYG and funded systems for mandatory earnings-related pension benefits, and it considers the funded system more suitable for voluntary pension schemes.

The specific challenges of pension reform related to the extension of personal coverage have to do with the large trends that have been influencing the economy and the labour market as well as with the specific requirements and needs of those that so far are not covered by any pension provision. The group of non-covered persons is very heterogeneous. In the developing countries they are, first of all, the self-employed, mainly in small and medium-sized enterprises as well as in the growing informal economy, both in urban and rural areas. There are also the still large groups of unpaid family labour, mainly working in agriculture and in rural areas.

A multi-tiered system characterised by diversification of financing and benefit mechanisms provides the greatest long-term income security. Usually there is no disagreement about a minimum guarantee for the poor (the first tier) and voluntary retirement saving (the third tier). It is generally also agreed that a closer contribution-benefit link, and proper incentives for contributions and transparency are desirable in the intermediate, mandatory insurance scheme (the second tier). According to Augusztinovics, the debate revolves around the institutional setting of the second tier: the method of financing (PAYG or funded) and the type of management (public or private). There are strong inter-linkages between these tiers. For instance, if a country has a well developed and sustained bottom tier, the part of the mandatory, contributory tier can be relatively smaller, and more emphasis can be put on voluntary arrangements.

9.5.1. Pension Reform and Coverage in Latin America

It is particularly in Latin America where reforms have changed the principles on which the financing and administration of pension schemes were based. The old principles of solidarity, redistribution, public administration, defined benefits and partially funded financial schemes were replaced by defined contributions, fully-funded individual capitalisation accounts, private sector pension-fund administrators (with separated financial statements), and a government guarantee for a minimum pension.

Structural reforms radically change the public system either by replacing it completely by a private one (the substituted model), or by introducing a private component in addition to the public one (the parallel model), or by creating a private system to compete with the public one (the mixed model). Five countries have so far adopted the substituted model: Bolivia, Chile, El Salvador, Mexico and Nicaragua. Colombia and Peru have applied the parallel model, while the mixed model exists in Argentina, Costa Rica Uruguay. Structural reforms are being considered in two other Latin American countries:

Brazil is looking at a mixed model and Honduras at a substituted model. One of the assumptions behind the structural pension reforms was that, if the private system is better than the public one, this will create an incentive to join the former and thus labour force coverage will increase. Before the structural pension reforms, the "pioneers", such as Argentina, Chile and Uruguay had the greatest coverage. The "intermediates", including Colombia, Mexico and Peru had coverage rates ranging from 20 to 45 per cent.

In some countries the self-employed can be covered on a voluntary basis, in which case a self-employed person would generally have to pay the equivalent of both the worker's and employer's contribution, i.e. about double the amount assigned to the salaried worker. The establishment of a minimum wage as a tax base does not correct the problem because a large majority of the self-employed have income levels that are below such minimum. Therefore, the heavy financial burden imposed on the self-employed becomes a significant barrier to coverage.

Only 10 percent of them are registered as members, mostly professionals with high incomes while only 4 per cent are active contributors. If, after beyond this relatively small group, it would be very difficult for other countries with larger groups of self-employed, peasants and informal workers to extend coverage to these traditionally under-represented groups. Pension reforms were supposed to reduce evasion and noncompliance in the belief that workers would have a strong interest in accumulating their pension savings.

Competition in the pension market is strongly influenced by the number of administrators. The number of administrators is fairly large in Argentina and Mexico, fair in Chile and Colombia (eight and six, respectively) and a few in the rest (two in Bolivia, two in El Salvador and five in Peru). In Bolivia, by 1998 there were only 350,000 insured and all of them were affiliated to one of only two administrators (deploy). In most countries there is a tendency towards a concentration between two to three administrators, who cover at least 75 per cent of the insured persons. Mesa-Lago points out that this concentration is not based on the lowest administrative costs or the highest return rates, but on the marketing and the number of sales persons.

Private pension systems charge commissions, the level of which is an indication of the efficiency of the systems. The commission is usually made up of two elements: one part is paid to the administrator for managing the individual account, the fund interest and the old age pension; and the other part is paid to a private insurance company against the risks of disability and death (except in Colombia and Mexico where these risks are covered by the statutory social insurance system).

Administrative costs of the private pension system are also high due to the transfer problem. Since insured workers or affiliates are allowed to choose the best administrator, they can move freely from one administrator to another with some restrictions: for example, they can move every six months, or do two moves per year. Pension administrators have created all sorts of additional attractions and benefits to raise the number of their members (gifts or additional electronic services to access personal information). They rely on sales persons whose work is to persuade the insured to change administrators and who, in return, receive a commission paid for each shift. It is in the sales person's best interest to encourage as many members as possible to change. As a result, the number of transfers is very high and has prompted public supervision agencies to impose additional constraints to the transfer of members.

Thus, the most important failures in pension reforms are the following: severe limits to the expansion of coverage, high transaction costs, evasion and noncompliance, and lack of competition. Some of these failures have then led to various forms of overregulation on the part of the government, such as the imposition on pension administrators to pay an annual minimum investment yield to the insured, the legal prohibition or restriction to invest in foreign instruments, and to prescribe methods to fix commissions to administer the pension fund.

The experience of Latin America seems, to some extent, to be repeated in the more recent experience of Central and Eastern Europe. A recent comparison of Hungary and Poland, both of which have introduced private sector managed pension schemes, show that administrative costs are high and that the real value of worker savings have declined during the first years of operation. The study also points to the substantial variation of the annuity pension benefits depending on the performance of the capital market at the time of retirement.

Moreover, it estimates the very high long-term transitional costs that the government has to pay for the transition from a PAYG to a funded system. Chile is still experiencing the transaction costs 20 years after the transition. In Hungary and Poland, the transitional financing costs are estimated to exceed 100 percent of GDP over the next 50 years and one percent of GDP until 2020 and two percent for many years thereafter respectively.

9.5.2. Examples of Extending Statutory Pension Schemes

Both funded and PAYG pension systems are faced with largely the same problem with regard to the extension of coverage, i.e. the fact that in many countries a large, and often growing, part of the labour force works in the informal economy. However, there are various ways in which statutory pension schemes can prepare the way for greater extension. As noted before, such efforts will be less effective, if the contribution and benefit structure of the statutory pension scheme is not adapted to the particular needs and contributory capacity of workers in the informal economy. Finally, the government may also set up, and partially finance, pension schemes that cover only particular groups, such as the self-employed or domestic workers.

In most developing countries the administration of social security systems has often been unable to deal with the special circumstances of the self-employed and casual wage workers. When statutory social insurance is extended to smaller enterprises, each new employer has to be identified, registered, educated and persuaded to comply with all the rules of the scheme in so far as they relate to the registration of existing and new employees and to the method and timing of the payment of contributions. Because casual workers work intermittently and irregularly for different employers, contributions are difficult to collect and the maintenance of up-to-date and correct records is administratively complicated. There is also some conflict with the underlying concept for the receipt of benefits, i.e. that of "replacement" income, in situations where the income to be replaced cannot always be determined clearly.

It is therefore necessary to gradually remove or reduce the legal restrictions that can cope with the extension. If a timetable is prescribed in the legislation, this will provide the discipline to ensure that administrative steps are taken to prepare for the extension of coverage, and it has also the advantage of avoiding further rounds of negotiation and political reflection. Administrative reforms are another important step to improve compliance and enforcement, for example by developing cooperation with other public agencies, such as tax agencies, to identify individuals and businesses that should be covered.

Moreover, improved governance supported by effective public relations and educational activities to increase awareness as to rights and obligations needs to be underpinned by compliance and enforcement procedures and powers that reinforce the mandatory character of the scheme. In some counties, such as the Philippines, the Social Security System scheme was developed to provide universal coverage but was restrained in its enforcement by a combination of weak public sector management and a soft compliance approach.

On the other hand, the example of Tunisia shows that good enforcement and a more correct estimation of self-employment income can lead to the effective extension of coverage. The inspection system of the National Social Security Fund carries out on-the-spot inspections as well as audits of large enterprises with a view to detecting under-declaration and fraud. Enterprises will face heavy financial penalties imposed by law. As in many other countries, self-employment incomes are often under-declared in Tunisia.

As a result, realistic income scales have been estimated for different categories of self-employed, taking into account the occupation of the insured persons as well as the size of the firm or farm. Self-employed persons have to pay their contributions on the basis of these scales, unless they can prove that they earn lower (or higher) levels of income. These measures, together with a thorough campaign to raise awareness among the employers' and workers' organisations, led in 1996 to almost 70,000 new affiliations within a period of two years.

In 1999 the Republic of Korea extended its National Pension Programme to cover the entire working population. This was the result of the philosophy on productive welfare, as adopted by the incoming president Kim. According to this idea, social policies are not just an instrument for greater economic competitiveness, but they also ensure that the basic social rights for each citizen are fulfilled. However, many temporary employees, mostly employed in medium- and small-scale firms, fail to pay their contributions. In addition, since the National Programme requires at least 20 years of contribution to provide eligibility for full pensions, it has so far mainly accumulated funds. Once pensions are being paid out from 2003, the fund is expected to run out in 30 years, unless there is a reform in the financing structure.

China is one country where a revision of the benefit and contribution structure has facilitated the entry of the self-employed and informal economy workers. Firstly, a clear distinction was drawn between the mandatory pension schemes for urban workers and the pension scheme for rural workers, the latter of which is government supported and provides for the voluntary participation of farmers. However, there are also considerable variations in the benefit and contribution structures of pension schemes for different groups of workers in the urban areas. It may also be possible to allow the self-employed earnings levels for different occupations.

Another way to adapt pensions to the priorities and contributory capacities of different groups of workers would be to design benefit packages for the self-employed and the informal sector which would range from a basic core of social protection obligatory for all gainfully occupied persons to a more comprehensive provision which would remain compulsory for certain groups of workers (from the formal sector). Survivors' and disability benefits would be the first candidates for such a core package.

Statutory social insurance schemes would have a comparative advantage in dealing with such benefits, because insurance against these risks requires a large pool of contributors. In this light, the Government of Malaysia is currently considering an ILO proposal for legislation of a compulsory scheme for self-employed workers. It would provide benefits similar to those for employees; and it would cover rehabilitation expenses as well as cash benefits for serious employment injuries and invalidity. It is proposed that the scheme be administered by the Social Security Organisation, but be financially independent from the scheme for employees.

Since extending or adapting the statutory pension scheme may not lead to the coverage of many additional workers, the question should be asked whether and to what extent it is feasible to design special schemes for the self-employed or other groups in the informal economy. There are essentially two ways of doing this. The first is to design a special public scheme that corresponds to the needs and circumstances of the excluded group, and that is administratively and financially distinct from the statutory scheme; it is financed wholly by the insured or partially, with a government subsidy. The second option is to encourage (and assist) the development of mutual support (or private sector) mechanisms covering occupational groups or communities.

Given the variety of developing countries, with regard to the level of economic development as well as to that of social security institutions, it is difficult to propose general policy conclusions. It may be possible to distinguish between two types of developing countries. The first consists of middle-income countries, some of whom have well-developed social security institutions. Such countries could aim at covering the population as a whole through the extension of the statutory social insurance programme. And secondly, there is the large group of low-income countries where a rapid increase in social security coverage can only be achieved through the setting up of social insurance schemes specially designed for different groups of workers from the informal economy.

9.5.3. Micro-Finance and Pensions

Traditionally, micro-credit institutions have focused on the provision of working capital loans for micro-enterprises as a means to break the cycle of poverty. Many of them have grown into MFIs, because a more holistic, integrated approach is needed to provide the full spectrum of financial services required by low-income households, not just micro-entrepreneurs. Life-insurance packages are often attached to business loans so as to guarantee the repayment of the loan, if the borrower dies, and in some cases to pay a lump sum to the survivors.

Within the context of their broader responsibilities, MFIs are now seeking to serve broader groups of clients and to expand their insurance services to health and asset insurance. To extend the availability of financial services to low-income communities, for various reasons the development of insurance products should probably come after the development of savings products. First, savings are more effective than insurance in reducing vulnerability to a variety of unpredictable or one-time social and economic events, such as expenditure for a wedding, the loss of business and sickness. On the other hand, insurance provides more appropriate protection for predictable events, frequently involving large losses, such as hospital expenditure, death, old age and disability.

Secondly, savings accounts are probably a more effective foundation for delivering insurance services than loans, because the credit-insurance link only provides coverage when the client has an outstanding loan. Finally, a savings-insurance link increases the likelihood that low-income clients with irregular income flows can access insurance, because they can either use their accounts to save the insurance premiums or pay the insurance premium with the interest gained on their savings. As a result, innovations that layer insurance with savings products such as the life savings products of various credit unions and SEWA's premium savings accounts are likely to be the more effective way of providing long-term coverage while minimising transaction costs.

Zeller suggests that there is a large role for MFIs in responding to risks of old age and death of family members through precautionary savings services (long-term deposits with higher interest rates) and life insurance. At the moment there are more examples of MFIs dealing with life insurance than with periodical old-age pensions. Bank Rakyat Indonesia provides life insurance that only covers the debt of borrowers. The Bangladesh Rural Advancement Committee (BRAC) pays out a life insurance to designated survivors. The 42 member during old age. While some micro-finance institutions provide precautionary savings, they mostly do so when they are registered as banks.

There are various mechanisms to extend the accessibility of life-insurance products, and eventually pensions, to low-income households. MFIs could play an important role in this process, because they are generally trusted institutions, and have already built up credit and savings channels for poor clients, frequently at a relatively low cost. On the other hand, they generally lack insurance expertise and often have a relatively small client base.

If they are large enough and have sufficient supervisory and management capacity, they may set up a separate business unit and hire in the required expertise. Otherwise, MFIs could act as an agent and out source the insurance part of the business or certain long-term activities of the insurance process to an insurer or specialised business. In addition, they may wish to out source risk through a re-insurer. The tasks of the MFI would then be to sell policies to clients in exchange for a commission. And in view of its relation of trust with the client, it would also service the policy, which involves verifying claims and submitting claims requests.

In this whole process the government will have an important, indirect role. Many of the regulatory standards established for commercial insurers serving high-income markets can unintentionally restrict the provision of insurance in small amounts to low-income customers. Through regulation and financial incentives the Government may also wish to influence the life-insurance, and eventually pension, benefits that are provided by the private sector. In fact, from a social security point of view, governments generally favour the payment of periodical benefits rather than lump sums.

The State has an inherent interest in periodical payments, because if the lump sum is not used well, the person in question may still come back for social assistance support that is financed from public money. For that and other reasons, the State might therefore be interested to subsidise such schemes, either by matching contributions or by technical support.

A large number of developing countries are planning or implementing major changes in their national pension schemes. Some are moving from PAYG schemes to fully-funded individual savings accounts, while others are moving from provident schemes providing lump-sum payments at retirement to a social security scheme providing periodical benefits. Pensions comprise three major contingencies, i.e. old age, disability and survivor ship. The extent to which various groups in the formal and informal sectors are concerned by these contingencies differs according to their specific work, income and family situation. More research is needed on the realities "on the ground" of formal pension provision as well as on the impact of old age, disability and death on income, assets and family relations.

It is particularly in Latin America where pension reforms have changed the principles on which the financing and administration of pension schemes is based. Pension reforms have not changed the substantial differences in coverage among countries, and overall coverage has probably declined over the past 20 years. The pioneers (Argentina, Chile, and Uruguay) cover 60-80 per cent, while the rest with a much larger informal economy cover less than 30 per reducing evasion and noncompliance, in the belief that workers would be more attracted by accumulated pension savings than by the benefits provided by PAYG schemes. Evasion and noncompliance may well have increased, and seem to be explained by excessive administrative costs and the so-called transfer problem. Nevertheless, both funded and PAYG pension systems are faced with largely the same problem with regard to the extension of coverage, i.e. the fact that in many countries a large, and often growing, part of the labour force works in the informal economy.

Approaches adopted by governments to integrate self-employed workers into the statutory pension insurance programmes have met with mixed success. The self-employed are usually not prepared to pay the "double", i.e. workers' and employers' contributions. However, some countries such as Tunisia have significantly increased coverage among the self-employed, in particular through the development of realistic income scales as the contribution base for different groups of self-employed workers. Some special schemes for these workers have also had success, particularly if the Government is willing to subsidise them and if such schemes can be supported by earmarked taxes. India, for instance, has achieved the successful coverage of about 400,000 mainly home-based beedi workers under the Employees' Provident Fund Act financed by an earmarked tax. China has also facilitated the entry of the self-employed and informal economy worker by adapting the benefit and contribution structures to the particular circumstances of urban and rural workers. Egypt has been one of the countries that has prescribed minimum insurable earnings levels for different occupations so as to provide the self-employed a degree of choice in their contribution liability.

Middle-income countries could aim at covering the population as a whole through the extension of statutory pension insurance programme. The low-income countries can probably achieve significant increases in pension coverage through intermediary institutions, such as MFIs. MFIs could play an important role in making life insurance and eventually pensions accessible to low-income households. They are generally trusted institutions and have already built up credit and savings channels for poor clients, frequently at a relatively low cost. MFIs could either manage the insurance business themselves or become an intermediary agent towards outside insurance companies. For both low and middle-income countries, some of the following conclusions may be suggested:

— Consider a revision of the statutory scheme to facilitate partial membership.

— Strengthen administrative capacity (compliance, record keeping and financial management).

— Undertake education and public awareness programmes to improve the image of the social security system.

— Extend coverage within a prescribed timetable to all persons working as employees except in special groups, such as domestic servants, family workers and casual workers

— Open up new "windows" and offer benefits that suit the needs and contributory tendency towards low and sometimes decreasing social security coverage capacity of non-covered groups.

References

Lee, E. 1998. *The Asian financial crisis: The challenge for social policy.* Geneva.

Lund, F.; Srinivas, S. 2000: *Learning from experience: A gendered approach to social protection for workers in the informal economy.* Geneva, ILO-STEP & WIEGO.

Márquez, G. (ed.). 1995: *Reforming the labor market in a liberalized economy* Washington, DC, Inter-American Development Bank.

Mazza, J. 2000: *Unemployment insurance: Case studies and lessons for the Latin American and Caribbean region.* Washington D.C., Inter-American Bank, Research Department Working Paper no. 411.

Mesa-Lago, C. 200. "Structural reform of social security pensions in Latin America: Models, characteristics, results and conclusions", in *International Social Security Review* 54(4), pp.67-92.

10

Human Security and Political Freedom in Modern Age

The concept of human security evolved as a result of the changes in security environment after the end of the Cold War. A combination of many factors led to its formation. A decreased threat of global nuclear war created a cognitive space for non-military threats to be perceived with greater intensity. At the same time, the process of democratization reached a new level as democracy spread to the developing countries. This meant also that individual human life and well-being received more attention and obtained more importance. Consequently, the role of human rights and freedoms and their implementation at the national and international level became much more significant. At the global level, one could observe a process of increasing globalisation, leading to shrinkage of space and time as well as the withering of borders. The role of physical distance has decreased, and technology has increased the speed of various transfers on the global scale. The meaning of national borders as cornerstones of national and international stability, has also decreased to a certain extent.

All mentioned factors opened space for increased development. On the other hand, an increasing number of internal violent conflicts erupted in Africa, Asia and Europe, leading to huge humanitarian crises, increasing differences in economic development between North and South emerged and the problem of terrorism gradually became a more serious and recognized threat. In such circumstances, the concepts of national and international security simply did not reflect the environment and the needs stemming from it. This is why a kind of intellectual 'revolution' started, aiming to provide the most appropriate and fitting concept that would make interpretation and analysis of security easier. Neorealist focus on states and military security proved to be increasingly narrow and unfitting.

In this respect, the narrow politico-military focused strategic studies evolved towards much broader security studies, encompassing also many non-military aspects of security. Prominent journals *International Security* and *Foreign Affairs* published two theoretically breaking articles both titled "*Redefining Security*". The first article, published in 1983 by Ullman, substantiated broadening of security to the economic and developmental issues. He questioned the utility of focusing on military security, since it conveys a profoundly false image of reality and causes states to concentrate on military threats and to ignore other and perhaps even more harmful dangers. He thought that such an approach actually reduces our total security. The second article was published later in 1989 by Mathews, substantiating broadening of security towards environmental, resource and demographic issues. Even the journal *Survival*, which was known for its neorealist approach, published an article on non-military aspects of security in 1989. Perhaps the most comprehensive approach to security after the end of Cold War was substantiated by the "Copenhagen School" led by Barry Buzan, Ole Waever, Jaap de Wilde and others. In their key publications such as *People, States and Fear, An Agenda for International Security Studies in the Post-Cold War Era, The European Security Order Recast: Scenarios for the Post-Cold War Era, and Security: A New Framework for Analysis*, its representatives defined security as an inherently multisectoral phenomenon consisting of military, environmental, economic, political and societal sectors. The Copenhagen School pragmatically combined traditional and emerging approaches in security studies. After 9/11, a concept of asymmetric threats became increasingly recognized and used by the scientific community worldwide. Asymmetry refers to the disproportionality between the threatening subject and the threatened subject, which refers mostly to terrorists on one side and the state and society on the other side.

What actually happened with the security at the conceptual level after the end of Cold War is simultaneous horizontal and vertical broadening. This is where the roots of human security are to be found.

Horizontal broadening refers to incorporating "new" non-military aspects of security, such as environmental, economic, demographic, criminal, terrorist, health, information, immigration and other aspects (or sectors and dimensions as called by some), while vertical broadening of security referred to incorporation of other non-state referent objects, such as individuals, local communities, groups of people by common ethnic, religious or ideological characteristics, global community, etc. It is this combination of non-military security dimensions and non-state referent objects that gave birth to the concept of human security.

The human security was finally conceptualized and presented to the global public in a *Human Development Report* in 1994. The concept has evolved since then, and today we can observe quite a number of seriously conceptualized definitions and theoretical approaches.

10.1. Concept of Human Security

The concept of human security should be clearly distinguished from the traditional and narrow concept of security. The former evolved in the nineties as a compensation for deficiencies of a traditional concept of security. Understanding of the term security has broadened along the vertical and horizontal dimensions. The "horizontal broadening" referred to including other security dimensions next to political and military, such as environmental, economic, health, social, etc., while the "vertical broadening" referred to including other referent objects next to the state. The individual became a key referent object in human security, differentiating it from the traditional approach.

The development of the concept of human security was deeply influenced by the political and security context after the end of the Cold War. Several factors created a cognitive space that was necessary for developing such a concept:

— decreased threat of global nuclear war,

— predominance of non-traditional and non-military threats,

— democratization,

— strengthening of human rights and freedoms in national and international policies,

— increase awareness of the importance of human life and well-being,
— globalization and related consequences,
— increase poverty and differences between developed North and poor South,
— increase number of internal armed and violent conflicts,
— spread of small arms and light weapons, as well as the issue of anti-personnel mines.

Because the above mentioned phenomena are unevenly spread around the world, they create slightly different input or context in the process of conceptualization of human security. Some regions have more conflicts, different social, cultural, economic and geostrategic context than other regions. This is why many (mostly similar, but slightly different) academic and political definitions of human security have been developed.

A comparison of conceptualizations of human security (along the perceived referent object, identified human values at stake, identified threats and means for providing human security) shows great similarity among concepts. Differences stem from slightly different contexts, which are mostly regionally conditioned. Comparison shows that all concepts stress that the key referent object is individual, while only some concepts also stress the centrality of human communities (e.g. ethnic groups, minorities etc.). The criteria for this selection is the vulnerability of individuals to traditional or non-traditional threats.

Comparison of human security approaches further shows a lower degree of unity regarding the identified human values. The values most often stated as "at stake" in human security situations are survival, safety, livelihood, freedom, well-being and dignity. For example, Bajpai stressed that the fundamental values at stake in human security are physical safety and well-being and individual/personal freedom. This brings us to the question of relationship between human security and human liberty and freedom, which will be addressed later.

A comparison of the concepts of human security regarding perceived and identified threats to individuals shows a great variety of potential threats. All approaches stress mostly non-traditional threats;

however traditional ones are mentioned and stressed by some as well. The threat spectrum includes the following threats:

— economic threats,
— food threats,
— health threats,
— environmental threats,
— personal threats,
— community threats,
— political threats,
— demographic threats,
— crime in all forms, including terrorism,
— natural disasters,
— violent conflicts and wars,
— genocide,
— anti-personnel mines, SALW, etc.

A difference among approaches in terms of giving different prioritization to different threats can be identified. Some approaches mention also the structural violence of different forms as a threat to human security. Freedom from fear is many times mentioned as a key element of human security. Freedom from fear is actually measured by the (opinion polls on) threat perception. Some approaches also mention an "acceptable quality of life". It is very important that many approaches understand the interconnection among threats (transborder interconnection and intersectoral interconnection). The latter refers to the fact that complex human security situations embrace a broad spectrum of more or less interconnected and correlated threats from different dimensions or sectors. This also means that extreme escalation of threat in one dimension leads to escalation of threats in other dimensions. For example, the wartime situation in Bosnia and Herzegovina was an example of extreme escalation of military threat that has lead to the escalation of economic threats (e.g. unemployment, economic crisis), environmental threats (environmental damage and pollution), terrorism, organized crime (e.g. looting during the war operations), health threats (e.g. unbearable health conditions), disrespect of human rights, etc. In this respect, we should support

Oberleitner's finding that individuals actually face an endless spectrum of potential threats.

One must also note that human security is directly related to the concept of international peace and security. The report by the UN High-level Panel on Threats, Challenges and Change entitled *A More Secure World: Our Shared Responsibility* makes a distinction between threats from non-state actors and states to human security as well as state security. Human security is in such perception put directly along the state security in national and international context. The panel proposed a comprehensive system of collective security that tackles both new and old threats, and addresses the security concerns of all states - rich and poor, weak and strong. The UN Secretary General confirmed in his introduction to this report that the UN strategies must be comprehensive and its institutions must overcome their narrow preoccupations and learn to work across the whole range of issues, in a concerted fashion. The report by the former UN Secretary General *In Larger Freedom: towards Development, Security and Human Rights for All* stressed the relationship between the rule of law and human security. The report stressed the rule of law as the all-important framework for advancing human security and prosperity. Yet, in many places governments and individuals continue to violate the rule of law, often without consequences for them but with deadly consequences for the weak and the vulnerable. In other instances, those who make no pretence of being bound by the rule of law, such as armed groups and terrorists, are able to flout it because the peacemaking institutions and compliance mechanisms are weak.

It is also very obvious that the UN broadened its understanding of the threat to international peace and security from conflicts among states to human security crises within states. Internal wars, genocides and other extreme violations of human rights can be treated as threats to international peace and security. The history of UN resolutions shows us that many of them (also within the 7th Chapter of the UN Charter) were adopted because of such situations and such interpretations. For example, Resolution 668 (1991) on Iraq stressed that suppression of civilian population represents a threat to international peace and security. The Security Council authorized the use of force in 1992 in Somalia and Haiti on behalf of civilian population and without the consent of the state. In Bosnia and Herzegovina, ethnic cleansing was labelled as violation of international humanitarian law and as a threat to peace and security. The genocide in Rwanda in 1995 was labelled in a similar way. Many related UN documents reflect the fact that international peace and security has an increasingly important human security aspect.

Comparison of understanding means for protection of human security shows that the state is actually the most important subject. Some approaches explicitly and some also implicitly stress the importance of non-governmental actors. The central goal of the human security agenda is to help the threatened people. Approaches identify two groups of means or measures: preventive and reactive. Preventive measures refer to all measures that aim to minimize the vulnerability of human beings, while reactive means are understood as secondary means for providing human security. The use of force is interpreted only as a last resort. The following means for providing human security are frequently mentioned:

— humanitarian intervention or humanitarian help,
— peacekeeping operations,
— peacebuilding,
— arms verification operations,
— respect for human rights and liberties,
— sustainable economic development,
— early warning,
— diplomatic missions,
— focused (smart) sanctions,
— preventive deployment of armed forces,
— preventive diplomacy,
— stronger civil society,
— empowerment strategies,
— assuring the minimal life standards, etc.

Approaches again differ in prioritizing these means. Many people claim that it is easier to ensure human security through early prevention than through later intervention; however it seems that this is not always considered in practice.

Our overview of means suggests that human security has become an inseparable part of national and international security policy performed by states, international organizations and non-governmental organizations. Human security plays a direct or at least an indirect role in formulating and implementing these policies.

10.1.1. Human Security and Human Sustainable Development

Human security approaches stress that the search for security must be based on human development. This is very important for human security as it puts it into a sustainable perspective. Actually, the sustainable development leads to environment where human security is less threatened because the emergence of violent conflicts is less likely. This is why the concept of human security is inherently and strongly connected with the concept of sustainable human development. This concept was formed in the second half of the eighties by the UN World Commission on Environment and Development and refers to the development that meets the needs of the present without compromising the ability of the future generations to meet their own needs. The commission defined this connection clearly by saying that sustainable development requires meeting the basic needs of all and extending to all the opportunity to satisfy their aspirations for a better life. In their view, a world in which poverty and inequity are endemic will always be prone to ecological and other crises. Similar thinking on inextricable link between development and security can be found in the already mentioned Report by the UN Panel on Threats, Challenges and Change. The report acknowledges that a more secure world is only possible if poor countries are given a real chance to develop. Extreme poverty and infectious diseases threaten many people directly, but they also provide a fertile breeding-ground for other threats, including civil conflict.

Human development is measured by the Human Development Index. This index actually measures the average achievements in a country in three basic dimensions of human development: a long and healthy life, knowledge and a decent standard of living. The strong connection between human development and human security brings us to consideration if conceptualizing the human security index would be possible.

Fundamental precondition for sustainable development is empowerment of people, referring to their education. By educating them, the key barrier to human development – human mind – can be surpassed. Means for achieving sustainable human development are rule of law, respect for human rights, economic development, social development, environmental development, creation of adequate norms and regimes. Many peace-building practices around the world reflect how development is connected to safety of people. Safe environment is a precondition for implementation of any kind of developmental projects, which further influence the well-being of population. Population with more satisfied basic needs is less likely to turn to violence in solving its problems.

10.1.2. Human Security Concept as a Challenge

Human security is a multidimensional phenomenon because it refers to a number of security dimensions (threats), almost all aspects of human life and a broad spectrum of means. This is why a multidisciplinary approach to human security is being shaped. Human security can be discussed from the perspective of human rights, security, law, humanitarian, economic, environmental, developmental and other perspectives or angles. For example, a Human Security consortium that was formed under the 6th Framework Research Program, financed by the European Commission, consists of a wide spectrum of research institutions, such as human rights studies, security studies, criminology and law. We can observe that a kind of "human security studies" is being shaped which is indicated by new human security research projects, courses in universities, conferences, HUMSEC journal, etc. Only a broad approach to human security can lead us to comprehensive and correct understanding of the human security situation.

One crucial problem arises from this "multi approach" however. The concept of human security actually refers to almost all security aspects (threats and risks). The question is how to build theory and implement it in the practice if it refers to everything. Such a broad concept actually lacks coherence and, consequently, focus. The problem of focus makes it difficult to implement the concept of human security in practice (in policy). This means that the concept of human security is theoretically well substantiated, attractive and modern; however it embraces almost everything, making it difficult to implement. The scientific community needs to operationalize this concept better if we want to avoid the inflation of this concept and the trap of broad understanding of security. Broad understanding of human security may be correct, but it is a labyrinth for which we need a better conceptual and political compass. What we perhaps really need is the development of a human security index, as already proposed and discussed by some scholars. Such index would enable the international community to monitor the human security situation in crisis areas and elsewhere systematically and permanently. It would give a clear benchmark upon which the preventive and reactive actions could be better prepared and more comprehensive. Already mentioned parallels with the Human development index could be valuable in addressing the challenge of conceptualizing and implementing the human security index.

The second problem stems from the fact that complex security environment created possibilities for faster interconnection among different categories (dimensions or sectors) of threats to human security. Human security crises are actually situations where threats from several dimensions escalate. They are strongly correlated. There is no one way or one mechanism for solving such crises. Many disciplines are involved, but they do not communicate enough with one another. There are no joint methodologies and also such need is not perceived and comprehended by most scholars. An interdisciplinary approach is currently the Achilles heel of human security. Interdisciplinarity in this respect refers to disciplines working together (not parallel) to achieve joint goals with joint methodologies. Also many actors that implement human security policy do not interact enough (OSCE, EU, NATO, OAS, G7/G8, UN, Human Security Network, Commission on Human Security, etc.). For example, the EU is looking for possible ways to increase human security in Kosovo in its new mission. The exploration of these possibilities should take into account the already existing activities of a large number of other foreign actors in Kosovo.

Complex security environments and corresponding human security situations and crises require optimal approaches. Partial approaches (by one actor) can be more or less efficient; however complex situations can not be solved by partial approaches. Interorganizational and interdisciplinary cooperation is therefore a necessity in the formulation of human security policy, decision making and implementation. We must take an additional step from our practice of broad initiatives and partitioned implementation to the practice of comprehensive implementation. A tool for this is better horizontal cooperation.

10.2. Challenge of Balancing Freedom and Security

Human security by its content opens the question of relationship between freedom and security. Concept and practice of human security is strongly connected to human rights. For some scholars, human security refers to the protection of personal safety and individual freedom. In the contemporary security environment, it seems that too many times a view on competing concepts prevails. Interpretations that we need to take sides in question of security versus freedom are prevailing. This is to a large extent stimulated by the intensive (legal or illegal) violations of human rights by states in the fight against terrorism. However, some scholars and politicians claim that the relationship should be understood in a more complementary manner. This is not a new thesis, as Benjamin Franklin already took this perspective in 1795. These are mutually supporting concepts because they are both human needs and human rights. Article 3 of the *Universal Declaration on Human Rights and Freedoms* states that everyone has the right to life, liberty and security of person. Kofi Annan also stressed the positive correlation among human rights, security and development in his report in *Larger Freedom: Towards Development, Security and Human Rights for All.*

In his opinion, the notion of larger freedom (that was introduced in his report) encapsulates the idea that development, security and human rights go hand in hand. He creates a triangle of interconnected elements – security, human rights and development. The former Secretary General argues that these three elements increasingly reinforce each other. This relationship has only been strengthened in our era of rapid technological advances, increasing economic interdependence, globalization and dramatic geopolitical change. Accordingly, we will not enjoy development without security, we will not enjoy security without development, and we will not enjoy either without respect for human rights. Unless all these causes are advanced, none will succeed.

Accordingly, the Human Security Concept refers to providing security within the limitations of respect for human rights. However, there are some limitations on human rights and freedoms due to some predefined interests of national and public security. This is the point at which the problems emerge, especially in the effective fight against the terrorism. Terrorism is a threat deeply incorporated in our societies.

According to the European Police Office (EUROPOL) altogether 498 terrorist attacks were carried out in the EU in 2006. The vast majority of them resulted only in limited material damage and were not intended to kill. A total of 706 individuals were arrested as suspects of terrorism in the same year. In the past several years, we have witnessed major arrests of terrorist suspects every month by European security services. The fight against terrorism has become a priority for many European and non-European states and international organisations. Basic security documents of these actors clearly reflect this priority.

The effective fight against terrorism obviously draws in large part upon the limitation of human rights and freedoms. This is due to prevailing preventive focus in fight against terrorism. The states are responsible for providing human security and also human rights. By defending some human rights, they obviously decrease some other human rights and freedoms. Finding a right balance is one of the biggest challenges of contemporary states and societies. This, however, is also a challenge of the Human Security Concept. The concept should be shaped and developed in a complementary way, balancing human security and human rights. This is not only a question of law and human rights experts, but a question of and for all disciplines dealing with human security. A better multidisciplinary dialogue should be developed within human security studies focusing on this question. The concept of human security should help to find an answer how to strive for acceptable (not maximal) level of security with minimal violations of human rights. More conceptual clearance would help various institutions within the states (e.g. police services, intelligence services, oversight bodies, political parties) and also international bodies, such as the EU. The process of establishing an Area of Freedom, Security and Justice within the EU can be successful only if the mentioned balance or equilibrium is found.

The process of finding a balance between human security and other human rights should at least draw upon the existing documents, such as the *Universal Declaration on Human Rights*, *European Convention on Human Rights*, *Guidelines on Human Rights and the Fight against Terrorism* and *Johannesburg Principles on National Security, Freedom of Expression and Access to Information*. These documents approve certain exceptions and situations in which human rights can be legally violated, however they also draw a strict line that can not be crossed by states in pursuit of security.

Looking at the critical examples in practice, we have no problem of identifying many cases where human rights were violated by organisations wanting to provide human and national security. But first, it should be clearly stated that sole terrorist attacks represent a gross violation of the human right to life. On the response side, we witnessed heavily militarized counter-terrorism, which is probably the first step in the wrong direction in addressing predominantly civilian terrorist threat. Definitions of terrorism are still not precise enough, leaving an open space for abuse by security services. Personal data exchange among countries is not necessarily subjected to the highest human rights standards, some states have been rendering their suspects to other states where human rights standards are not adequate, proactive stimulations for committing a criminal and terrorist act by European and US police services were identified, profiling terrorists can lead to religious or ethnic discrimination, pre-charge detention periods are increasing, violence used by states in crisis management operations outside Europe and US is not subject to the same limitations as at home, the concept of enemy combatant has been misused, Guantanamo bay detention camp proved to be a place where torture was used to extract information from suspects, where suspects are being held without temporal limits, and military commissions (courts) were used to trial detainees, etc.

Telecommunication and internet providers needed to prolong the storage time for communications that took place among users, universal data bases are being created for data mining purposes, simultaneously creating worries on how to control access and prevent misuse of personal data. Some terrorist suspects were detained in Europe by the CIA at secret locations, where torture and other illegal practices were most likely used. This list of disputable or critical practices simply does not end. This fact just proves our statement that balancing between human rights and security is one of the most important challenges of the human security studies community.

10.3. Technical Foundation of Human Security

Besides the evolution of the concept of human security and practice, the concept of critical infrastructure protection is gaining importance. The concept is focusing on threats to and protection of critical infrastructures, such as:

— energy (oil and gas production, refining, treatment and storage, electricity generation, transmission of electricity, gas and oil, distribution of electricity, gas and oil),

— information and communication technologies – ICT (e.g. Internet, provision of fixed telecommunications, provision of mobile telecommunications, radio communication and navigation, satellite communication, etc.),

— transport (road transport, rail transport, air transport, sea transport),

— water systems (provision of drinking water, control of water quality, control of water quantity),

— food (provision of food and safeguarding food safety and security),

— health systems (medical and hospital care, medicines, serums, vaccines and pharmaceuticals, bio-laboratories and bio-agents),

— financial systems (payment services/payment structures, etc.),

— state infrastructure, (ministries, relevant objects) etc.

These are all important systems that consist of objects and processes vital for human society. Vitality refers to criticality for normal functioning of human society. Many authors understand critical infrastructures as networks of mutually connected elements upon which normal functioning of society depend. Some authors stress that societal dependence from these systems is increasing.

Threats to critical infrastructures are, in fact, the same or at least similar to threats to human security. Critical infrastructure can be damaged, destroyed or disrupted by three categories of threats:

— disasters (broad spectrum of more or less coincidental events coming form system external environment),

— intentional attacks and

— failures (due to internal malfunctions in systems).

Damaged, destroyed or disrupted critical infrastructure for any reason directly or indirectly affect or even threaten human society, state and individuals. Human vulnerability in this area is increasing together with increasing dependence on vital support systems. We can identify plenty examples where human security was threatened also because of the malfunctioning of critical infrastructures. Most bigger terrorist attacks destroyed beside human lives also critical infrastructure. 9/11 was an attack against financial, military and political centres. The London and Madrid attacks involved rail infrastructure. Terrorist hijacking of airplanes involve air transport infrastructure. Natural disasters, such as hurricane Katrina and the tsunami in Asia, led to such destruction of critical infrastructures that human lives (not to mention well-being) were threatened. These events triggered the biggest humanitarian operations of the recent past. Europe and America have witnessed some big electric blackouts in the past ten years, which caused economic damage. Some serious humanitarian crises (e.g. Sudan, Kosovo, Macedonia in time of conflict) alarmingly showed that critical infrastructure is extremely important for human security. The worst case scenario regarding the "millennium bug" or Y2K included seriously disrupted human life due to potential malfunctioning of multiple critical infrastructures (financial, information, transport, energy and other infrastructures).

Despite such importance of critical infrastructures, the concept of human security has not addressed this problem at all. The problem is the predominantly technical orientation of scientists dealing with critical infrastructures and predominantly non-technical orientation of disciplines dealing with human security. These disciplines and approaches are not really capable of looking ver the self-imposed boundaries to strongly connected problems. Human security has many non-technical aspects; however, the unaddressed technical aspect is increasingly important. This has also serious effects on practice, especially formulation and implementation of human security measures. Interdisciplinarity and comprehensiveness proved again to be the Achilles heel of human security.

10.4. Freedom from Fear vs Freedom from Want

In an ideal world, each of the UNDP's seven categories of threats would receive adequate global attention and resources. Yet attempts to implement this human security agenda have led to the emergence of two major schools of thought on how to best practice human security — '*"Freedom from Fear"*' and '*"Freedom from Want"*'. While the UNDP 1994 report originally argued that human security requires attention to both *freedom from fear* and *freedom from want,* divisions have gradually emerged over the proper scope of that protection (e.g. over what threats individuals should be protected from) and over the appropriate mechanisms for responding to these threats.

Freedom from Fear — This school seeks to limit the practice of Human Security to protecting individuals from violent conflicts while recognizing that these violent threats are strongly associated with poverty, lack of state capacity and other forms of inequities. This approach argues that limiting the focus to violence is a realistic and manageable approach towards Human Security. Emergency assistance, conflict prevention and resolution, peace-building are the main concerns of this approach. Canada, for example, was a critical player in the efforts to ban landmines and has incorporated the "Freedom from Fear" agenda as a primary component in its own foreign policy. However, whether such "narrow" approach can truly serve its purpose in guaranteeing more fruitful results remains to be an issue. For instance, the conflicts in Darfur are often used in questioning the effectiveness of the "Responsibility to Protect", a key component of the Freedom from Fear agenda.

Freedom from Want — The school advocates a holistic approach in achieving human security and argues that the threat agenda should be broadened to include hunger, disease and natural disasters because they are inseparable concepts in addressing the root of human insecurity and they kill far more people than war, genocide and terrorism combined. Different from "Freedom from Fear", it expands the focus beyond violence with emphasis on development and security goals.

Despite their differences, these two approaches to human security can be considered complementary rather than contradictory. Expressions to this effect include:

— Franklin D. Roosevelt's famous Four Freedoms speech of 1941, in which "Freedom from Want" is characterized as the third and "Freedom from Fear" is the fourth such fundamental, universal, freedom.

— The Government of Japan considers Freedom from Fear and Freedom from Want to be equal in developing Japan's foreign policy. Moreover, the UNDP 1994 called for the world's attention to both agendas.

— Surin Pitsuwan, current Secretary-General of ASEAN cites theorists such as Hobbes, Locke, Rousseau and Houme to conclude that "human security is the primary purpose of organizing a state in the beginning.". He goes on to observe that the 1994 Human Development Report states that it is "reviving this concept" and suggests that the authors of the 1994 HDR may be alluding to Franklin Roosevelt's Four Freedoms speech without literally citing that presentation.

Although "freedom from fear" and "freedom from want" are the most commonly referred to categories of human security practice, an increasing number of alternative ideas continue to emerge on how to best practice human security. Among them:

— G. King and C. Murray. King and Murray try to narrow down the human security definition to one's "expectation of years of life without experiencing the state of generalized poverty". In their definition, the "generalized poverty" means "falling below critical thresholds in any domain of well-being"; and it is in the same article, they give brief review and categories of "Domains of Well-being". This set of defition is similar with "freedom from want" but more concretely focused on some value system.

— Caroline Thomas. She regards human security as describing "a condition of existence" which entails basic material needs, human dignity, including meaningful participation in the life of the community, and an active and substantive notion of democracy from the local to the global.

— *Sabina Alkire.*Different with those approaches seek to narrow down and specify the objective of human security, Sabina Alkire pushes the idea a step further as "to safeguard the vital core of all human lives from critical pervasive threats, without impeding long-term human fulfilment". In a concept as such, she suggests the "vital core" cover a minimal or basic or fundamental set of functions related to survival, livelihood and dignity; and all institutions should at least and necessarily protect the core from any intervention.

10.5. Human Security and Development

Human security also challenged and drew from the practice of international development. Traditionally, embracing liberal market economics was considered to be the universal path for economic growth, and thus development for all humanity. Yet, continuing conflict and human rights abuses following the end of the Cold War and the fact that two-thirds of the global population seemed to have gained little from the economic gains of globalization, led to fundamental questions about the way development was practiced. Accordingly, human development has emerged in 1990s to challenge the dominant paradigm of liberal economy in the development community. Human development proponents argue that economic growth is insufficient to expand people's choice or capabilities, areas such as health, education, technology, the environment, and employment should not be neglected.

Human security could be said to further enlarge the scope for examining the causes and consequences of underdevelopment, by seeking to bridge the divide between development and security. Too often, militaries didn't address or factor in the underlying causes of violence and insecurity while development workers often underplayed the vulnerability of development models to violent conflict . Human security springs from a growing consensus these two fields need to be more fully integrated in order to enhance security for all.

The paper *Development and Security* by Frances Stewart argues that security and development are deeply interconnected.

Human security forms an important part of people's well-being, and is therefore an objective of development. An objective of development is "the enlargement of human choices". Insecurity cuts life short and thwarts the use of human potential, thereby affecting the reaching of this objective.

Lack of human security has adverse consequences on economic growth, and therefore development. Some development costs are obvious. For example, in wars, people who join the army or flee can no longer work productively. Also, destroying infrastructure reduces the productive capacity of the economy.

Imbalanced development that involves horizontal inequalities is an important source of conflict. Therefore, vicious cycles of lack of development which leads to conflict, then to lack of development, can readily emerge. Likewise, virtuous cycles are possible, with high levels of security leading to development, which further promotes security in return.

Further, it could also be said that the practice of human development and human security share three fundamental elements:

First, human security and human development are both people-centered. They challenge the orthodox approach to security and development i.e. state security and liberal economic growth respectively. Both emphasize people are be the ultimate ends but not means. Both treat human as agents and should be empowered to participate in the course.

Second, both perspectives are multidimensional. Both address people's dignity as well as their material and physical concerns.

Third, both schools of thought consider poverty and inequality as the root causes of individual vulnerability.

Despite these similarities, the relationship with development is one of the most contested areas of human security . "Freedom from fear" advocates, such as Andrew Mack,argue that human security should focus on the achievable goals of decreasing individual vulnerability to violent conflict, rather than broadly defined goals of economic and social development. Others, such as Tadjbakhsh and Chenoy, argue that human development and human security are inextricably linked since progress in one enhances the chances of progress in another while failure in one increases risk of failure of another.

10.5.1. Relationship with Human Rights

Human security is indebted to the human rights tradition (the ideas of natural law and natural rights). The development of the human security model can be seen to have drawn upon ideas and concepts fundamental to the human rights tradition. Both approaches use the individual as the main referent and both argue that a wide range of issues (i.e. civil rights, cultural identity, access to education and healthcare) are fundamental to human dignity. A major difference between the two models is in their approach to addressing threats to human dignity and survival. Whilst the human rights framework takes a legalistic approach, the human security framework, by utilizing a diverse range of actors, adopts flexible and issue-specific approaches, which can operate at local, national or international levels.

The nature of the relationship between human security and human rights is contested among human security advocates. Some human security advocates argue that the goal of human security should be to build upon and strengthen the existing global human rights legal framework . However, other advocates view the human rights legal framework as part of the global insecurity problem and believe that a human security approach should propel us to move above and beyond this legalistic approach to get at the underlying sources of inequality and violence which are the root causes of insecurity in today's world.

10.5.2. Gender and Human Security

Human security focuses on the serious neglect of gender concerns under the traditional security model. Traditional security's focus on external military threats to the state has meant that the majority of threats women face have been overlooked. By focusing on the individual, the human security model aims to address the security concerns of both women and men equally. Women are often the worst victims of violence and conflict: they form the majority of civilian deaths; the majority of refugees; and, are often the victims of cruel and degrading practices, such as rape. Women's security is also threatened by unequal access to resources, services and opportunities. Human security seeks to empower women, through education, participation and access, as gender equality is seen as a necessary precondition for peace, security and a prosperous society.

Human security seeks to address underlying causes and long-term implications of conflicts instead of simply reacting to problems, as the traditional security approach is often accused of doing. "The basic point of preventive efforts is, of course, to reduce, and hopefully eliminate, the need for intervention altogether," while an investment in rehabilitation or rebuilding seeks to ensure that former conflicts do not breed future violence. The concepts of prevention and rebuilding are clearly embraced as the "responsibility to prevent" and well elaborated in "The Responsibility to protect report of the International Commission on Intervention and State Sovereignty."

10.5.3. Human Security Approach

While there are numerous examples of the human security approach in action, two notable global political events with direct ties to the human security agenda include the development of Responsibility to Protect (R2P) principles guiding humanitarian intervention and the passage of the Ottawa Treaty banning anti-personnel landmines.

The application of human security is highly relevant within the area of humanitarian intervention, as it focuses on addressing the deep rooted and multi-factorial problems inherent in humanitarian crises, and offers more long term resolutions. In general, the term humanitarian intervention generally applies to when a state uses force against another state in order to alleviate suffering in the latter state.

Under the traditional security paradigm humanitarian intervention is contentious. As discussed above, the traditional security paradigm places emphasis on the notion of states. Hence, the principles of state sovereignty and non-intervention that are paramount in the traditional security paradigm make it difficult to justify the intervention of other states in internal disputes. Through the development of clear principles based on the human security concept, there has been a step forward in the development of clear rules of when humanitarian intervention can occur and the obligations of states that intervene in the internal disputes of a state.

These principles on humanitarian intervention are the product of a debate pushed by United Nations Secretary General Kofi Annan. He posed a challenge to the international community to find a new approach to humanitarian intervention that responded to its inherent problems. In 2001, the International Commission on Intervention and State Sovereignty (ICISS) produced the "The Responsibility to protect", a comprehensive report detailing how the "right of humanitarian intervention" could be exercised. It was considered a triumph for the human security approach as it emphasized and gathered much needed attention to some of its main principles:

The protection of individual welfare is more important than the state. If the security of individuals is threatened internally by the state or externally by other states, state authority can be overridden.

Addressing the root causes of humanitarian crises (e.g. economic, political or social instability) is a more effective way to solve problems and protect the long-term security of individuals.

Prevention is the best solution. A collective understanding of the deeper social issues along with a desire to work together is necessary to prevent humanitarian crises, thereby preventing a widespread absence of human security within a population (which may mean investing more in development projects).

The report illustrates the usefulness of the human security approach, particularly its ability to examine the cause of conflicts that explain and justify humanitarian intervention. In addition, it could also act as a paradigm for identifying, prioritizing and resolving large transnational problems, one of the fundamental factors that act as a stimulus for humanitarian intervention in the first place. However, human security still faces difficulties concerning the scope of its applicability, as large problems requiring humanitarian intervention usually are built up from an array of socio-political, cultural and economic problems that may be beyond the limitations of humanitarian projects. On the other hand, successful examples of the use of human security principles within interventions can be found.

The success of humanitarian intervention in international affairs is varied. As discussed above, humanitarian intervention is a contentious issue. Examples of humanitarian intervention illustrate, that in some cases intervention can lead to disastrous results, as in

Srebrenica and Somalia. In other cases, a lack of clarity as to the rules of when intervention can occur has resulted in tragic inaction, as was witnessed during the Rwandan genocide. One example is of a successful humanitarian intervention and also of humanitarian principles being applied is East Timor which, prior to its independence, was plagued with massive human rights abuses by pro-Indonesian militias and an insurgency war led by indigenous East Timorese against Indonesian forces. A peacekeeping mission was deployed to safeguard the move to independence and the UN established the United Nations Transitional Administration in East Timor (UNTAET). This not only dealt with traditional security priorities, but also helped in nation building projects, coordinated humanitarian aid and civil rehabilitation, illustrating not only a successful humanitarian intervention but also a effective application of human security principles.

In contrast to the traditional security discourse which sees security as focused on protecting state interests, human security proponents believe that Anti-personnel mines could not be viable weapons of war due to the massive collateral damage they cause, their indiscriminate nature and persistence after conflict. In particular, they argue that Anti-personnel mines differ from most weapons, which have to be aimed and fired since they have the potential to kill and maim long after the warring parties have ceased fighting. The United Nations has reckoned that landmines are at least ten times more likely to kill or injure a civilian after a conflict than a combatant during hostilities. The effects are also long-lasting. The ICBL estimates that anti-personnel mines were the cause of 5,751 casualties in 2006. Whereas traditionally, states would justify these negative impacts of mines due to the advantage they give on the battlefield, under the human security lens, this is untenable as the wide-ranging post-conflict impact on the day-to-day experience of individuals outweighs the military advantage.

The Ottawa Convention, which led to the banning of anti-personnel landmines, is seen as a victory for the Human Security agenda. The Ottawa Convention has proved to be a huge step forward in the 'Freedom from Fear' approach. In Ottawa, the negotiations were moved outside traditional disarmament forums, thus avoiding the entrenched logic of traditional arms control measures. According to

Don Hubert,an advocate of Human Security from the Canadian Department of Foreign Affairs, the main reason for its success was a multilateral focus. While INGO's like the UN and the ICRC remain the key players along with middle power states like Norway and Canada, its actual power and push comes from the involvement of a host of civil society actors (NGOs) and the general public. Human Security proponents believe that this treaty has set new standards in humanitarian advocacy and has acted as a landmark in international lawmaking for a more secure world.

Critics of the treaty, however, caution against complacency on its success. Many states, they point out, have neither signed nor ratified this convention. They include China, Russia and the United States who are major contributors to the global weapons trade. Second, even though there were a diverse group of civil society actors, the real influence on the treaty came from the ones in the 'global north'. Third, cynics may argue that the success of this campaign stems from the fact that these weapons were outdated and of limited military value and this treaty just helped to accelerate a process that would have happened anyway.

References

Paris, Roland. 2001. Human Security - Paradigm Shift or Hot Air? In: *International Security*, Vol. 26, No. 2.

Thomas, Caroline. 2000. Global governance, development and human security the challenge of poverty and inequality. London and Sterling, VA: Pluto Press.

Tadjbakhsh & Chenoy, Human Security: *Concepts and implications* , London: Routledge, 2006.

Hampson, F., 2002. *Madness in the multitude: human security and world disorder,* Ontario: Oxford University Press.

Thomas, C., 2001. "Global governance, development and human security: exploring the links," *Third World Quarterly,* Vol. 22(2):159-175.

Shahrbanou Tadjbakhsh, *Human Security : The Seven Challenges of Operationalizing the Concept*, "Human Security: 60 minutes to Convince", UNESCO, September 13, 2005-09-14, Paris France.

Bibliography

Acton, John D. 1907. *The History of Freedom and Other Essays*. London: Macmillan. p. 4.

Andreas Schedler, Larry Diamond, and Marc F. Plattner, eds., 1999. *The Self-Restraining State: Power and Accountability in New Democracies* Boulder, CO: Lynne Rienner Publishers.

Andrew Puddephatt. 2005. *Freedom of Expression, The essentials of Human Rights*, Hodder Arnold.

Arno Tausch, (Ed) 2003. "The Three Pillars of Wisdom? A Reader on Globalization, World Bank Pension Models and Welfare Society" Nova Science Hauppauge, New York.

Augusztinovics, M. 2002. "Issues in pension design", in *International Social Security Review* 55(1), pp. 21-35.

Baeza, C.; Montenegro, F.; and Nuñez, M. 2002. *Extending social protection in health through community based health organizations: Evidence and challenges.* Geneva,ILO-STEP.

Brett, Sebastian. 1999. *Limits to tolerance: freedom of expression and the public debate in Chile*. Human Rights Watch.

Chaabane, M. 2002: *Towards the universalization of social security: The experience of Tunisia* . Geneva, ILO; Extension of Social Security, ESS - Paper No. 4.

Derick W. Brinkerhoff, 1999. "Identifying and Assessing Political Will for Anti-Corruption Efforts," Working Papers no. 13, *Implementing Policy Change* project, USAID, January.

Devereux, S. 2000. *Targeting social protection programmes: Case study examples of issues.* Easthampstead Park Conference Centre, Inter-Agency Workshop on Social Protection, 22-23 March.

Dror, D.M.; Jacquier, C. 1999: "Micro-insurance: Extending health insurance to the excluded", in *International Social Security Review.* Geneva, ISSA, Vol.52, No.1, pp. 71-97.

Eyerman, Joe. 1998. "Terrorism and democratic states: Soft targets or accessible systems." *International Interactions* 24(2):151–170.

Fearon, James D. 1998. Commitment Problems and the Spread of Ethnic Conflict. In *The International Spread of Ethnic Conflict*, ed. David Lake and Donald Rothchild. Princeton: Princeton University Press pp. 107–126.

Guibault, Lucy; & Bernt Hugenholtz . 2006. *The future of the public domain: identifying the commons in information law*. Kluwer Law International.

Hampson, F., 2002. *Madness in the multitude: human security and world disorder,* Ontario: Oxford University Press.

Iannaccone, Lawrence R. 1992. "Sacrifice and Stigman: Reducing Free-Riding in Cults, Communes, and Other Collectives." *Journal of Political Economy* 100(2):271–292.

Krueger, Aland B. 2007. *What Makes a Terrorist: Economics and the Roots of Terrorism*. Princeton: Princeton University Press.

Lee, E. 1998. *The Asian financial crisis: The challenge for social policy.* Geneva.

Lund, F.; Srinivas, S. 2000: *Learning from experience: A gendered approach to social protection for workers in the informal economy.* Geneva, ILO-STEP & WIEGO.

Marlin, Randal . 2002. *Propaganda and the Ethics of Persuasion.* Broadview Press.

Márquez, G. (ed.). 1995: *Reforming the labor market in a liberalized economy* Washington, DC, Inter-American Development Bank.

Marta Lagos, 2001. "How People View Democracy: Between Stability and Crisis In Latin America," *Journal of Democracy* 12 January.

Mazza, J. 2000: *Unemployment insurance: Case studies and lessons for the Latin American and Caribbean region.* Washington D.C., Inter-American Bank, Research Department Working Paper no. 411.

Mesa-Lago, C. 200. "Structural reform of social security pensions in Latin America: Models, characteristics, results and conclusions", in *International Social Security Review* 54(4), pp.67-92.

Messel, E. 2001: *Social protection strategy.* Geneva, ILO; paper presented to an ADB seminar in Tokyo.

Modigliani, Franco. 2004. *Rethinking pension reform* . Franco Modigliani, Arun Muralidhar. Cambridge, UK ; New York : Cambridge University Press,

Muralidhar, Arun S. 2001. *Innovations in pension fund management* / Arun S. Muralidhar. Stanford, Calif.Stanford Economics + Finance.

Norton, A.; Conway, T.; and Foster, M. 2001. *Social protection concepts and approaches: Implications for policy and practice in international development.* London, Overseas Development Institute; Working Paper 143.

Ortiz, I. (ed.). 2001. *Social protection in Asia and the Pacific.* Manila, Asian Development Bank.

Panda, P. 1998: "The elderly in rural Orissa. Alone in distress", in *Economic and Political Weekly.* Mumbai, June 20th, pp. 1545-1550.

Paris, Roland. 2001. Human Security - Paradigm Shift or Hot Air? In: *International Security*, Vol. 26, No. 2.

Peter Middlebrook , 2009. *When the Public Works: Generating Employment and Social Protection in Ethiopia.* Lambert Academic Publishing.

Reynaud, E. 2002: *The extension of social security coverage: The approach of the International Labour Office.* Geneva, ILO, Extension of Social Security, ESS - Paper No. 3.

Rodrik, D. 1997: *Has globalization gone too far?* Washington DC, Institute for International Economics.

Ron, A. 1998: "Health care in Asia and the Pacific: increasing the focus on social health insurance", in *International Social Security Review* Geneva, ISSA, Vol.51, No. 2, pp.17-37.

Ron, A.; Abel-Smith, B.; and Tamburi, G. 1990: *Health insurance in developing countries. The social security approach.* Geneva, ILO.

Sabates-Wheeler, R. and Kabeer, N. forthcoming: *Gender equality and the extension of social protection.* Geneva, ILO, Extension of Social Security (ESS) paper series).

Sankaran, T.S. 1998: "Social assistance: Evidence and policy issues", in W. van Ginneken (ed.) *Social security for all Indians.* New Delhi, Oxford University Press.

Schleberger, E. 2002: *The universal pension scheme in Namibia.* Geneva, ILO, Extension of Social Security, ESS - Paper No. 6.

Shahrbanou Tadjbakhsh, *Human Security : The Seven Challenges of Operationalizing the Concept*, "Human Security: 60 minutes to Convince", UNESCO, September 13, 2005-09-14, Paris France.

Standing, G. 1999. *Global labour flexibility. Seeking distributive justice* London, MacMillan Press.

Tadjbakhsh & Chenoy, Human Security: *Concepts and implications* London: Routledge, 2006.

Thomas Carothers, 1999. *Aiding Democracy Abroad: The Learning Curve* Washington, D.C.: The Carnegie Endowment for International Peace, p. 101.

Thomas, C., 2001. "Global governance, development and human security: exploring the links," *Third World Quarterly,* Vol. 22(2):159-175.

Thomas, Caroline. 2000. Global governance, development and human security the challenge of poverty and inequality. London and Sterling, VA: Pluto Press.

Thuy, P; Hansen, E.; and Price, D. 2001. *The public employment service in a changing labour market* ILO, Geneva.

WHO. 2001. *Macroeconomics and health: Investing in health for economic development.* Geneva.

World Bank, 2000: *World Development Report 2000-1. Attacking poverty.* Oxford University Press.

Yun-han Chu, Larry Diamond, and Doh Chull Shin, 2001. "How People View Democracy: Halting Progress in Korea and Taiwan," *Journal of Democracy* 12. January.

Zeller, M. 2000. "The safety net role of micro-finance for income and consumption smoothing", in Lustig, N. (ed.) *Shielding the poor. Social protection in the developing world.* Washington DC, Brookings Institution Press and Inter-American Development Bank.

Index